PITCH INVADERS

Stella Orakwue is a journalist and television producer. A former senior television news journalist at ITN, she now runs her own independent production company which has produced documentaries for British television. She has an emotional attachment to all things red and white, and lives in north London.

Critical acclaim for PITCH INVADERS

'Firmly points the way for a wider debate'
The Independent [Book of the Week, sports section]

'A provocative, important book'
All Sport & Leisure Monthly

'The book is much more thought-provoking, controversial and therefore interesting than the usual dross served up in sports books. If you have an open mind then give it a go' *Cardiff Western Mail*

'I read this book in one sitting and, boy, does she know her football. In this brilliantly insightful but ultimately unsettling account she tackles all the sacred issues that most black pundits moan about, and white ones secretly believe. [Stella Orakwue] is . . . a clear and far-sighted analyst of one of the most socially complex games on the planet' *Untold*

'Imagine what a team Orakwue and Mr Mellor would make if they got together'   *FourFourTwo*

'A worthwhile cause'
        The Express [Book of the Day, sports section]

'A welcome and very forthright account of the treatment of black footballers in the modern game'
        Sports Collector

'Leaves very few stones unturned. Brilliantly and exhaustively researched . . . it is stirring stuff'
        Yorkshire Evening Post

'Some thought-provoking evidence'
        Match of the Day Magazine

'This is a book that I'm sure lots of black professional footballers would like to have written. On the surface it's exploring the trials and tribulations of being a black footballer in 1990s Britain, but at a deeper level it's really about the state of race relations in this society. A thoroughly enjoyable and informative read'   *Alarm*

'Excellent. The book . . . is provocative. It has to be because it tackles head-on racism in football and proves that it is still very much alive both on and off the pitch. Thought-provoking and disturbing'
        Bolton Evening News

Stella Orakwue

PITCH INVADERS

The Modern Black Football Revolution

VISTA

A Vista paperback
First published in Great Britain by Victor Gollancz in 1998
This paperback edition published in 1999 by Vista,
an imprint of Orion Books Ltd,
Wellington House, 125 Strand, London WC2R 0BB

© Stella Orakwue 1998

A CIP catalogue record for this book is available
from the British Library.

ISBN 0 575 60341 0

Printed and bound in Great Britain by
Guernsey Press Co. Ltd, Guernsey, Channel Isles

For my father, PWJ Orakwue.

Acknowledgements

I would like to thank Lynn Patterson for being a great friend and a rock of solid support. Tony MacKintosh for his encouragement. Jon Holmes, who didn't put my fax in the bin. Richard Wigmore, who opened the door. Special thanks to my editor, Ian Preece, who listened and waited and read and demanded and argued . . . And Tom and Naciye Sadat and family for being great pick-me-ups, excellent football analysts, and for letting me use their brilliant drycleaning shop as my wardrobe.

Contents

Introduction

Andy Cole didn't start it. But, for a few months, he became its most public face. History was made, hysteria fermented, when he was sold for £7 million in January 1995. Britain's most expensive player: a black man.

By August, and the start of the 1995–96 season, Stan Collymore had gone for £8.5 million. Les Ferdinand: £6 million. Reorder. Collymore, Cole, Ferdinand: the three most expensive in the country. Three black men.

What a difference a couple of decades make. In the 1970s, too many managers believed that black wannabe-footballers were an exotic breed who didn't have enough 'bottle' to play the game. They would freeze in the winter, pine for that African or Caribbean sunshine.

Today, even a club like Everton, regarded by many black football fans during those wilderness years as an excellent example of a club employing only white players, has a black footballer. In the 1996 season, all the Premiership teams had at least one black player; many had two, three or more, who played regular first-team games. Except Blackburn and Sunderland. They didn't have any blacks in their squads. It was ironic that Blackburn, with an all-white team, became Champions in the same year that black players were making football history by becoming the most highly valued players in Britain.

Our black players have slowly integrated into the game they adore, and many unbiased people do admire them for their resilience, stamina, power, pace, verve, originality and goalscoring abilities. But all is not as it seems.

I wanted to write this book after I came home from Arsenal's victory celebrations at Highbury following their win over Parma in the European Cup Winners' Cup in May 1994. Standing outside Islington Town Hall I watched, amazed but uplifted, as I witnessed the adulation poured on to Ian Wright by the thousands of people there. He hadn't even played in the Final. And it wasn't just because he was the team's top scorer and had helped them get there in the qualifying matches; it was more than that.

We loved him for being one of us, a regular guy. When he made his emotional speeches from the Town Hall balcony he spoke our language, drank our kind of beer, held it the way we did. When he mucked about – almost dropping the trophy at one point – we lapped it up. He was black. The people there were mostly white. But he belonged to all of us: black and white; man and woman; adult and child.

In my mind, the crowd's acceptance and acknowledgement of this simple fact appeared to be proof indeed that our lives as black people in this country had reached a crucial stage. Most white people now know that the majority of black people here aren't going 'back to their own countries'; they aren't going back anywhere. They are here for good. Here to stay. Even if a growing black minority do wish they could up and go to that Caribbean or African land of their dreams, it remains a hazy dream, like some white people's dreams of a new life by the sea, in somewhere like Australia. Our lives are intermingled: many of us are now friends, colleagues, business partners, employers, employees, next-door neighbours, lovers, husbands and wives.

The silent but visible integration of black and white in British football parallels that in British society – and it's happened during the same timespan. But how does this integration work in people's everyday experiences? Is it solid? Is it only a cover for insidious practices and prejudice? If Ian Wright had been one of the black Chelsea players who 'screwed up' the '94 FA Cup

Final against Manchester United, would he, like they were, be blamed by some people I overheard for being a 'crap black footballer'? Why weren't those Chelsea men just players who had had a bad game? Why were they all of a sudden 'black players'? Colour raised its head sooner rather than later, which made me want to know how concrete were the changes in white football's attitudes towards black players.

And could you, by searching for the answers to that, also find out where the strengths and weaknesses lie in today's relationships between white and black Britons?

I realized that despite their current professional and financial success, our top black footballers have been unable to shake off the stigmas, stereotyping and racist labelling attached to the one thing they share in common: the colour of their skin. The criticisms, sniping and attacks levelled at them are exactly the ones thrown at the black communities they came from, and which many still have roots in.

They remain outsiders who have to contend with attitudes no white player comes up against. People who are judged not on the basis of their individuality but on the basis of concocted group characteristics enshrined in mythology.

The players are regarded as unruly, naïve, lazy, ill-disciplined, brutal, useless, having attitude problems, lacking in technical skills, lacking in managerial skills. It seems that money, skill, fame and even adulation from a mainly white fan base can't help you escape the white legacies of your black skin. Getting to the top of the pile makes no difference – it can even make it worse.

And that's what fascinated me. Getting to the top is supposed to be the best means of getting out and getting rid of all that racial hassle. Getting to the top is supposed to prove that racism is dying. Isn't that why 'successful' blacks are held up or paraded to more lowly members of their race? False proof.

I wanted to know whether the black Premiership players – the footballers at the acknowledged top of the game – were, in the 1990s, regarded and treated as their white counterparts were. Or would the New Racism – the coded, sophisticated, reconfiguration of racist attitudes for the needs of nineties' people facing a new century – find and attack them at the top?

New Racism. How does it work? Today you can take somebody to court if they attack you physically because you are black; sue them if they've kept you out of employment because you are black. But as a consequence of those hard-won successes, the ball game has literally moved: today's battles against racism no longer revolve exclusively around the judicial system. Instead, the daily interpersonal relationships between black and white is now the new arena for the fights against racist practices and thinking. And that means we're in an environment where you can't legislate because New Racism is in people's hearts and minds. For example, a black person has the same fiery temperament a white person has; or he or she is as difficult as the white person next to them; or they have off-days as white people have off-days – there is no law, no courtroom where judgement can be passed on those who will criticize the black man or woman whilst excusing or commending the same behaviour in those who are white. And, as a result, New Racism has physical, mental and economic consequences for black people. Repeated and sustained criticism of a black person's personality or performance can lead to voluntary resignation or constructive dismissal, inability to find new work, lack of money, physical stress and psychological trauma.

Having the right to express complex personalities is still off-limits for blacks, as they are corralled into a mental arena patrolled and policed by nervous, insecure whites. The fundamental right to be assessed as a human being with a life of ups and downs is still a long way off. Within a year, Cole was to be damned as worthless by the public and the press both in skill

10

and valuation because he was not scoring; but Alan Shearer and Robbie Fowler were, and are, entitled to their periods of drought, their values left intact, their talent still lauded.

Whether or not those involved in football – be they reporters, managers, officials, players or fans – are racially motivated, one of the themes of this book is that the manner of sports reporting, team selection or general conduct often gives rise to that perception in black communities. Nowadays, what black people want to see in the media and on the pitch is not only justice being done but being seen to be done.

Andy Cole's painful search for his lost confidence and form won't end it. Stan Collymore's 'difficult' and 'problem boy' tags won't end it. Les Ferdinand's exclusion from representing his country at major championships like Euro '96 won't end it. There will not be a return to the days when black players simply didn't feature in football, their abilities dismissed or disregarded. Just as black people in Britain are here for good – whether anyone likes it or not.

But as I watched Cole's miserable stagnation, nourished, aided and abetted by those who felt uncomfortable with his new status at the top and longed for him to fail; as I observed how his pain provided many white observers with private pleasures, I wondered if this is the best the future can hold for Britain's blacks. More of you may be able to get to the top but none of you will be able to escape the New Racists.

I have analysed the views of black players as expressed to white reporters and writers in interviews and news conferences, and the views of white sportswriters on black players. There were three reasons why I decided to quote and examine what people have gone on the record as saying. First, the newspapers, especially the tabloids, are where most white fans will get their information about black footballers. Indeed, the output of the media is mostly responsible for forming the views and opinions of the majority of Britain's white population on black Britain. What are black and white being fed? We look in their mirrors (the media's) and don't see ourselves. Secondly, when a black person makes an observation which a white person finds unpalatable, the black commentator is often accused by white critics of 'making it up', or of 'generalizing' and 'exaggerating' – until, that is, a white person makes the very same statement. Then it acquires, miraculously it seems to me at times, validity and status. To avoid accusations of 'they didn't say that', or 'I don't believe he wrote that, I bet she's made it up', I therefore decided to analyse what was already on the record and in the public domain for those who cared to look. Thirdly (and probably what I found most depressing – but understandable), more black footballers are confident nowadays about talking about overt racism (for example, racial abuse from white fans), and that willingness is a sign of some progress from the eighties (even if it seems odd to me to observe the large white appetite for hearing how awfully black players were treated in the past). However, black players are still extremely reluctant to discuss how they are treated *today* by the football clubs, Establishment, and industry. They back away from going on the record about how they are perceived and portrayed racially, and how that has affected them professionally and personally. This is the New Racism in action. But again, there are strong hints and glimpses in media interviews and statements – for those who have not been blinded by colourblindness. The mention of colour in our new Britain continues to provoke the old response of acute discomfort amongst the white majority; and a don't-want-to-talk-about-it, worried one from 'successful' blacks. But, surely, the most dangerous people are those who claim to be colourblind? What they claim not to see, they cannot change.

Stella Orakwue, May 1997

Born in a Slum – But the Slum Wasn't Born in Me

The teacher turned abruptly. The red in his cheeks, whipped up by the freezing wind, darkened. The small, intense black boy stared back at him defiantly, his pitch-black eyes challenging a reaction. A few of the other boys examined their boots; a couple hugged themselves protectively. The rapid silence made the youngsters in the opposing team, just a few yards away, look round. All of them knew what was coming next. They'd been here before.

In the staffroom, the teacher often described those determined, sometimes hostile eyes as 'arrogant'. 'Arrogant little sod! He always thinks he's right,' he told a colleague. But this game was one confrontation on the field too many. No 11-year-old was going to talk to him like that.

'What did you say?' the adult barked.

The boy glared at the teacher. 'Why should I come off? The ref's always after me. He's useless. He never did anything about all those other fouls the others did, but he came after me for my one. Now you've gone and backed him up by taking me off. It's always my fault, and I didn't do anything. The rest of the team are useless. I'm the only one playing properly. Why should I come off? I'm not coming off.' His attitude said it, but he didn't bother: the ref was only after me because I'm black.

The gamesmaster shouted, 'You're nothing but a bloody pain in the backside. You'll do as you're bloody well told. If I hadn't substituted you, you idiot, you were only going to be sent off, backchatting a ref like that. You're not the only player in the side.' Even if, as they both knew, he was the best one.

That imaginary boy was not Ian Wright, Andy Cole, Paul Ince, Stan Collymore, John Fashanu or any other prominent black footballer, and no such schoolmaster existed. This fictional account is based on an amalgamation of reports and is intended to show what a typical black footballer was supposed to be like as a schoolboy.

Andrew Cole's teachers thought he was a very difficult boy. Later, his coaches and managers thought he was a very difficult young man. When he became England's most expensive player in 1995, worth £7 million, nobody expected it. Very few in the sports world liked it. Because they didn't like him.

Cole wasn't alone, but he didn't know it at the time he was growing up in the rougher parts of Nottingham. As he was being suspended from school, standing up to teachers, or getting into fights in and out of school during the 1980s, the other black boys and black teenagers who would go on to form the richest group of black people in British history (when *Business Age* first published listings of rich sportspeople, black footballers appeared as if from nowhere), were doing exactly the same.

Andy Cole is an all-rounder. At school he was first class at basketball and cricket, and he could run too: he was the fastest boy in his year in the 200 and 100 metres. But if he was brilliant at all those activities, he was even better at football. Even in junior school, he was the best footballer in Nottingham.

And like the other black boys and teenagers, football was his salvation. It made him, and them, millionaires, catapulting them away from the African and Caribbean communities many had their roots in; communities where a life of crime, drugs and prison sentences had been predicted by those who thought they knew what boys filled with such 'attitude' and 'arrogance' would become.

In Cole's case author Robin McGibbon described in the *News of the World*, in 1994, how a school's gamesmaster recalled: 'I got the feeling that if Andrew hadn't made it at football, he would have been a pimp.'

Another said: 'We rarely had a problem with his football. The problem was: would he keep his nose clean? He was from a deprived area and mixing with the wrong crowd. They were apparently involved in petty theft and vandalism. We were worried he would be lured into it.'

West Ham isn't a pretty part of east London. But schoolboy Paul Ince knew its rough and ready areas very well. Almost as well as the route to West Ham United's training ground at Chadwell Heath. He was always there, pleading to be given a chance. Eventually, he was. John Lyall was manager at Upton Park when he met the 12-year-old Ince. He signed him for the Hammers two years later.

'He used to come round with his mates and watch us train virtually every day,' Lyall told the *Daily Mirror* in April 1995. 'One of them would always pluck up courage to come over and ask if they could borrow a ball. They would play all day. I remember him scoring a goal from forty yards. And you could throw the ball at any part of his body and he could control it.'

The skinny, enchantingly pretty, fair-skinned boy – a true Eastender who was born not too far away in Ilford and had the Cockney accent to prove it – was taken on on schoolboy forms. But for his first manager, that was just the beginning of the involvement with his prodigy's life off the training field.

John Lyall looked up from his desk. 'They're not here again?'

''Fraid so,' his assistant said, shooing in two police officers.

'Where is he?' Lyall demanded. No names were needed – the coppers could only be after one person.

Thinking back, years later, Paul Ince admitted to the *Daily Mirror* in February 1995, 'I could easily have finished up in jail, running with a gang or living as a deadbeat. My unruly behaviour has often landed me in trouble. At school I was caught lifting a couple of pounds from a teacher's purse and letting off fireworks in the woodwork class. Suspension was my middle name.'

In April he revealed to the *Mirror*: 'John gave me about eight last chances, but one day the police came to the training ground and he took me to one side and gave me a real slagging off. I realized then that that was really my last chance.'

In 1993, during a tour of the United States, Paul Ince became the first black captain of an England team. Two years later, valued at £7.5 million, Manchester United's self-appointed 'Guv'nor' ('Every side needs players who moan, nag and drive the team. That's me') was transferred to one of the world's biggest football clubs, Inter Milan. He was their first black player. Not many of the Italian club's fans saw this as progress.

Andy Cole got to know Ryan Giggs well because they were both in the biggest team in the land, Manchester United. When Paul Ince was at Manchester United, he was Ryan's best friend. Ryan Giggs is black. The only problem is that he doesn't look it, and hardly anybody in the sportsworld, television commentators or newspaper journalists, mentions it. That's because the sports-media is 99.9 per cent white. But I've not met a black person in England who doesn't know and isn't immensely proud, even if they're not sure he's proud of his black blood.

The following article appeared in the *Voice* in October 1994: 'Football star Ryan Giggs is under fire from black members of his family because he does not acknowledge them in his biography, published this week. *Ryan Giggs – My Life* barely mentions his black relatives in the 125-page book and they are saddened by the exclusion. Joanna Wilson, Ryan's aunt, told the *Voice*: "Ryan has completely denied his African side and that is sad. The black members of his family have been just as influential in his upbringing as his white relatives. He seems to be ashamed." Both Ryan's father's grandfathers were black merchant seamen from Sierra Leone, who landed in Tiger Bay, Cardiff, and married local girls. Joanna, 33, is distraught at Ryan for what she saw as him effectively turning his back on his grandparents, Winnie and Danny Snr, who dote on him. "He has upset us all," she said. "Last year he met Nelson Mandela but failed to mention to him his African heritage. Why can't he publicly announce the African part of himself?"'

Two mixed-race women wrote to the paper the following week to express their disgust at the article. 'Who gives anybody the right to class people of mixed race simply as black, especially as Ryan Giggs is from a varied multiracial background? His grandfathers on both sides were black. What saddens us is that our existence as mixed-race people seems to be ignored. We are expected to deny that we are of mixed race (we do not mean just black or white) and are usually grilled or toasted to see "which side" we're on. Why is our existence such a problem and an issue to many black people?'

MY AFRICAN ROOTS BY RYAN GIGGS was the *Daily Star* headline in April 1997. 'Soccer star Ryan Giggs has told his thousands of fans: "I'm BLACK – and proud of it." The Manchester United idol spoke of his roots for the first time in a TV documentary, in which his dad reveals their West African ancestry. Millionaire heart-throb Ryan, 23, says bluntly: "I have never, ever forgotten the fact that I'm black. My dad's black and the majority of my family are black – and I'm very proud of the fact."' The documentary was screened on the BBC in Wales.

It's pathetic, really, that as a race, we still cling to the thought that just a drop of the black stuff makes somebody one of us. We can then claim him or her: their talent, their money, their intelligence, their fame, in fact anything they have that we want to make us feel better about ourselves. Whether those people are

17

alive or have been dead for a thousand years doesn't matter, they're black and so are we, however diluted the connection.

I have met white people who are more aware and well-informed about black people's perspectives on many issues (without being patronizing) than many mixed-race people I know. But because they're white and don't have enough melanin, however right-on they are, there's always the nagging suspicion that they'll betray you when you've just started to trust them, or come out with something truly dreadful and unforgivable about black people that will hurt simply because it was so unexpected. (And I thought I *liked* them.)

A high number of this country's black footballers are of mixed-race parentage. Usually with a white mother and a black father. Surprised at the combination? Not if you're a black female. Our black men were the first to expound on 'love is all around', or 'it doesn't matter if you're black or white', decades before Wet, Wet, Wet and Michael Jackson. Very often for love, read sex. Black females are now humming the same tunes. Miscegenation is all around me and everywhere I go.

One side of Ryan Giggs' family comes from one of the oldest black settlements in this country, Cardiff's Tiger Bay. The only other place I've ever seen so many mixed-race people is Liverpool. I was seventeen, and with a coachload of black teenagers who'd travelled up there for a dance. I was shocked at the skin shades bombarding me – none of them even close to being black (*we* were black), but they weren't white people either. What were they? Weren't there any black people in Liverpool?

'The launch of Liverpool's Transatlantic Slavery Gallery confirms the often denied fact that the traffic in African slaves was the cornerstone of the city's overseas trade between 1730 and 1807,' wrote the *Weekly Journal* in November 1994. 'If Britain gave birth to the trade that enslaved Africans, the city was the European capital of that trade – a trade which helped to enrich some of the leading merchant families of Liverpool and provided employment for thousands. Of the 11,000 ships which sailed from England to Africa in the eighteenth century, about 5300, nearly half, departed from the port of Liverpool. Now, the city that houses Britain's oldest black community has become home to the first slave gallery at the Maritime Museum on the Albert Dock. A local woman walked into the gallery with a neck brace cradled in her arms. The brace was a punishment device used on runaway slaves; it circled the neck and had spikes protruding to inhibit sleep and delay the progress of the escapees. A similar device was already on exhibition. But this one, the woman explained, had been handed down through her family. Through three generations of Liverpudlians, straight from the source – a direct link with the present day.'

Ryan Giggs once declared himself 'the best-looking black man at Manchester United' in a feature *Touch* magazine ran which included him in a speculative all-black team. But you have to see him next to his brother, Rhodri, to realize that he is black in the first place, because if Rhodri is, and he certainly looks it, then Ryan must be – but he doesn't look it at all.

I've collected dozens of pictures of Giggsy and studied all the usual giveaways: nose (hardly flat at all); lips (thin); hair (straight not straightened); colour of eyes (they look kind of hazel brown in the colour photos – jury out: many blacks have hazel eyes); and, of course, skin shade (say no more). Conclusion: Ryan could join the National Front. His very expensive feet were formed in black and white worlds, but the black side is revealed on a need-to-know basis.

'Ray Wilkins has paid Torquay United £350,000 for the man who has been tagged "the black Ryan Giggs",' was a piece in the *Sun* in July 1995. 'The QPR boss signed Caribbean ace Gregory Goodridge, 24, after he impressed in a pre-season match between Rangers and Barbados.'

White world and black world. The origins of today's stars lie in both camps. They are either the offspring of men and women who came to Britain during the mass wave of black immigration in the 1950s and 1960s; or they are the offspring of black men who got involved with local white women in Britain.

It shouldn't come as a surprise that so many white people still call those in the latter group 'half-caste', but, unfortunately, it does. One or two are genuinely unaware that the term gives offence today, but will pick up on the silence and query if they've said something wrong. Many more do it deliberately, in defiant maintenance of ignorance. Like the way they use the term 'coloured' instead of 'black'. Or Afro-Caribbean instead of African-Caribbean. Black people who use the term half-caste, do so to wound and insult. Like when we use the phrase half-breed.

So what should we call these people whose black and white worlds collide inside their own bodies? Especially in an age where a black British cricketer goes crazy at being called a negro. Mixed-race is very widely used; there's also biracial (a bit American, but beginning to catch on here); transracial; multiracial; multiethnic . . . and let's not forget black – but only if it isn't chosen just because an individual has been turfed out by their white world.

No, not calling them anything (for I can hear all those liberal voices giving me their 'they're just people, members of the human race' theme song) isn't good enough in a world where race matters very much indeed. Oh, unless you're white, when of course it doesn't matter, it's terribly unimportant and people should just get on with their lives because we've all got the same opportunities now, irrespective of colour – and, by the way, do you know how tough their (white) lives are?

When I look at the backgrounds of our late century's black football stars, I see my own and my friends'. All of us have had to live in two or more worlds. In accordance with the belief that those who look at other people's lives should also open up, here's my background.

I've always lived in a black and a white world. They run simultaneously, but often stressfully, even if moving around between the two comes easy to me because I was brought up in England since the age of four, went to a nearly all-white secondary school, and work today in a virtually all-white industry.

Within the two worlds I grew up in, there were several mini-worlds. In my black world I was an African and lived until I was 19 as part of a traditional African family, with all the extended relationships, or so-called relationships, that entailed. My friends outside school were from the Caribbean, but were mostly Jamaican. At sixth-form college in central London, my friends were mostly from the Caribbean islands or were London-bred Africans.

There were three other black girls in my year at my Islington secondary school, and a couple of others dotted the upper years. I can still name each one of my eleven-year-old classmates: the crazy ones, the funny ones, the too-clever-by-far one, the snob, the one with the big tits, the one we all knew was on her way to being a lesbian, the very pretty ones, the one who must be kicking herself for having broken up with Gary Kemp (who later formed Spandau Ballet) and the one who said she would commit suicide at 29 because there was no point in living after that.

My white world: as a child, my white friends were working-class whites who also lived in Islington (I used to have a broad Cockney accent, and it comes back when I'm angry, together with language I can't remember acquiring). At secondary school, my mates were still mostly from the white working class who'd managed, like me, to get into a grammar school. It wasn't until I started working as a television news journalist, after university, that I encountered the great and the good of the white middle classes.

I'm Nigerian, I'm African. I share a Caribbean-British heritage,

I'm a Londoner (north), I'm sort of British, but never English. None of these descriptions fits properly on its own.

I'm working class, but yes, if you strap me down and extract all my teeth without an anaesthetic and using a blunt razor, and then threaten to carve my eyes out with a star screwdriver, I'll mumble that I accept I'm now also a member of the black middle classes – but only because of the kind of work I do, and the pay you can get, and maybe because of the kind of pastimes I enjoy now (but that could be age, you know), and maybe it's because a lot of the people I hang out with are black and white middle class (but I met a high proportion of them through my work, and that's when the class rot sets in).

I've always lived in these worlds. White and black. A mixed-race existence without being of mixed-race. 'Born in a slum, but the slum wasn't born in me.' One of Reverend Jesse Jackson's *bon mots* which, typically, gets to the heart of the matter. Looking back, was I really raised in a slum? Yes, in the very early years: the pest-ridden council estates of Islington in the sixties and early seventies. Was it a ghetto? Not quite: Hackney in the mid-seventies and early eighties. Hackney is nearly 50 per cent black. So mixed-race but strictly segregated Liverpool scared the life out of 17-year-old me, and still makes me feel uncomfortable.

Ryan Giggs' parents are Lynne Giggs and Danny Wilson. She's white; he's black. Lynne's mum and dad didn't want black Danny (then a building-site labourer) hanging around their little blond girl, but that didn't stop the pair producing Ryan. Ryan *Wilson* was born in Cardiff in November 1973 to this teenage mum and dad. They weren't married. Rhodri followed four years later.

Black Danny is invariably described by white writers who deign to mention his existence in pejorative terms.

By the way, what is not so frequently mentioned is the fact that he was also an excellent rugby player who played for Cardiff and Wales, and played rugby league for the Manchester club, Swinton. One writer grudgingly admitted that Ryan was always going to be a footballer of one kind or another since he'd inherited 'natural ability' from his dad.

Ryan said of his father: 'I used to watch him every week and he was great. Everybody who saw him says that. He has just been stupid. He could have been right at the top and he threw it away.'

Danny Wilson thought he'd hit the big time when he got the job with Swinton. Sports have traditionally been seen as a means of escape from the 'ghetto' for black men. Look at America. Here, with football being the national game, it's football that has been used as a means for several black players to escape from the 'inner cities', that euphemism for both black people and for all things rotten with Britain for the last two decades. Maybe the double euphemistic meaning is deliberate.

From all accounts, Ryan Wilson's 'troubled' home life should have turned him into a juvenile delinquent. It seems that following a disappointingly unfulfilled life in rugby league, Danny Wilson wreaked havoc on his family, forcing Lynne, who was working as an auxiliary nurse and a barmaid to make ends meet, to obtain a court order barring him from their home in Swinton. After that, Ryan changed his surname to his mother's maiden name, Giggs.

Today, son and father don't see each other often. A determined-sounding Ryan has no public regrets about this. 'I've always thought that, at the end of it, he's my dad and we had a lot of good times. I get on with him. But I'm not going to let myself get close to him again. I don't want to see him because it hurts too many of the people who mean most to me. It hurts my mum and grandparents, so I just don't see him . . . He knows it's his own fault things are the way they are.'

So while Ryan has opted publicly (you can't go more public

than disowning your father's name) for the white side of his family, Danny is back where he came from: with his black family in the black and white world of Tiger Bay.

Broken homes and single-parentage are supposed to be the main backgrounds of black people, our most prominent achievement in white people's eyes for what passes for black family structure. Drinking in a Docklands wine bar one evening, the talk turned to divorce. A young, middle-class white girl was explaining how she felt about being the product of divorced parents. I admired her for standing up for herself and insisting that she hadn't been damaged by her parents' separation.

Suddenly, the male executive among us turned to me and said: 'You know all about that, don't you, Stella?'

I was confused. What was he on about? Why had he jumped on me out of the rest of the group? It took me a couple of seconds.

'My parents were married for nearly thirty-five years,' I replied coldly.

'Oh,' he said, and turned away.

I was the only black person in the group, so, naturally, I must have come from a 'troubled' background, and known all about broken, split, divorced and single-parent families.

John Barnes' family background would probably have given that man apoplexy. How can he be a middle-class black footballer if he comes from that island-home of the broken black family, Jamaica? And his father, Ken Barnes, a Colonel in the Jamaican army! God forbid! Not surprised he can't play with all the baggage he's carrying.

Barnes is probably the most distinguished of all the black players with a Caribbean heritage. But he has also suffered more than the others for having such a strong link with those islands, as opposed to this island. But, despite the barrage of personal and professional attacks he's had to sustain, he's still an easy-going fellow, patient and very focused, helped no doubt, by having re-created his own middle-class nuclear family background with his wife Sue and their children.

John Fashanu, like John Barnes, is not just a millionaire, he's a multimillionaire. But Barnes has made his fortune through the business of football, without all the frenetic outside business activities 'Fash the Bash' adores and excels in.

'When I was a kid, someone asked me who I preferred, George Best or Bobby Charlton. I said Tiny Rowland.' John Fashanu and his big brother (by a year) Justin headed up British football's West African posse in the late eighties and early nineties. John and Justin. Chalk and cheese. One straight; the other gay; John worth at least £6 million, Justin still to make his pile. But if it hadn't been for Justin, John wouldn't be in football. Norwich signed John on the back of Justin's early massive success. Today their lives couldn't be more different.

But publicity, lots of it, is something that the brothers do have in common. And once again John leaves Justin behind. Although Justin was pleased not to have featured in the match-rigging scandal which dogged John since 1995 – he has now been acquitted – John desperately backed away from giving Justin public support when he decided to come out as a homosexual.

John Fashanu's father is Nigerian, his mother is from Guyana; but he calls Sam Hammam, the owner of Wimbledon, the club he personified for nine years, his real father ('My Lebanese dad'). He went to Nigeria to find his father when he was 18; the last time the two had met, he was a baby. Fashanu was born in Kensington, West London. He and Justin were put into a Dr Barnado's children's home when their mother couldn't cope on her own with four young children after their father returned to Nigeria.

But, as John discovered to his great financial advantage later, there's nothing that Nigerians love more than the return of the

Prodigal Son (Fash hardly knew the country) as a star (England international) ready to do business (make them rich as well as him or herself).

He loves it. 'I know all the right people. I mean, I know practically everyone in the world. I'm a high-profile black footballer and I'm a television star. I have so many contacts that I'm more a politician than a footballer.'

It's the way that John has utilized his African contacts which has made him one of the richest footballers in the UK, and sentenced him to incredible rumour-mongering, malice and unremitting *schadenfreude*. The Nigerian billionaire, Chief MKO Abiola, was known as Fashanu's 'godfather'.

Fashanu's business interests are many and varied and include property management, construction, television and acting as a sports agent for African footballers. And then there's sportswear. He's the sole distributor for Admiral sport and fashion wear in . . . Nigeria. When did he find the time to fit in football? 'I'm 65 per cent businessman, 35 per cent footballer.'

Not bad for a Barnado Boy – the tag which inevitably comes up when you mention Fashanu. Yes, he did spend some time in one of Dr Barnado's establishments, but from the age of 2, until he was 18 years old, he lived with a middle-class couple, the Jacksons (an engineer and a woman who drove ambulances during World War Two), in an isolated village in the Norfolk countryside. Betty Jackson, an ever-supportive woman, is still 'Mum'.

The 'Black Pack' was a group of black footballers who partied and premiered hard in the eighties and early nineties. Fashanu was very involved in initiating the lads' night-outers. John Barnes and Paul Ince were fully paid-up members. Later, so was Ian Wright. Ian Wright always does things later than everybody else, but he also wastes no time in catching up and taking over.

Ian Wright is a raggamuffin. The Arsenal and England striker is hard-core West Indian through and through – well, as hard core as you can get if you were born and brought up in south London.

Don't mess with him, though, and he might, only might, leave you alone. Fashanu jokingly nicknamed him 'Mr Angry'. His other nickname is 'Satch', as in Louis Armstrong's Satchmo. Like the great African-American jazz trumpeter, Ian loves his music: ragga, reggae and soul. And he loves to sing – he's even released a record, although Satch's and Satchmo's styles are slightly different.

The late-starter didn't get into the professional game until he was 22. Before then he earned his keep by working in a series of manual jobs, starting off as a plasterer. Because he started so late, he's made his million faster than the other black football millionaires in the UK.

His motivation each year is the Golden Boot, he told the *Daily Mirror* in September 1994, the award given to the player who has scored the most goals that season. 'That's what I go for and I know if I score enough goals at the end of the season, I'll get it. How do I keep myself motivated to score goals? Because there are a lot of good forwards out there trying to be number one.

'I'm a winner – that's all I'm interested in. I'm so intense about being the best that when I look at the Olympic Games, silver and bronze mean nothing to me. Being number one means everything. You should get gold for winning and nothing else. My philosophy is winner takes all.

'I'd like to be remembered as a great, someone who said he wanted the best and got it. It's nice to be liked. That's good, because I'm not a bad guy. But most of all I just want to be the best. I drill that into my children. "Be the best," I tell them. "Win, win, win. But always do it within the rules."'

Andy Cole, just like Ian Wright, who was to be his idol in

the game, hated losing, hated even coming second. An old teacher remembered how young Andy burst into tears, ripped off his shirt and refused a runners-up medal when his side lost a cup final. With the happy-loser mentality dominating English culture, the boy was punished for not wanting to come second, for not swallowing the 'it's the taking part and not the winning that matters' English philosophy.

When black men cracked open the door of British football, they found often that it was their physical build and perceptions of their 'natural abilities' (speed, strength and stamina), as opposed to how skilfully they read the game, which determined where managers deployed them. Their intelligence on the pitch was dismissed as 'flair', something instinctive, intuitive, unpredictable, mercurial and unreliable. It was therefore more common to find them as forwards ('natural pace', 'pace and power', 'a big strong powerful lad', 'he is quick', 'quick and strong' are common descriptions of black strikers), or in defensive positions. (Although we used to be accused of being 'naïve' in defence, that now is applied to African football teams – I got sick of hearing it from television commentators during the 1994 World Cup.) It took black British footballers much longer to break into the midfield, seen as the 'engine room' of the team, where the qualities of organization, intelligence and vision were needed in order to orchestrate play and distribute passes. It was a position of responsibility and control. No wonder that Paul Ince, as we know, liked to be called the guv'nor when he made the job his own at Old Trafford and for England. Of the new crop, Arsenal's young Senegalese-French player, Patrick Viera, is universally regarded as outstanding. John Barnes could and can lay off a pass as neatly and accurately as if he were joining two dots with a ruler, but admiration of that is never divorced from cries of woe for his 'lost pace'. 'You're black, why can't you run any faster, John?' I feel they're saying.

The figure of 25 per cent – of black players as a proportion to white in all four divisions of the Football League – is often bandied about. However, I make the figure between 12 and 15 per cent. Nobody knows the exact number. The Professional Football Association refuses to note whether a player is black or white in its records because, as they put it to me, 'there's no need to'. What you refuse to see you cannot change. However, it's strange how quickly and accurately white people can count the number of black people in jobs if they covet those jobs or feel, whether it's true or not, that the figures are getting too high. In my first job, I was one of three or four black people scattered in various editorial positions in a company of nearly a thousand: 0.3 or 0.4 per cent of the workforce. In the pub one evening, a white woman from a non-editorial department said blacks in the company were 'taking their jobs'. How people hate to discuss colour, unless . . .

It reminds me of the surprise expressed when, following the release of figures from the 1991 Census, which recorded ethnicity for the first time, it was realized that there were, rounding up the figures, just 900,000 African-Caribbean (including 500,000 Black Caribbean and 212,000 Black African) people in the UK out of a total population of 55 million. 1.6 per cent black. We always knew we weren't that many, but the view of one white acquaintance – 'I always *thought* [my italics] there were a lot more black people here than that' – neatly sums up that of the majority of whites. Why? Feeling swamped? 94.5 per cent of this country is white; 5.5 per cent is made up of minorities.

Where does the football industry get their much-quoted '25 per cent black players' from? Is it feeling and believing rather than seeing and counting?

An examination of the 92 Football League clubs' team photographs from August 1995 shows that on average most English teams have only two or three black players out of squads averaging twenty to twenty-five members.

Of course, some clubs (Aston Villa, Coventry City, Wimbledon, Liverpool, Walsall, Crystal Palace, Birmingham City) have at least double the average number of black players. But there are others (Burnley, Rotherham United, Norwich City, Scunthorpe United, Sheffield United) who have just the one solitary figure. And more than a dozen who have no black registrations at all. The majority of these all-white clubs are in the North: Blackburn Rovers, Sunderland, Barnsley, Darlington, Grimsby Town, Hartlepool United, Rochdale, Stockport County, Tranmere Rovers, York City. But Peterborough United, Ipswich Town and Hull City didn't have any black players, nor, strangely, given their location, did West Bromwich Albion.

'Given their location.' There is a sentiment that it is far easier for clubs in areas where the greatest number of black people live – the South-East (where 45 per cent of all blacks live) and the Midlands – to have black players in their teams. That is true upto a point, but what's that saying about horses and water . . . ? Compare West Brom's zilch with Walsall's seven black players and Coventry's eight. Same pool of talent, but who's drinking from it? And in these market-driven days, with considerable TV money around, most teams, certainly those in the upper divisions, can afford to buy in what they need and what they haven't trained themselves.

It will be interesting to see what will happen to the footballing opportunities for young home-grown blacks if the trend to buy from abroad, especially from Europe, continues. Young blacks in non-footballing jobs already find it far more difficult to obtain employment in England than the white person they went to school with. But will white and black homegrown trainees fare equally in the rush to employ cheap European imports?

What's deemed our 'natural pace' is highly valued here; as is our 'natural strength'. One of the dismissive comments made about black footballers by white commentators is: 'All they ever do is score goals.' That is to say their overall play is suspect, and the rest of the team (white) is forced to carry them. But it is a typical New Racist reaction: as soon as black expertise is demonstrated in a difficult area, that area is downgraded. The goalposts are moved.

Have you ever come across a club or a fan who didn't want strikers to be goalscorers? Isn't it the job of attackers to ram it in the back of the net? Clubs give hefty bonuses per goal scored as an incentive to their strikers. And pity the poor forward who suffers a drought, or loses 'his pace'. There is nowhere to hide.

Two powerful urges drive black footballers: an almost pathological need to be the best, to be first; and the equally fearsome need to be respected. In some ways, it's the desire to be respected that sustains the fire in their bellies, driving them on. In a world where black men still do not get respect for being black or for being men, then for the ones whose extraordinary talent forces the world to take a close look, what they demand in return is respect.

John Fashanu puts it like this: 'My life is about respect. I have worked many years for respect.' For him, the business and the football had just one aim. Many blacks understood instinctively why track stars Linford Christie and Colin Jackson called their management company 'Nuff Respect'. One white journalist said it was a 'rather naff name'; other white writers never fail to throw in a cheap jibe whenever they refer to it.

Showing Their True Colours

He was the colour of burnt oak, with tiny, dark, freckle-like spots sprinkled across his cheeks and just underneath his eyebrows. 'I support,' he said, banging his glass on the table, 'the team with the most black people in it.' Then he smiled, as if to say, that'll teach them: if they want me to say I'm on their side, they know what to do. He and I cracked up; he knew I understood his smile. I too had screamed and yelled for Cameroon in their World Cup '90 tie against England that Sunday evening.

I've heard the sentiments that man expressed many times from black people. But what if Cameroon had been playing against my north-London Premiership club? The answer is simple: no dirty tackle would have been too dirty if it meant that that geriatric, Milla (who's he think he is, anyway?), was taken out of the game as early as possible – anything to prevent such a calamity as a Cameroon win. My domestic team fields a couple of black players per game. For many of the years my father supported them, they didn't have any.

The sight of black bodies appearing on a sports pitch or occupying a spectator's seat is, for many, like a psychological migraine made especially for white English heads. Who do you support? Why? Do you support England? Why do you? Why don't you? Where do your loyalties lie?

To black faces those questions mean: we can see you're black, and you're obviously speaking with an English accent, but where do you really come from, where do you really belong? Where do your loyalties lie?

Where do you come from? Where do you belong? What do you call yourself . . . ? We detest it when we are asked these questions by white people. Yet black people ask it routinely of themselves. It is at the crux of the psychological trauma eating away at far too many of us: our physical presence here versus our mental detachment.

A trauma made even worse by the inner knowledge that for the vast majority of black people in England, they are too *English* to have a home anywhere else in the world; that if they were cradling a gurgling newborn and thinking of names, it would be Sharon not Shola, Adam over Ade every time; and that the loudest flag-waving, book-quoting Afrocentrics have white English mothers or girlfriends, or have never been near 'the Motherland'.

We detest it when these questions are put to us by whites because it is rare to find an occasion when the reason has not been to exclude black people. It is always clear when the line of questioning is not natural curiousity about a person's background. Bigots who believe mistakenly that their class, education and expensive clothes have hidden their racism, have a little song and dance. Then I become very generous with my lies:

'Where do you come from?'

'North London.'

'Have you always lived there, then?'

'Yep. Years.'

'Where were you born?'

'North London.'

'Oh, how nice. But where do your parents come from?'

'North London.'

'No, I mean where were they born?'

Where do your loyalties lie . . . ? The point is that it's hardly ever done the other way round: it's not assumed that a black-skinned person may actually be from these isles instead of from those faraway islands or continents. It's rarely assumed that you or your parents could possibly be born here. I never fail to subject my white questioners to exactly the same line of interrogation. It is very amusing to see how they are visibly irritated by the fact that you haven't grasped that simply being born here makes them English; or that simply because they weren't born here doesn't mean they can't call themselves English. You see, they are white.

The concept of a black Englishman or woman has yet to be grasped by the nation. We have yet to find a forward-looking definition of Englishness which claims black people and gives them room to become cultural stakeholders in UK Limited; a definition of Englishness that is not linked to white skin colour. Despite widespread racism in the US an African-American is an American – you try to tell him or her that they belong anywhere else. How awful it is for the thousands of black people born in England, and the millions who will be in the future, to feel that they are English through and through and yet they are denied everyday acceptance as Englishmen and Englishwomen because a black skin isn't part of England's national equation.

In Africa, people of English descent have not allowed skin colour to prevent them from demanding acceptance as nationals of majority black-populated countries. But, unbelievably, I have met white South Africans and white Kenyans who had emotional problems with the concept of a black English person. It's a refusal to let go what's dear to them (glorious, whites-only memories which, they believe, constitute their true heritage, something that can still be part of their children's future if things stay as they used to be), whilst everybody else makes the personal sacrifices and compromises in an attempt to get as many people as possible included in the future.

There are no black Englishmen or women. Except in the world

of sports. There, English men and women can be any colour the managers, coaches, selectors, administrators feel like, as long as they win. Any colour as long as it eventually leads to gold and green: medals and money.

'British is best' read a tabloid newspaper caption under the picture of happy victors, Darren Braithwaite (black), Tony Jarrett (black), Linford Christie (black) and John Regis (black), winners of the 4×100 metres relay in the '94 Athletics World Cup. All four had one hand held high in salute and acknowledgement of the cheering home crowd at Crystal Palace; their other hands clutched the edge of an enormous Union Jack, large enough to drape across four taut shoulders like an outsized cape.

The Union Jack includes anyone who's got the passport and is a winner. If it leaves many blacks uncomfortable to see members of their race wallowing in it, at least that's preferable to England's St George's flag, with its WASPish country-club membership requirements. Englishness (cultural rights) is the problem, not Britishness (residential rights).

If black people are not visualized as being English people, any black person who becomes a member of an English team, a representative of England, is condemned to a professional (and often personal) life of hellish experiences. Not only have they had to work harder than most of their teammates to get into the team in the first place – harder because they have faced not just physical requirements, but psychological ones – but once in, the job of continually having to prove how good you are, and how much you justify your place, merely intensifies. If you are nearby when anything goes wrong, you alone will be blamed despite the failure of the entire team.

Underlying this sorry state of affairs is fear and insecurity. The fear of losing what one group of people had all to themselves once upon a time, long ago. The fear that new entrants are turning out to be so good that if something, anything, isn't done to control their entry, then all will be lost, and the new entrants will become the dominating force.

The new entrants could end up taking the majority of the places in the team if they are not kept out by one means or another. Just like in the workplace, if barriers aren't erected to keep black people out of jobs they can do as well as the next white person, they could end up taking jobs which could have gone to a white person. The best foundations for racism are, and always will be, economic ones.

Olympic athlete Linford Christie kept the tills ringing at race meetings in Britain and around the world. If the England football team had the equivalent of five Linfords panting to be chosen for the line-up, they wouldn't all get picked. Because that would mean five places lost to the white candidates who were also vying for a place.

And, more importantly, what would it look like having an England team which was half black? A nightmarish prospect for some, no doubt. For some, there is also the fear that if you have blacks in your club or national squad, it's an acceptance that they really are in this country to stay.

Another European and former colonialist country, Holland, points the way to how things could go in the future (unless the situation is controlled). The Dutch have made good use of the swamp of footballing talent which descendants of their former colony, Surinam, have brought to Amsterdam and other parts of the Netherlands. There are far more blacks in Britain than there are Surinamese descendants in Holland, yet the Dutch regularly field more black players than the English. Caribbean-English and African-English are just as enthusiastic about the game – and could be just as talented – as black Dutchmen, who are trained in greater numbers.

The all-conquering Ajax club in Amsterdam has been known to field six black players. These Surinamese descendants, 'An ideal synthesis of South American flamboyance and European efficiency,' as David Endt, a former Ajax player, was quoted as saying in the *Daily Telegraph*, have helped to make the club a European legend, admired worldwide. Would English Northern clubs, and England, be prepared to pay such a colourful price to get the same result?

Some black male dancers once told me that the reason it was so difficult for them to break into ballet was because ballet teachers and artistic directors saw ballet as a whites-only art form, and they weren't about to let blacks with all that 'natural ability' get a foothold there. And what would a 'line' of white ballet dancers' bodies look like with black bodies in it? Consequently, black dancers are generally pushed into other forms of dance like jazz or musical theatre. They can have that. That's more their scene.

Former England manager, Graham Taylor, fielded teams which were half black (if you left out the goalie) for the 1994 World Cup qualifying campaign. His squad included Des Walker, Carlton Palmer, Paul Ince, Les Ferdinand, Ian Wright, and his protégé, John Barnes. He would often play two black strikers together: Ferdinand and Wright. England didn't qualify. And Taylor is probably the most vilified national manager this country has ever had. His team selections, and one single player in particular, bore the brunt of the attacks.

But all black players have had to pay the price for England's non-appearance in the 1994 World Cup. Taylor's mix and match approach gave everybody in the squad a chance: he really was colour blind and practised real equal opportunities; he didn't do the equivalent of inserting a false sentence at the bottom of a job advertisement merely to comply with the law, as one look at thousands of offices around the UK (virtually all white) would verify.

However, Taylor was hammered for his technical approach.

By October 1993, wrote David Lacey in the *Guardian*, the critics had managed to crack the England manager's veneer of amiability: 'Every time the team plays a different way I get criticized for it,' Taylor said. 'I'm accused of not knowing my mind. I'm accused of being unsettled. I'm accused of not having experience. It's a load of nonsense.'

But, as Lacey put it: 'When the England manager announced the squad for Rotterdam he supported his argument about the near impossibility of achieving a settled side with statistics showing that in equivalent periods of their management his predecessors had found it equally difficult to field unchanged teams. Taylor worked out that, between them, Alf Ramsey, Don Revie, Ron Greenwood and Bobby Robson had achieved it only seven times in 173 matches. Without our knowing whether changes were forced or unforced and what options were available, this evidence is superficial ... international managers tend to be judged more on the changes they make than those they eschew.

'From time to time Taylor has chided critics for their lack of faith in the versatility of the English footballer. "All good teams are adaptable," he said after the victory against the Poles. "All good teams meet what is required of them at any one particular time. Let them decide the formations." Rotterdam will prove the relevance of these words to an England side which will have to function without its natural focus, Gascoigne, giving Taylor the chance to show how flexible, and how imaginative, his own concepts really are. The critical knives are being resharpened, although if Taylor picks Palmer, he will be the most popular Englishman in Holland since Field Marshall Montgomery.'

But when the proverbial hit the fan, as in any real workplace where blacks are employed, the criticisms and abuse were directed at the black players' performances. They were the failures, whilst it was felt the rest of the team – the whites – had done the best job they could given the situation, i.e., the manager they had to put up with. These black men were playing under the most punishing and debilitating scrutiny, and also with the full knowledge that a section of England's support would rather a team with so many black players didn't qualify for the World Cup.

Taylor's successor, Terry Venables, evoked the good old Hovis-advert days of cobbled streets and cutie-pie white kids taking the freshly baked loaf back to mum in their all-white neighbourhood. (Apparently these bread ads were filmed around the corner from Ewood Park.) Venables actually fielded all-white England teams in internationals. For most of his time in charge of the national squad, the three most expensive and talented strikers in the country, Collymore, Ferdinand and Cole, were mixed-race and black, and born and bred in England. Venables was 'watching', 'progress-following' and 'monitoring' them.

To be monitored until they collect their pensions? Les Ferdinand was at the height of his powers at 28 years old when he was bought by Newcastle as a replacement for the Manchester United-bound Andy Cole. But apart from a brief appearance as a substitute for Alan Shearer, he hadn't had an England call-up for nearly two years. He was so despondent he believed his international days were over.

When he eventually got a call-up for the squad in October 1995, Newcastle's deputy manager Terry McDermott was forced to say: 'It would have been an injustice if he had not been included. There's no way that a manager from Brazil, Argentina, or wherever, could ignore a player of his calibre.' He didn't play. He was called up for the Euro '96 squad by Venables. Again, this remarkably gifted striker didn't play in a single match.

The England coach's first sporting memory was going with his dad to watch West Ham play Doncaster Rovers at Upton Park when he was very small. 'Charlie Williams,' Venables told the *Daily Telegraph* in 1994, was 'one of the very few black players around at the time, [he] was at centre-half for

Doncaster. He was a good player and a character. Many years later I saw he'd become one of The Comedians [the stand-up comedy show].'

Venables, who collected two England caps under Alf Ramsey during his playing days in the 1960s, is on record as saying: 'If you want to win major Championships, you must have players who feel strongly about their country. If I feel playing for England is secondary to some players, they will become secondary to me ... The 1966 World Cup winners had a lot of patriotic people in the team. People love their country in different ways. Alan Ball kept saying it and you knew he meant it. Bobby Moore and Bobby Charlton typified another spirit, another Englishness.'

In that interview with the *Sun* in 1994, Venables said he could still remember very clearly how wonderful it felt the day he was picked for England: 'I was in my car and the news came over the radio. I drove straight to my mum's café. I don't know if she had heard, but she knew within a second of me getting through the door. That call-up meant everything. It was why you played in the park, and all the hard work throughout your career was justified.'

Fed up with rejection after rejection by Venables, Cole had thrown a major wobbly in October 1994 after being excluded from the squad to face Romania at Wembley. The following exchanges were covered by virtually every newspaper. Venables said Keegan, Cole's Newcastle manager, had influenced his decision. 'I had a conversation with Kevin last week about several of his players and I was told that Cole wasn't 100 per cent fit for this level of competition, and that renders all other considerations irrelevant. If he's going to be considered and judged, he's got to be fit. I should be able to take the word of his manager about whether he's fit or not. I'm looking at him as well as a lot of other players very closely, and only their form and fitness will alter my judgements. He's done very well, there's no doubt about that, but he has looked restricted in his last couple of matches.'

Cole was fuming. The *Independent* reported him as saying: 'I have done as much as any centre-forward in the squad. I outscored them last season and this season I have scored 11 goals in 11 games. If Kevin Keegan tells me tomorrow he has pulled me out that is fair enough, but he has said nothing to me yet and I don't think he would have done so without telling me. That's not his style. This is the fourth time I have been left out, but the first time it has got to me. I'm gutted. I don't think shin splits is the reason for it. I have played every game this season and though I am only 80 per cent fit, I do not think it is showing. Why am I not in? Your guess is as good as mine.'

Keegan replied: 'Cole isn't fit to play for England. It's simple – the lad can't train because of his shin injury and that means he couldn't do himself justice with England.'

A month before the bust-up, the *Sun* said that Venables had to deny that he had been put off Cole by talk of his relationship with George Graham when the striker was at Arsenal. The teenager hadn't got along with the strict disciplinarian, nicknamed the Ayatollah by the squad. 'It's not true that George has said anything to me about Andy Cole,' Venables said. 'People suggest I'm saying one thing publicly and another thing privately about Cole – but that's also not true. I don't talk to many people about players – I keep most things to myself. I wouldn't mislead anyone on this subject.'

In the black newspaper, the *Voice*, Ron Shillingford wrote: 'Venables has included the out-of-form Tottenham pair Darren Anderton and Teddy Sheringham in the squad, which indicates that he is showing favouritism to players he used to manage. That bias was exhibited again a month ago when Venables invited the injured Paul Gascoigne to accompany the England squad preparing for the match against the United States. The Lazio midfielder is still recovering from a broken leg and will not play again until next year. The invite was supposed to give the injured Gascoigne "a lift".

'There has always been suspicion of a black quota system operating in the England squad. Cole's exclusion raises that suspicion again. At the time of going to press, he has not even been invited to attend the squad session, though he desperately needs "a lift" too. There was a question mark over his fitness because he has been suffering from shin splits, but Venables could still have picked him for the experience of being in the squad.'

Would Cole's inclusion have meant that the 'quota' was over-subscribed? That October 1994 squad already included Ince, Barnes, Ferdinand and Wright. By Euro '96 Barnes was out, Wright was out, Ferdinand was out in that he never played; Ince was back in after a year out of favour.

In March 1995, with Alan Shearer injured, Venables had to look at other strikers. Apart from Chris Sutton and Matthew Le Tissier, the contenders were all black. But Les Ferdinand was unfit, and Venables apparently didn't fancy Stan Collymore or Ian Wright. The England coach, looking at his sheet for the friendly against Uruguay, had to call for Cole.

The papers reported Cole's excitement. 'I got a call from England [!] on my mobile phone when I was out driving with my girlfriend, and that was that. I was shocked but thrilled to be called up. I didn't expect that to happen until next season. It has been an incredible few months for me, but I don't expect to be in the team.'

England's most expensive footballer at the time couldn't believe he'd made it after such a long wait. It was the call every player hopes and dreams of during his career. But with people like Malcolm Allison advising Venables, Cole still had something to overcome. Allison was the man who checked out strikers for the England coach. Here he is on Cole: 'Ferguson [the Manchester United manager] has just bought £7.5 million worth of problems. I've watched Cole many, many times, analysed his game, done a count on him, and the facts all add up to the same conclusion. When he's not scoring, he's doing nothing. You're playing with ten men . . . It got ridiculous. He would do nothing, then score and the whole stadium [St James' Park] was chanting his name. He did score some great goals, too, but the team was doing all the graft, not him.'

Andy Cole had scored 68 goals in 84 matches for Newcastle United: a club record. He'd also won the Golden Boot for his 41 goals in the '93–94 season. Most managers and football officials would be delighted with a striker who scored so many goals, but not, apparently, if his name's Cole. In that instance it seems you have to run around the pitch like a headless chicken, work your butt off in training, collapse from exhaustion, and have a demeanour so gentle that Mother Theresa would puke.

Would Cole be called up more if he'd been more creative on the field but hardly scored? No – as was revealed when he hit a dry spell at Manchester United. His detractors couldn't wait to say that Cole needed to put some more away before he had enough class to play for England, that he would have to become a more consistent goalscorer. It was as if his £7 million price tag, instead of conferring respect, merely brought out the vitriol in his critics.

His first England call-up in March 1995 – two months after his chart-topping sale to Manchester United – meant that Cole was forced to attend a press conference. 'Yesterday, as he faced more than a dozen journalists,' the *Independent*'s Glenn Moore noted, 'there was a wary look in his eyes and an arms-folded, lean-back defensiveness about his posture.' What a surprise; I wonder how those white journalists would have felt if they were on their own in a room filled with their black critics. The *Guardian*'s David Lacey commented on 'his rather odd mixture of bravado and humility, sometimes in the same answer. For example: "You can say that I've got a lot to prove, but I've got a lot to learn as well. That's what it's all about, learning. The team I'm playing for now will make me a better player. I'm proving that now."'

'When I went to Manchester United,' a frustrated Cole said in the *Telegraph* in 1995, 'every paper said Andy Cole was not worth two bob, never mind £7 million. People must remember that Andy Cole didn't set the fee. The fee was set between Alex Ferguson and Kevin Keegan. If Kevin Keegan thought I was worth £6 or £7 million, it's entirely up to him. People say I only score goals, but I have been getting involved in all-round team play. I always knew I could do it, now I am starting to prove it. The manager wants me involved in all-round play; at Newcastle, Kevin Keegan just wanted me to score goals. But I know I will still be judged as a goalscorer. I will miss chances, I am entitled to, but scoring goals is what I do best. I want to keep scoring goals and keep playing well. I want to be the best in the country.'

Allison had also dismissed Ian Wright for scoring 'goals galore' for Arsenal 'but, strangely, not for England'. When Alan Shearer failed to score in several internationals for England – for nearly a year – but continued to score for Blackburn, not so many people regarded this as 'strange'. They waited patiently for the return of his form however long that would take.

With black players already characterized as difficult, temperamental, unpredictable and risky to have, Ian Wright, who is a human being who happens to have a short-fuse personality, found a multitude of critics willing to question his patriotism and commitment under the guise of footballing criticism. They couldn't use the place-of-birth code question though, because Wright was born in England. So out came the England-shirt code.

The speculation increased in September 1993, as we neared

the climax of the World Cup qualifiers. Mihir Bose, writing in the *Sunday Times* about England's 3–0 win over Poland, claimed, '. . . there must be a worry about Ferdinand's striking partner. Wright, having started the night as the senior man whose place in the side was unquestioned – interestingly, he did not emerge for the pre-match kick-around – left Wembley looking a bit like football's equivalent of Graeme Hick. We know he can play, but can he play when he pulls on an England shirt?'

In a match report on an Arsenal–Ipswich game in which Kevin Campbell scored a hat-trick, journalist Martin Searby commented: 'We have had Ian Wright, the single, the CD, the video, but so far he has failed by some margin to be anything like a hit in an England shirt. He is so gifted, it is a mystery. Perhaps, like Campbell here, he merely needs an easy goal to get him going.'

These pieces seem to echo the old chestnut about whether black players have difficulties playing for England.

'If he can do it for Arsenal, why can't he do it for England?' cried Chris Lightbown in a *Sunday Times* article sub-titled: ON THE ENIGMA WHO HAS TROUBLE SCORING FOR HIS COUNTRY. 'What hums for Arsenal, stutters for England,' Lightbown wrote. 'Wright has scored 61 goals in 86 games for Arsenal, but only one goal in 13 games for England . . . But not only has Wright failed to score goals for England, he has not come close, suffered bad luck or even looked like scoring on most of his international appearances. What is the problem and can it be solved by Wednesday [the day of the England–Poland game]?

Lightbown answered his own question: 'The problem is that the better Wright plays for Arsenal, the less likely he is to score for England. On a technical level, this is quite straightforward. Arsenal's system usually means their forwards have plenty of space to run into when they attack, a perfect formula for Wright, whose speed and positioning sense take him towards international class. But England tend to attack at a slower rate, which means opponents' penalty areas are crowded by the time he reaches them. Too many bodies in the way blunts his rapier thrusts.

'Then there is the matter of temperament. Arsenal tolerate Wright's outbursts because they believe the fire stoking such behaviour sparks goals like that against Everton. Douse the fire and you subdue the talent, runs Arsenal's thinking. But things don't work that way for England. This is partly because the full panoply of the FA and national expectations falls on the shoulders of England players, but also because England place a premium on predictability. With less time to get to know each other's styles, England players need to be sure of colleagues' ways. A weakness such as, for instance, Stuart Pearce's slowness in getting back to defend after his forward runs can be accommodated if it is understood.

'But Wright's weaknesses are unknown, which is the key reason for the dichotomy between his club and country performances. Precisely because he can score unpredictable virtuoso goals, Wright remains somewhat unpredictable, even to players working alongside him every week. Organizing his sparks would douse his fire, which would subdue his talent.'

As Wright pointed out in *Today*, two years after England failed to qualify: 'I've never played in an England system that would benefit me. I've had to come back and work in areas that I don't have to for Arsenal. Of the 11 games I've started, look at how it's gone. It hasn't been beneficial to the way I play – they don't knock the ball over the top where I go. It's very frustrating.

'You want to do well when you play for England, but after a while I thought, They're not using me to my best potential here. Then people ask me how come I don't score goals for England like I do for Arsenal? It's not for lack of trying. There are players who have played for England who I know are not as good as me. But it's all about luck and when you get your chance. You can't turn England down. If they want you to play in a more defensive role, you can't say, "I'm not going to do that."'

Do England managers and their aides, in their discussions about black players, worry about that mysterious virus that I'm going to call white shirt/black skin, or WSBS? Did they, and do they still, think a black footballer will just stop scoring goals once he pulls on a white shirt?

There may have been no racism or quota system in the team selection process and there are many perfectly reasonable criteria which have to be fulfilled. Nevertheless, the perception of many black writers and football fans was that a racial motive, whether actual or subconscious, played a part in selecting the line-up.

When he finally got into the squad, Venables' conversion to the Cole cause was a wonder to behold. 'I'm delighted to have Andy Cole with us, to see him at the highest level for the first time.' Next, he likened him to that saint, Gary Lineker; and then he said: 'At Newcastle, he [Cole] *was asked to play in a certain way* [my italics], spearheading the attack and getting into the six-yard box, with people like Robert Lee and Peter Beardsley left to do the job around him. He is now playing in a bigger area with United, moving wide and dropping back. His link-play has been a lot better. There are similarities between Andy and Gary. In the end, *Gary learned* [my italics] to work back and come deeper, take the ball back into the box and score. If someone is not scoring goals, he has to do something else and Andy is well capable of that.'

Golly gosh, a 23-year-old was going to be given the chance to learn new tricks after being asked to play a certain way. A certain way which continued for a long time because it was extremely successful. He was going to be given the chance to fine-tune his abilities and develop new ones. He was at last going

47

to get the fair play that any white young male with his talent would have got automatically.

At a Bisham Abbey news conference Cole said he'd dreamed of an England call-up since he was 10 years old: 'I've always felt it was my destiny to play for my country. I think I've proved I'm good enough. I had a tough time when I was younger but I've kept plugging away.'

At the Uruguay game, first Nick Barmby – one of Venables' former Tottenham boys – came on for Peter Beardsley and made his England debut, and then in the 71st minute Cole was called on to replace Sheringham, and got his first cap. The *Guardian*'s David Lacey reported: 'For Cole the setting could not have been better. Called late into the squad after the injured Alan Shearer's withdrawal, he now had the opportunity to impress on Venables his potential as an England matchwinner. Two chances fell his way. He missed them both, and although Wembley roared its sympathy as his header rebounded from the crossbar, at this level that counted as profligacy.' Tut, tut, typical. Cole had had a massive 19 minutes 'at this level' and already he'd been labelled profligate. No assessment was made of Barmby's contribution to the match – maybe it was felt that as he'd only spent 25 minutes in the game, it wasn't long enough to start judging, labelling him.

Here is David Lacey on the 0–0 England–Colombia match in September 1995: 'Alan Shearer has now gone a year without scoring for England but, the way he played last night, more goals should not be far distant. He hit the bar and the intelligence with which he used his speed and strength to disturb the opposing centre-backs confirmed him as England's best central striker.' Shearer played a full 90 minutes and hit the bar – but it was clearly the bar's fault that he missed. Cole's 19 minutes was all he got under Venables.

There's only a year between Andy Cole and Alan Shearer, but the way the two highly skilled strikers are regarded couldn't be further apart. Why have a Delroy when you've got the real Roy of the Rovers? All the players competing for places knew that Shearer's was the first name on the England manager's list when the squad and first eleven were being drawn up.

According to Patrick Barclay, writing in the *Observer*: 'Certainly he [Cole] bears little comparison with the remarkable Shearer who, though only a year his senior at 24, has the full range of a centre-forward's skills, including the ability to hold the ball and build play. If Venables wants to keep intact the system for which he has shown a preference, using just one full-time front runner, with midfielders supporting, the argument for a fit Sheringham is strong. But that option may not be available and Cole could find himself back in partnership with Beardsley against Uruguay, the last visiting country to win at Wembley.'

For the country's black strikers, Shearer is the man whom they all have to compete against. For a long time it appeared that, for the newspapers, they couldn't play with him; but neither could they dislodge him in favour of themselves. Shearer and Ferdinand were played together by Venables when Ferdinand was finally given a game because of injuries sustained by Teddy Sheringham. But it apparently didn't work out during their one game together for England as strikers. Andy Cole is also apparently considered to be incompatible with Shearer upfront for England. And so was Ian Wright.

Contrast the position at club level. In his one year in the No.9 shirt at Newcastle, Ferdinand established himself as a formidable centre-forward – he scored 15 goals in the first 14 games alone; and a hat-trick in October 1995 equalled a post-war eight consecutive scoring games for the club. By the end of that season, Ferdinand had scored 25 League goals and 4 in the Cup. When Shearer joined Newcastle in August 1996, Kevin Keagan was enthusiastic about the potential for playing him and Ferdinand together: 'I think they will make a terrific strike-force. I think they can take each other to the places they dream about going.' But the *Times* reporter, Peter Ball, noted: 'There is no doubt, however, who is going to be the senior partner. Despite his modesty, Shearer likes his own way and has already taken over the No.9 shirt, with its special place in Geordie folklore. "I would play in any number shirt for Newcastle United, but the No.9 at Newcastle is something very special and I've always wanted to wear it," he said. "I've mentioned it to the manager, he mentioned it to Les and Les has been very kind and given it to me."' As he'd been doing it justice for a year, the shirt must also have been very special to Ferdinand. By early May 1997, in their first season together, Ferdinand's League and Cup goal tally was only 18 (13 League); Shearer's was 27 (24 League) making the two strikers the best partnership in England using League goals as the benchmark. But Shearer partnered by Sheringham (when fit) is still preferred internationally. As Jonathan Pearce wrote in the *Daily Mirror* in December 1995: 'Ferdinand has blistering pace, he's deadly in the air, slick and quick on the ground and makes direct runs into areas where he can receive service. But against top quality Continental defences, those areas are few and far between. Alan Shearer has a little more guile when he drops deeper and will conjure goals for himself. Both need Teddy Sheringham to play off. He brings others into the game magnificently and the Sheringham–Shearer partnership looks most likely to succeed.'

As far as England fans and the English media are concerned, Alan Shearer is the football King of Kings, Lord of Lords, and conquering Lion of England. This young man, who hit them in game after game for all-white Blackburn Rovers before his world-record £15 million move to Newcastle, can do no wrong, even when he's not scoring.

Alan Shearer is supreme because he touches raw emotions in

white English fans. Emotional memories of a lost England. An article in the *Guardian* daydreamed: 'When describing Alan Shearer it is tempting to give life to the dead language of football appreciation . . . But other terms spring to mind, each redolent of some half-imagined yesteryear when hair was short, showers were cold and plain folk were poor but honest, wanting nothing more from life than a daily slice of Hovis and good sing on a grimy terrace on a Saturday afternoon . . . [Shearer] resembles the very model of the classic working-class sporting hero and suits the language to match: still only 24, Shearer is "upright", "clean-limbed", "well-made"; everything legend demands an English centre-forward should be.'

Michael Parkinson reminisced in the *Daily Telegraph*: 'When I tell Shearer that he reminds me of the heroes of my youth – Nat Lofthouse, Wally Ardron, George Robledo – he understands the compliment. He wears the No.9 on his back like they did; he is built to the same specification. He has strong legs, a big backside, wide hips. His boss, Kenny Dalglish, was made the same way, and he could play a bit. He doesn't mind sticking his head in where it might get kicked.'

If it wasn't for Paul Ince, an East End boy like Venables, the line-ups in all the England Euro '96 games would have been all-white. As mentioned, Les Ferdinand was part of the squad at Bisham Abbey training camp but was not in the team. Here was a man who had been voted the Players' Player of the Year. The *Mail on Sunday*, calling him 'the surprise winner', said: 'Ferdinand's triumph, ahead of David Ginola and Peter Beardsley, plus Fowler, Shearer and Nottingham Forest's Steve Stone [all white] from a six-man shortlist, has to be considered one of the biggest shocks in the 23 years of the PFA award.'

Not as big as the shocks coming Ferdinand's way in the three months following that award (given partly for his blistering goalscoring form with Newcastle). Just a few days after the ceremony in March 1996, he found that Venables was placing him fourth in line for a place as the premier striker against Bulgaria at Wembley. Alan Shearer, Teddy Sheringham and Robbie Fowler 'are all favoured ahead of Ferdinand by coach Terry Venables as the build-up begins to the European Championships,' wrote the *Mail on Sunday*. And we all know what position Venables gave Ferdinand that June. And very comfortable it was too.

Even though he hadn't scored in his previous ten England games by the time of the March '96 Bulgaria game, Shearer was still Venables' number one. He even made excuses for him. 'When he is given the right service, Shearer will finish it off. [Oh, so it was the rest of the team's fault.] His failure to score has genuinely not concerned me,' said the England coach in the *Mail on Sunday*. He was sticking to his 'Christmas tree' single-striker formation (a lone striker supported by players breaking forward from midfield) and that striker was Alan Shearer.

A few months earlier, the *Daily Telegraph*'s Henry Winter had written: 'Assuming Venables ignores the two-predator lobby, which would be a great pity, then Ferdinand is not expected to displace Alan Shearer, despite the Blackburn man's recent absence of international goals. Shearer's barren spell reflects more on the system than any tailing off of his acknowledged capabilities, which have sustained his club through recent travails.' If only Ian Wright, who was hammered for not scoring for England as he did for Arsenal, had had equally considerate responses.

Britain's blacks were furious about the way Ferdinand was being treated. If proof were needed that even superlative talent doesn't get you anywhere – that there must be hidden agendas at work – here it was. What more did Ferdinand have to do? Bleach his skin?

In the quarter-finals of Euro '96, when England played Spain, Venables fielded yet another all-white team. The only black who got on the pitch was the child mascot led out by the captain, Tony Adams, before the game. (Paul Ince was sitting out a one-game ban; David Platt had replaced him.) The little black mascot got a pat on the head before running off the pitch.

Outraged English blacks felt they'd been hit on the head with a hammer. Already uncomfortable with the notion of supporting an England which doesn't support their presence and their right to work here, many told the *Voice* black newspaper that they had cheered Germany in the Euro '96 semi-final. If it were truly a level playing field, then there would always be several black players on Wembley's green and pleasant turf. Sporting ability is colour blind, and it hurts when this is prevented from being shown. Better to cheer the all-white German team than a team which is a good representation of a country of racial hypocrites.

Why were we so shocked and dismayed? We knew an all-white national team was on the cards, because it had happened before in spite of a plethora of black talent. The first time was against Colombia at Wembley in September 1995. (Seaman; Neville, Adams, Howey, Le Saux; Wise, Redknapp, Gascoigne, McManaman; Barmby, Shearer.) None of the 'new youngsters', the 'Tel's Tots' – Nick Barmby, Jamie Redknapp, Steve Howey, Gary Neville, Steve McManaman – were black. I wondered as I watched the game on television that cold, wet and thoroughly depressing Wednesday night, what the England coach's decisions signalled to all the black football youngsters, potential England tots, out there – let alone the nation's top three signings: Collymore, Cole and Ferdinand. Collymore and Coventry's John Salako had been included in the squad, but when Collymore pulled out because of an ankle problem, Ferdinand was snubbed again by not being called up. Salako wasn't used. The only team with black faces was the Colombian's – until Barnes replaced Redknapp in the 75th minute.

Even Paul Ince had been told not to bother jumping on a plane from Rome. The *Daily Mirror* reflected: 'Paul Ince: he has developed in five years from bit-part player to one of Europe's most dynamic midfield talents. Don't worry about his absence tonight – that's Terry's rap over the knuckles for skipping the Umbro Cup. Ince is Mr Indispensible [sic] and is like three players in one. Never mind ball-winners, passers and runners – Ince is all three. Add the explosive long-range shooting, and he's the ultimate example of the all-purpose modern player.' But within three months they'd got used to not seeing Ince playing for England, and in a December 1995 'Man-by-Man Guide To England's Euro '96 Campaign' Ince was left out altogether. (In the same guide Ferdinand was described as: 'A straight replacement for Shearer and will only play if Shearer doesn't. Strong in the air and a very direct player – *a great substitute to have* [my italics].')

Ince had skipped the Umbro cup in June because Venables had earlier dropped him from an international shortly after the player's court appearance on assault charges connected to the Cantona affair. Ince felt he could have done with the public show of support which playing him would have illustrated. Venables spent a year being annoyed that the midfielder had dared to show his annoyance with him.

Venables went on to field an all-white team in Oslo the next month. (Seaman; Neville, Adams, Pallister, Pearce; Wise, Redknapp, Lee, McManaman; Barmby, Shearer.) This time, even the subs were white: Stone and Sheringham. And even the *Sun* was forced to dub the 0–0 result WE DID IT SNOREWAY, to note, 'in the second half England mustered not one shot on target. Not from Alan Shearer, from Teddy Sheringham [or] from four of the brightest midfield players in the Premiership,' and to ask, 'Would it have been different had Les Ferdinand been allowed to do more than just make up the number at training yesterday? We shall never know,' the paper concluded. 'But what is certainly true is that Venables made a rod for his back the minute he refused to even name the Premiership's leading goalscorer as one of his five substitutes.' In November, we had another all-white performance against Switzerland (Seaman; Neville, Adams, Pallister, Pearce; Lee, Redknapp, Gascoigne, McManaman; Sheringham, Shearer). Steve Stone, on as an early substitute for Jamie Redknapp, engineered the 3–1 victory.

All white on the night in September . . . October . . . November . . . and then for the whole world to see in June '96.

One or two white writers have said in public what many whites believe in private, namely that if you have a team entirely composed of white English, then these people will play with a blazing determination; a gut-fuelled innate patriotism, not an acquired one. A patriotism which is in the blood. Any black English in this set-up would only be driven by an individual ambition to further his own career, and at best could destabilize the team, affect its spirit; at worst the black English could be the enemy within, subconsciously working against the interests of the team and rooting for the other side.

Even a black English player born here couldn't be fully trusted because, the argument went, he would suffer from conflict between loyalty to his country of birth, and to his race and culture. Therefore for an England team to win, there would have to be a racial and cultural basis to team selections. Basically, a candidate would have to be white. National qualification (just a passport) would not be sufficient to guarantee instinctive patriotism and a visceral commitment.

Robert Henderson's infamous July 1995 article in *Wisden Cricket Monthly* on racism and national identity in cricket quoted journalist Matthew Engel: ' "It cannot be irrelevant to England's long-term failures that so many of their recent Test players were either born overseas and/or spent their formative years as citizens of other countries. In the heat of Test cricket, there is a difference between a cohesive team with a common goal, and a coalition of individuals whose major ambitions are for themselves . . . There is a vast difference between wanting to play Test cricket and wanting to play for England."' For cricket read the other national sporting activities (football, athletics) that contain qualified blacks. People did.

And Henderson had an even more pressing enquiry: 'What of those players raised solely or largely in England? Well, liberals tell us this should not matter one whit. An Asian or negro raised in England will, according to the liberal, feel exactly the same pride and identification with the place as a white man. The reality is somewhat different. It is an entirely natural thing to wish to retain one's racial/cultural identity. Moreover, the energetic public promotion of "multiculturalism" in England has actively encouraged such expressions of independence. However, with such an attitude, and whatever his professional pride as a cricketer, it is difficult to believe that a foreign-born has any sense of wanting to play above himself simply because he is playing for England. From what, after all, could such a feeling derive? Norman Tebbit's cricket test is as pertinent for players as it is for spectators. It is even possible that part of a coloured England-qualified player feels satisfaction (perhaps subconsciously) at seeing England humiliated, because of post-imperial myths of oppression and exploitation. An article in the August 1991 WCM entitled "England's Caribbean Heritage", by Clayton Goodwin, a white English journalist with particularly pronounced Caribbean sympathies, lends credence to such a view. Mr Goodwin argues that children born in this country of West Indian parents do not feel part of English society and, consequently, tend to identify only with sporting heroes who share their own physical race. Significantly, no white or Asian sporting figure supported by this group is mentioned in the article, although many negroes are. A few quotes will give the flavour: "Naturally, those West Indians who came here as immigrants have a nostalgic respect for their 'home' region – longing for the lost 'good old days' is not solely the white man's preserve. Their children, humiliated and made to feel inferior in every aspect of their day-to-day life, will relish the chance of using the success of others sharing the same physical attribute [blackness] for which they are downgraded to show, however vicariously, that they do have worth. You can't blame the put-upon black people of Britain for feeling similar justifiable pride when Viv Richards and his team, who in other circumstances might be regarded as 'second-class citizens' like themselves, have put one over on the heroes of their detractors."'

My concern in all of this is for the black player. Being born in England hasn't lessened the racially motivated slights and attacks on England-capped Les Ferdinand, Ian Wright, Andy Cole, Stan Collymore and Paul Ince. The people who pose the 'Who do you support, where do your loyalties lie?' questions with respect to team sports are talking about skin colour, pure and simple, not nationality. The subtext is: we cannot rely on you, you will let down the side; you may even betray us.

England football managers have a responsibility to ensure that black England fans do not suspect that on-form black England players have been left out of the line-up because of doubts surrounding commitment, patriotism, instinctive loyalty and passion for their country. Black England certainly mustn't be left thinking that black players have been left out because they are black.

In January 1996, Richard Williams, writing in the *Guardian* about Venables' decision to quit, speculated about the reasons a Venables-must-stay campaign wasn't started. 'The first, and most delicate, was his apparent reluctance to allow the national team to reflect the ethnic balance of most English League clubs in the mid-nineties. Most Premiership teams now take the field with two, three, four, five or even six black players. Yet since he dropped Paul Ince, who left Manchester United for Italy in the summer and has since failed to reproduce his best form, no black player has been an established member of Venables' team. Almost twenty years since Viv Anderson became the first black to wear the England shirt, Venables' refusal to give wholehearted backing to the talents of players such as Les Ferdinand, Andy Cole and Stan Collymore has seemed to constitute a retrograde step, perhaps the result of age breeding a mistrust of mercurial flair and a disinclination to deal with difficult temperaments when honest, uncomplaining journeymen are readily available.'

We're always difficult, aren't we? Also, it would be nice to think that the absence of black players from Venables' line-ups was a major reason for the sports world being unmoved about his departure, but I think not. As a general comment, when white support (or white wellbeing) is thought to be at stake, black interests get ditched fast. No contest. No principles. No honour. If people had wanted Venables to stay, any perception that he may have been reluctant to use black players wouldn't have entered into their calculations.

'New Labour', 'new era', 'new beginning' was the message the party trumpeted during the 1997 General Election campaign. However, it seems that for New Labour that meant avoiding the fact that important issues they talked about – unemployment, education – affected Britain's black communities disproportionately. They didn't mention that. They didn't take a stand about what they intended to do about the terrible inequalities in these areas because they were worried that that might scare off the white natives. Why didn't they think that in their 'new era' people might want to do something about blighted and destroyed black lives? They didn't want to take the risk. But how big a risk would it have been? They had had a massive lead in the polls for months on end and eventually got a landslide. No, funnily enough, when it came to black issues they suddenly didn't want to ask people to change their attitudes for the better. 'Time for a change' didn't seem to apply to how British society viewed and treated black lives. Indeed, the party descended to usage of the bulldog in one of its election broadcasts – an image blacks associate with racists.

And in our new Britain we still have an FA which has failed to take action when white players racially abuse black ones. Upset black feelings and oppressed black lives don't seem to count for much in our new era.

England expects. But what, exactly, does England expect of those with black skins wearing its national colours? The answer is England expects more, much more, than it would even dare to hope for from one of its white players. And this extraordinary double standard permeates not just the football Establishment, but also the watching England fans – the white ones.

As a black spectator, you cannot avoid hearing the unspoken message to the black players from the white hooligan element: 'We've had to let you into this hallowed team, and you're out there now, but if you fuck up, you bet your life we'll let you know about it.' They don't have to fuck up to be told about it. They don't have to fuck up more than once to suffer the equivalent of a lynching.

The white hooligan is the embodiment of the traditional racist, an Old Racist, if you like. We all know what they are capable of – we've seen it many times – and that such behaviour and beliefs are despicable; we can all say that and it's acceptable that they are unacceptable. However, you don't have to be a hooligan to be a New Racist. A New Racist would no more think of calling Barnes or Ince or Wright a nigger than to call his own mother that. But in newspaper articles, remarks made by television reporters and commentators, and the sniping and blaming away expressed by fans at the end of a game, there will be a nasty imbalance in the attention, criticism and treatment which is directed at black players. This can be just as damaging psychologically as being called a nigger.

The New Racism also allows people to let themselves off the hook by blaming many examples of racial woes, divisions and inequalities on 'institutional racism'. But there is no such thing. I've always been perfectly happy in a government building, in a large corporation, in a private members' club, in a hospital, until the prejudices and discriminatory practices and comments of a white person become focused on my presence. People practice racism, not bricks and mortar. Institutionalized racism means lots and lots of *individuals* allowing their prejudices to get the better of them. Uriah Rennie, the Football League's only black referee, told the *Observer* in February 1995 how he'd: ". . . been locked out of grounds because they don't think I'm the referee; and I've been directed to the players' changing rooms rather than the officials' room. Obviously it is because I don't fit the image in terms of age and colour. It is comical really, but it brightens the day.'

Black players have that most inhuman of all tasks facing sports people: to perform at the most punishing level of excellence each and every time they appear on a pitch. They must not fail, they must not underperform, indeed, they do not have the right to such demonstrations of their humanity – that's for everybody else. But it is precisely this extraordinary pressure on black players in England teams which makes them underachieve: this constant, unrelenting, debilitating pressure under which no human could be expected to perform to his or her best.

For John Barnes, the verbal lynching went on for season after season, international after international. The fact that he could still tie the laces on his boots and pull on that white shirt in the face of it all was a testimony to the man's incredible fortitude, dignity and unshakeable self-discipline.

'Underperformance', 'underachievement', 'Brazil', 'Brazil', 'Brazil', is typed in endless columns and reports about how Barnes wasn't up to scratch during this match or that game. The virulent racism he faces from the chanting white England fans is often dismissed as 'booing'; the racists described as 'boo boys'. Much of what is written about Barnes is racism in code.

John Barnes, with 79 appearances, is England's most capped black player. And the most punished for that honour. He has fine-chiselled features, and speaks in a clipped, rapid-fire delivery. John Barnes is many things: serene, confident, strong, highly intelligent, extremely rich and hugely talented. But John Barnes isn't English. He wasn't born in England, his parents weren't born here, his grandparents weren't born here. John Barnes is Jamaican. He was 13 when he came to this country from Jamaica, where his relatives still live, and which he visits nearly every summer. John Barnes is a Jamaican who is married to an English woman, and they have half-English, half-Jamaican children. Where does John Barnes feel he belongs? Where do his loyalties lie? Jamaica versus England: who would he support?

The sports media and many white English fans don't think he puts his heart and soul into internationals. And these attackers believe that because he spent his 'formative' years in Jamaica he has problems when he puts on a shirt with the three lions on.

Barnes distinguished himself in English club football for Watford and Liverpool, but his detractors say something happens to him when he puts on an England shirt. It's almost witchcraft, he loses his abilities. He's under a spell, he can't play. He's too laid-back. How can a Jamaican pour his heart and soul, not just his technical prowess, into an England shirt? That bulldog spirit is only really present in real Englishmen – white Englishmen, that is. The guts, tenacity and sheer determination that most black players have doesn't seem to count. The fact that many white England players' commitment can be called into doubt is rarely mentioned.

An individual black player's commitment and character doesn't seem to count because the general perception of black people in the minds of those who control football today is still entangled with ways of thinking about Africa and the Caribbean, which were formed during colonialism. Now, we may be in Europe, we may be playing more countries than ever before in international contests, but black players are still having to combat an insular, conservative Football Association over-endowed with a negative historical legacy of the abilities of black people and the capabilities of black nations. So even today, a black player may still be considered lightweight however passionate and committed a performer he is.

Barnes' problems began with the brilliant England goal he scored against Brazil in Rio in 1984. From that moment onwards he was expected to reproduce that dazzling performance on a regular basis. Barnes, unlike other squad members, was not going to be allowed off-days, sustained injuries or weight problems.

And more often than not, whenever he didn't come up to scratch, he was no longer John Barnes, England player, but John Barnes, Jamaican-born. As Linford Christie (who also came to England as a youngster from Jamaica) recalled: 'As a winner, I'm from Great Britain. If I'm beaten, I'm an athlete who runs for Great Britain. When I lose, sometimes I'm known as a "native of Jamaica".'

But Barnes never scored another goal like the one in Rio. And for that he was to be damned.

The attacks on Barnes reminded me of those on so many black professionals I know, and of my own experiences. Black professionals are expected to perform outstandingly on a daily basis without showing any human frailties. In a sense, to justify and prove ourselves on a daily basis; whilst excuse are made for underperforming or less talented white colleagues, and their mistakes understood and dismissed.

Voice newspaper columnist, Tony Sewell, doesn't understand, either, why we put ourselves through this torture. 'I have always found it disturbing when black people say they have got to be twice as good as their white counterparts to get a job. This makes going to work more akin to a court case where you are constantly trying to disprove your guilt. This must take many black pros to the brink of a mental breakdown. The idea of having to prove your "professionalism" has always been an issue ever since black people wanted to do more than be British Rail ticket inspectors.'

After a working life spent mostly in the company of white people, I now realize that real equality in Britain will have arrived only when black people have the privilege of obtaining and keeping a job when they are as ordinary – even as mediocre – as the numerous white people they will often be forced to share their working lives with.

Even the one or two commentators who said they knew they expected too much from Barnes couldn't get over their unease with him for making them feel that way. John Barnes was the focus of their criticism for everything wrong with the England game in the late eighties and early nineties. He was the man they had stuck on top of the bonfire. 'John Barnes?' wrote Jimmy Greaves, TV pundit, former player and writer. 'He is associated with the bad old days when the same old team played the same old way and brought back plenty of nothing from every tournament they visited.'

White England players have had less serious injuries than Barnes' injuries which dogged him over consecutive seasons, affecting his workrate, fitness and form badly. But whilst Barnes was being attacked for getting fat and not being able to run a 100 yards in under 10 seconds, white players like Paul Gascoigne got tea and national sympathy when they were laid off, or, like Alan Shearer, when they hit a bad patch.

What made matters worse was that when Barnes was playing according to their superhuman standards, he was wearing Liverpool's colours. Why did his skills seem to work for Liverpool, critics wanted to know, and not for England? Again, as with Ian Wright, Barnes explained, in Liverpool's club magazine, that it was like asking experienced players to be proficient in opposing types of play: 'I get asked that question every week. The comparison is best illustrated by taking Peter Beardsley and putting him in the Wimbledon team and expecting him to play as well as he does for Newcastle.

'At Newcastle, they play the ball to his feet and he uses it. At Wimbledon, the ball would be knocked over the top for him to chase.

'When I was playing for England I was expected to beat three or four players. If I didn't succeed, I probably wouldn't see the ball for five or ten minutes, and I felt I had to do better, even if it meant beating six players.'

Barnes said in the *Observer*: 'When you play for England, the opposition more often than not has the majority of possession, whereas when I played for Liverpool in the old days, we dominated teams so much I used to get the ball about 30 times in a match, and sometimes I took on the full-back and at other times I laid off. With England if you give the ball away, you know you're not going to get it back for a while. So I got myself into a bit of a situation where if I got it I wanted to do something really spectacular, and I would lose it. So the next time I would try something twice as spectacular, which is not the thing to do.'

'I want John to simply play on the left of midfield and give us a little passing and control,' said Graham Taylor in the *Evening Standard* in 1993, discussing his next match a few weeks after San Marino. 'His role is somewhat changed to what it was against

San Marino. But if they boo him again, he just has to play through it. He's not the sort to turn away from a challenge.'

Not that everyone thought he played well for Liverpool in the 1990s. Jimmy Greaves once began his *Sun* column: 'John Barnes walks into a paper shop in Liverpool. The newsagent's wife turns to her husband and says: "That's John Barnes." "No, it's not," he replies. But she insists. Finally he plucks up courage to enquire: "Are you John Barnes of Liverpool?" Barnesy says: "Yes." "So, do you know Ian Rush?" questions the newsagent. Barnes replies: "Of course I do. We're teammates. Why do you ask?" "I was just wondering," says the newsagent. "Has it ever occurred to you to pass to him?"'

Barnes had the last laugh, though. By 1997 he was the pass-master. His new midfield role made him king of ball distribution for Liverpool. Sky television analysed his passing for one game and it was nearly 100 per cent accurate. But his midfield success has been marred by his diminishing appearances in an England jersey.

In September 1994, after some tough running sessions on holiday in Jamaica and back at home in Cheshire, he got that call from Venables for an England friendly against the United States. He hadn't had an England call-up for well over a year.

'If I had got fit and lost my ability then my career would be over. But I knew my ability hadn't changed – I was still the same player as always. It was just a question of getting my fitness right to bring it back out. I never thought an England return was impossible, I never thought I was out of the frame for good. I always felt if I got it right, I would be knocking on the door after a couple of months. I'm surprised to be back so soon – but I'm not surprised to be back.'

The press were very unpleasantly surprised, however. Why had Venables telephoned somebody who in their eyes was a 30-year-old has-been who had 'let them down', had 'betrayed' them? Jimmy Greaves wrote: 'Say he plays next Wednesday and does well. What has it proved? A friendly? At home? Against America? Does this erase the 50 or more matches in which he has failed to impress?' And in a sideswipe at Venables for picking Barnes: 'The new broom was meant to sweep clean – not rearrange the dirt.'

The headlines could be summed up by one in the *Sun*: TERRY'S GONE ALL BARNESY BARMY! Venables wasn't really taking any chances anyway: 'What can I lose by picking him? It's not as if America can knock us out of the World Cup, is it? It's not the end of the world.'

For Barnes, though, the pressure was, yet again, inhuman. As he confessed to *Today* in September 1994: 'I couldn't believe how I felt. I was really nervous and I was in that sort of state from the moment I knew I was going to be playing.' But the nerves weren't shaking because of fear of the game – he'd already turned out for England more than 70 times. No, Barnes was petrified about the reaction of an English crowd at Wembley to his appearance in an England shirt. He is the only England player to ever be abused at home by England supporters. For the 'boo boys', Barnes' England career has become entwined with Graham Taylor's legacy. And for those whose hatred of Taylor is deep, Barnes represents all that they feel about the Taylor era.

In the end, Barnes did play well. 'I desperately wanted to do well this time . . . I knew I had to produce a performance, and I think I did. But more important, I showed I was fit to wear the shirt of my country.'

But the crowd didn't see fit to stop the abuse. Barnes, as ever, was diplomatic. He, like too many senior and therefore isolated blacks in white-dominated professions, tries to play down racist behaviour. 'If they [the fans] had crucified me, that would have been it. It would have been all over as far as England is concerned. You can't disguise being under that sort of pressure. It is strange making your 74th appearance and realizing you're still on trial.

'There was an awful lot of scepticism about me playing again, and I hope I have now answered that. A lot of it was unfair. It hurt, but it didn't surprise me. I have always judged myself on my contribution to attack – and against the Americans I was pleased with that.'

The lynch-crowd thought they'd burned him out after their hate campaign, which culminated in the first-class display of racism put on at Wembley in 1993 when England played San Marino. But he'd bounced back. They still barracked him, though. Nobody 'boos' the England captain, David Platt, when he plays below par. Yet Barnes gets 'booed' when he's playing well.

Barnes is perennially accused of underachievement. Many black people outside the football world are accused of being low achievers and bad performers in the workplace. But the worst underachiever is the country itself, England. It, more than any other entity, deserves low marks for the lack of fulfilment of black aspirations in important spheres like education, jobs and housing.

There is a mentality akin to schizophrenia in many white people's attitude to blacks trying to achieve in their lives or their professions. Often it appears that many whites don't know whether to hate it more if a black person is talented and go-getting, or when that black man or woman is incompetent. To a large extent the black person who is incompetent, slothful or lazy (in modern parlance: 'laid-back' – a description virtually always applied to blacks) is a superb creation of the white mind over centuries. Lack of employment opportunities, deliberately inferior education and poor-quality housing have given birth to some blacks who fit these descriptions as closely as some whites do.

John Barnes, though, is of course a product of the middle classes. His father was a colonel in the Jamaican army, and maybe it's Ken Barnes who needs to be credited for the resilience of his son. But Barnes' toughness was not appreciated by England fans and some sports journalists. It was almost an affront to see him trying to keep going despite their best efforts to send him screaming to the nearest asylum.

Barnes typifies the experience of many black British who've managed to enter the senior echelons of a previously all-white profession. They, like him, find that you can be inside, but that doesn't mean that you have been included. You will be monitored and your every move examined. You will need to prove on a daily basis that you deserve to be where you are. You will be the subject of petty racial jibes and attacks until the sheer number of these occurrences starts to have a debilitating effect on your confidence, health and therefore job performance. The result being that you are unable to perform to your own self-imposed and far higher standards.

And when, despite this harassment, you somehow manage to rebuild yourself mentally and physically, as Barnes did with self-discipline (employing new training methods paid for by himself and performed in his own time) and a new tactical approach, the result is often that you'll be hated even more. But the 'boo boys' haven't been able to destroy Barnes. He refuses to go quietly. Left out of Terry Venables' swansong squad for the 1996 European Championships, he became part of one national television team analysing the games, and still appears as a TV summarizer today.

What his tormentors had put him through during the previous years, they would have been unable to cope with themselves. This knowledge of their own failure if faced with similar challenges fuels the continuing hatred of Barnes and a sullen disrespect for his service to England.

As Tony Sewell pointed out: 'For many black professionals playing for England in high-profile jobs demands a call above duty. Often this has nothing to do with "courage" or commitment, the usual attributes that you would associate with a professional. It demands acting like a "good nigger" and smiling graciously in the face of racist taunts.'

It matters to black players to play for England. They want to play for England. Or for Ireland. The former Republic of Ireland manager, Jack Charlton, profited from the likes of Paul McGrath, Phil Babb and Terry Phelan.

The Irish Football Association, according to the *Guardian*, once described their citizenship rules like this: 'The way you do it is you get the birth certificates of your grandfather and grandmother, then you get their marriage certificate to make sure and then you get the birth certificate of the relevant parent of the player – make sure it matches the grandparents' name – and then you get the parents' marriage certificate and then you get the player's birth certificate.'

English commentators make wry, jealous comments, but there are no gripes about the lack of determination and commitment by black skins in green shirts.

It could be argued that it matters to black players to play for their nation perhaps more than it matters to white players. From Viv Anderson – the first black England player, back in 1978 – onwards, every black player knows how special it will be if he plays for England. Only one has so far reached the pinnacle. Paul Ince was terrifically proud to have captained England, even if it was only for one game. And it was against the Americans. And England lost 2–0.

It mattered to Barnes to play for England. But at the end of the day most fans care more about the performance of their League team than the England team. They would rather see their club finish well than England win an important international. In a Premier League survey of fifteen thousand football supporters in 1995, more than three-quarters thought success for their club was more important, or much more important, than success for the national side.

Tackling the Opposition

His brother held up one end of the ten-feet-long banner. STOP THE CRIMINAL JUSTICE BILL it screamed. This dark, chocolate-skinned young man had his eyes focused on a point most people couldn't see. His lips were set so tightly, he was almost pouting. He had been on numerous demonstrations and protests, but was standing as upright and determined as if he were a novice. I was fascinated by the picture on the T-shirt he was wearing proudly: surely that smiling, confident face, looking very much like an eternal Ph.D student's, wasn't a true reproduction of the features the entire country knew so well?

Didn't the demonstrator's brother really look like, at best, a huge, grizzly bear; and at worst, a monster: half black man, half animal? Where was that half-cocked, obviously high-on-drugs manic grin? The infamous picture of George Silcott's brother had been taken in a police station. Any police photograph of an arrested suspect has the same effect on human features as one of those photo-booth pictures taken after a drunken night's lark.

Winston Silcott, who has had his conviction for the murder of a police constable during the Tottenham riots of 1985 quashed, doesn't look anything like the demon we have thrust into our faces by the popular press every time his name is mentioned. As his brother's T-shirt shows, there are other photographs available. But why show the truth when a false image can maintain prejudice? Black men, especially ones cleared of killing white men, aren't supposed to look intelligent. The image of the big, violent, rampaging, black bogey man who is uniquely programmed –

because he's black – to rob, rape and murder (in no particular order) is still a very potent image in the 1990s. Potent and acceptable.

An angry, shocked United States couldn't believe what it was hearing and reading. Hearts went out to Susan Smith, the young white mother whose faltering voice described how her two baby boys, aged three, and fourteen months, had been hijacked in her car at night and driven off. Her children were found dead. She said the murderer was the black man who had hijacked her car. Susan Smith's story was believed for a very long time by a very large number of people. She didn't even have to provide any evidence – her word was good enough.

But there wasn't a black man. No black man killed two white children. Susan Smith murdered her babies by strapping them in the seats of her car and rolling the vehicle into a lake. She, a white woman and mother, did it. Not a black man. Why was it so easy for people to believe her lies that a black man had committed the crime? Or perhaps the question should be: why is it *still* so easy for white people to believe criminal lies about black people, especially black men?

As the *Voice* newspaper reported in November 1994: 'Britain has not been immune to such cases, either. The most notable incident occurred over a year ago involving two white youngsters, one of whom claimed to have been attacked by a black man who poured a flammable fluid on his face. The boys' imaginative description had all the hallmarks of the black stereotype that is constantly bandied around by the mainstream media. They claimed he had been 5ft 11in, with a scar across his nose and right cheek and a thin moustache, and was probably drunk or on drugs. He was also meant to be aged 30 to 35, sporting a gold tooth and zig-zag-patterned haircut. The graphic description was what made this case even more disturbing. How two boys, one aged 7, and the other aged 8, could conjure up such a vivid picture of their would-be attacker was the question that was never fully answered. The injured boy's mother subsequently launched a tearful plea on television and in the newspapers for help to catch the man who had supposedly maimed her son. The truth, however, eventually came out when eyewitnesses told police that they had seen the children messing around in the park with a can of petrol and matches.'

So much for the perennial hope that 'the children' will make it all nice and rosy and different in 'the future'. South London teenager Stephen Lawrence was murdered in April 1993 at a bus-stop by racist white boys of his own age-group – not racists from his parents' generation. Who was responsible for bequeathing the hate? Who will be in 'the future'?

Many whites regard black men as big, violent, loudmouthed, uncontrollable, frightening characters who, when not knocking their wives, girlfriends and children around, are beating and killing other innocent people. Black male dominance of the world of boxing appears to them to be in the natural order of things. A heavyweight champion like Mike Tyson is merely demonstrating the animalistic behaviour which, in their books, characterizes the black race. Tyson was once pictured stripped to his underpants frolicking with a 14-stone tiger – his pet. The report began: 'He's big, brutal and could kill a grown man with just one blow – and the tiger is a bit of a handful too.' Just where do you draw the line at depicting blacks as animals, and continuing to feed racist imagery?

And, even if violence isn't immediately apparent – the black guy may be grinning and dancing away; cracking endless jokes, he may be the soul of the office or the shop floor; he may be a mild-mannered man – then it's not hard for whites to be convinced that violence is just beneath the surface. Because violence is in 'their nature', even if they don't look the part. Let's not forget that *Time*, a highly prestigious, mass-circulation American international news magazine, darkened bronze-coloured O. J. Simpson's face for its cover picture. The thinking, many blacks felt, was that the blacker (and thus more menacing) the handsome and normally light-skinned Mr O. J. looked, the more likely it would be believed that he'd murdered a white woman and a white man.

The demon image which the outside white world still continues to hold of the dangerously violent black man doesn't just spill over into football, it dominates the way the game perceives and judges black players and the black communities the majority of them come from. You can have as many white murderers, rapists and robbers as you like, but these white men retain their individuality, creating bad images only for themselves. Even their families remain unsullied by their crimes, sometimes going on to benefit by writing the 'brother/son/husband-I-never-knew' type of book. Certainly the white communities they come from are left untarnished.

As the number of black men entering League clubs became noticeable in the late 1970s and early 1980s, the terminology black people are accustomed to hearing when their 'street' (where, apparently, we all come from) lives are being described crept into the world of football. Behind the use of certain words and terms is the fear of the dark, unstable, unfathomable world of the black male and his unpredictable temperament, which has endangered football right at the source where it was created: England.

Instead of the entry of black players into the game being a phenomenon to be applauded and used beneficially by all involved in football, by the mid-1990s their numbers are having the same effect which mass black immigration has had on the country at large. There is very limited real integration and understanding between black and white; and the old prejudices pertaining to blacks are being faithfully restructured by whites to

avoid head-on criticism in the more pluralist and more hypocritical 1990s. In other words, the New sophisticated Racism – perfect for the times.

The following words are rarely unused when commentators
and writers (nearly all white and male) are discussing black footballers: 'menacing', 'predator', 'marauder', 'aggressive', 'brutal',
'hot-headed', 'argumentative', 'lethal', 'volatile', 'belligerent', 'ter-
rifying', 'fearsome', 'frightening', 'powerful', and, of course, 'big';
yet simultaneously black footballers are often 'lightweight', 'ill-
disciplined', 'laid-back', 'half-hearted' and frequently 'happy' or
'smiling' (Dwight Yorke is always 'smiling').

This letter from a south-London mother appeared in the black
newspaper, the *Weekly Journal*: 'Operation Eagle Eye has certainly [been] in full swing in my neighbourhood. How do I
know? Because my 12-year-old son and his friends were stopped
four times last week while going about their daily business. On
the last occasion I went to the police station concerned to lodge
my complaint and was told by some young whippersnapper:
"Well, madam, your son does look big for his age," to which I
lost my cool and hurled a string of abuse. I was then ejected
from the station, which only served to worsen my anger. But I
deviate a little, my main point is to express my dismay at the
continuing stereotyping that affects our sons, many of whom
'look big for their age'. Regardless of their physical presence
young boys should not be singled out for police attention just
because they do not conform to what white people think 12-year-
old boys should look like.'

'Big, bad Devon White isn't out to win any popularity competitions – he just wants to score goals,' said the *Mirror* report on
a match between Notts County and Bournemouth in September
1995. 'White, 6ft 4in of raw aggression, found himself in the
middle of controversy as he clearly handled before grabbing his
first goal. But he snapped: "There's always controversy about my

goals. No one likes the way I play." The big man also converted a late penalty.' I didn't know what colour the Notts player was – until I read that report. No, it doesn't mention his colour. It didn't need to. Because, when we are tall, our build – together with our fabled strength – becomes the main focal point.

A common feature of articles on black footballers is the insistence that the man in question would be inside prison doing a long stint if he hadn't been saved from a life of crime by the game and its white authoritarians. For every Paul Ince who admits he had a 'wild past' ('. . . I could have finished in jail, in a gang, or a deadbeat') there are dozens of black players with very ordinary pasts. But we rarely hear about them; that's not what we are supposed to be about.

A January 1995 *Sunday Mirror* article on Birmingham's Ricky Otto began: 'Ricky Otto goes into the biggest match of his life [up against Liverpool in the FA Cup third round] admitting: "If I wasn't playing professional football I would be one of three things – dead, hooked on drugs, or serving life in prison!"' Surely this saved-from-the-jaws-of-prison past equally applies to more than a few white players – they are the majority, after all – but you never hear about that. Indeed, although the reporter said, 'Otto is angry that he cannot shake off the bad-boy reputation which has dogged him since spending three years of his four-year sentence in Brixton and Wandsworth prisons,' he then went on to focus the long article on nothing but Otto's prison period, with (in case we got a bit bored) dashes of 'street' theft recollections, knife fights and stabbings in Hackney before the player became a 'jailbird'. What kind of a player was Otto? I never found out. It wasn't in the article. Oh, apart from the aside that Otto 'has set his sights on doing some serious harm to mighty Liverpool when they visit St Andrews'.

'Doncaster winger Jamie Lawrence,' began a *Today* newspaper report in the same month, 'joins Premier League Leicester today, just 18 months after finishing a four-year jail term for robbery with violence. Lawrence, who could cost £200,000 in a package deal, is Leicester manager Mark McGhee's first signing as he bids to avoid relegation. But Lawrence, born in Balham, south London says: "When you've been banged up you can handle anything else in life. I've always been totally up front about my past and don't see any point in trying to hide it. Sure, I've taken stick from opposing fans, but I've just ignored it and got on with my game." Lawrence was spotted in Albany Jail, Isle of Wight, by Ambrose Mendy, who arranged trials with Southend, Wimbledon and Millwall. He then joined Sunderland and made his debut at Middlesbrough, where the fans chanted "thief" and the Ayresome Park disc jockey played Elvis Presley's "Jailhouse Rock". But after joining Doncaster on a free transfer, Lawrence made an immediate impact, with McGhee saying: "I've checked his background and I don't see any worries. If he's got any problems then I just hope he gives them to opposing defences from now on."' That was the sum total of the article. What kind of a player was Lawrence? Didn't get a clue. But we did find out he could handle relegation because being inside taught him how to do that. The photo caption read: 'Lawrence ... prison term'.

Football is a dirty old game. Dirty, nasty, violent and always physical. And many men 'play dirty', use violent tactics to win. As former manager Howard Wilkinson put it in *Today* in February 1995: 'I think a football field is a violent place. You can accept the blows and the throw-ins not given, but not the character who sets out by use of excessive violence to hurt. It has now become formalized. It has blended in with the game.'

White, not black, footballers are the most violent men on the pitch. But, frequently, their 'misbehaviours' are seen as incidents committed by naughty men, silly boys, loveable rogues. The attitude being: 'Tsk, tsk, there he goes again – he's a one, isn't he! Bit of a nutter!' The old guys, like 1970s Chelsea 'hardman' Ron 'Chopper' Harris are remembered fondly through misty eyes. His successors . . . well, the photograph, now a classic, of Vinny Jones looking like a caveman and gripping an agonized Paul Gascoigne's balls was even used by British Telecom in their campaign to advertise yet another change of telephone codes. One to remember indeed. Somehow, I don't think John Fashanu, Vinny's long-term teammate at Wimbledon, trying to break off Gazza's testicles would have caused as much amusement.

Vinny Jones is probably the white player with the most violent reputation and extraordinary disciplinary record in current English football. If headbutting needed a sponsor, it should be Vinny – you associate the man with the act. His roll call of dishonour in the League includes ten sendings-off in nine years; numerous bookings; and it was Vinny who got an FA fine of £20,000, plus a suspended six-month ban, for taking part in the making of a video called *Soccer's Hard Men*.

But this hard man only really got a vitriolic press when he tried to bite off the nose of a tabloid reporter. 'As a joke,' Vinny offered in mitigation, adding, 'Because I'd had a bit too much champagne, I probably bit him a bit too hard on the nose, but it was meant as a bit of a prank.' It took that incident for the *News of the World* to cancel his column with them, and for the other papers to lay into him. How dare he attack one of theirs.

Vinny is joined in the white 'cheeky chappy . . . helluva character . . . likeable rogue . . . nutter' stakes by players like Neil Ruddock, Roy Keane, Dennis Wise, Julian Dicks and Duncan Ferguson. Ferguson deserves special attention. Known to his friends and sportswriters as 'John Wayne' (or a 'deplorable rascal', a 'diamond with rough edges', a 'big daft lad'), he has the honour of becoming the first player to receive a custodial sentence for an attack against another player on the football pitch. He'd headbutted an opposing player, Raith Rover's John McStay, in April 1994, when he was playing in the Scottish Premier Division for Glasgow Rangers. One of Scotland's leading judges, Judge Hope, upheld his three-month sentence and told him: 'A footballer who assaults another player on the football field is not entitled to expect leniency from the courts just because the incident occurred in the course of a football match.'

Stamping on opposing players, headbutting, elbowing, late and dirty tackling, and just sheer physical intimidation are not strange tactics to many white players. And that's just the on-field activities. Dennis Wise was acquitted of charges of assaulting a taxi driver and his black cab in a fracas outside a private club owned by Terry Venables. And Duncan Ferguson doesn't limit his assaults to fellow players: he's also got past convictions for attacking a football-supporting postman who was on crutches, an off-duty policeman and a fisherman. These drink-related crimes gave him his jokey nickname: 'Duncan Disorderly'.

The tactic of raising elbows to head-height when players are challenging each other in the air (flying elbows) is so widespread, with even Graham Kelly, the FA's chief executive, saying 'you can see such things 200 times a week', that I find it breathtaking that it has become identified with a single black player because of one unfortunate incident.

There is really only one black man whom fingers can point to justifiably for repeated involvement in violent incidents on the pitch. Step forward the leader of the Black Violent Tendency: John Fashanu. Or Fash the Bash. Or Bashanu. Or Big Bad John. The outlaw black player who, for most of his career, played for Wimbledon, the country's outcast team, and the one everyone hates to play. (But remember, his foster mother loves him.)

It's ridiculous but true that one black robber, one black rapist, one black murderer will be used by powerful white individuals to stigmatize the entire black race and ferment the innate fears and prejudices of ordinary whites. As Fashanu says: 'I'm 6ft 3in, big and black – I'm bound to get stitched up.' He was called the most physically fearsome forward in Britain – a silly description. He's tall, but he has a slim build. He does not look threatening unless it's in your mind. Certainly not as threatening as, say, Neil Ruddock or Julian Dicks. But, as Ron Atkinson put it, 'He frightens defenders out of their skins.'

'I am quite happy to call Fash my rottweiler,' Atkinson said, when he brought the forward to Aston Villa, 'and put him up in the front line to give my side a bit of snarl.'

Just as one black murderous thug indicts all black men in the eyes of whites, has Fashanu's individual reputation for involvement in violent incidents coloured the way other black players are regarded by the football industry?

Fashanu says of himself: 'I am a physical player but I do not go out to deliberately injure opponents.'

Most of the black players in the modern game were born or raised in Britain. They trained here, so they play a very similar game to white players born or brought up in Britain. The English game is renowned for being a very physical one. As Fashanu put it in *Today* before a game with the glamour boys of Manchester United in November 1993: 'Nobody can match Wimbledon for the powerful, physical, uncompromising image that we like to project. We are the masters. And we will fight with vigour for each other because we are aware that games against Manchester United are normally very physical despite their reputation as a flair team.

'They have gained respect for attractive, open football. But they also have some tough players like Bryan Robson, Paul Ince, Steve Bruce and Mark Hughes. It makes me laugh when people say United aren't physical. How can you say a player like Mark Hughes isn't physical – people are scared of him precisely because of his channelled aggression. Of course, I am condemned for the same approach.

'They say I'm always involved in putting it about, but when was I last at the centre of a controversial incident? About a year ago, and just about every player could be accused of the same thing . . . I go out there and make my presence felt. I am uncompromising, physical and committed. But that is exactly what I am paid to do.'

Unfortunately for Fashanu, and for Gary Mabbutt, just a few days later his elbow clashed with the Spurs captain's face.

But it is clear that the reputation for violence and bad discipline that hangs over black players is there because managers, coaches and referees cannot shake off the feelings which link these players to black inner-city communities supposedly riddled with crime, violent fathers and disruptive domestic backgrounds. The 'that's what you can expect from them' element.

There is certainly a cultural element to the game – but it is between nations and continents. And every nation blames every other nation for bringing the game into disrepute: the world is full of dirty foreigners who play a dirty game. Glenn Hoddle, Chelsea's then manager, tried it on when he was about to face the Spanish side, Real Zaragoza. He said he was preparing his players (obviously thoroughly timid chaps) for Zaragoza's dirty tactics and physical game. That Latin temperament means all sorts of intimidatory tactics on the pitch, you see.

Some of the tackles you see in games between African countries can leave you gasping. Ditto for South America. However, in England in particular the cultural card is displayed for footballers with the same nationality, and given a colour angle. Different clubs have their own styles of the national game; but black players are all said to play the same way at whichever club they belong to: dirty tackles, dodgy elbows, dissent. Football is full of fouls, but let a black player commit one and all hell breaks loose.

Ron Atkinson also said of Fashanu: 'He goes in where angels fear to tread.' You could add: and often leaving his opponents in a hell of a mess behind him. Fashanu says he has his own personal 'style'; players who had to play opposite him say they expected tough confrontations, tough battles – it's a war. A West Ham defender said: 'You look at the calendar and go: "Oh no, it's Wimbledon!". Fash's game is based on aggression, and if you take that away I don't think you would end up with a lot.' But aren't all players' games based to a degree on aggression? Or is white aggression good; and black aggression bad?

After Gary Mabbutt shattered his cheekbone and nearly lost an eye – the pictures were horrific – following the aerial collision with Fashanu's elbow in November 1993, Gordon Taylor, the chief executive of the Professional Footballers' Association, said Fashanu's protestations of innocence weren't good enough. 'It's no longer sufficient,' he fumed, 'to say there was no intent. The use of elbows is dangerous and reckless. It is akin to dangerous or reckless driving.'

In the *Sunday Mirror* that month, Blackburn defender Kevin Moran, who was left with a broken nose after a clash with Fashanu, summed up the prevailing attitude towards the black striker. 'You can't keep saying sorry. Fashanu has got to ask himself why it always seems to be him. I'm not talking about individual cases, but how often when this business crops up is the name of John Fashanu on the end of it? You can't just keep saying it was an accident. It's a man's game and we all know accidents happen – but Fashanu does seem to be involved in an awful lot of accidents. He's a strong guy and he does put himself about a bit, but you can't keep getting away with saying, "I'm a big fellow and these things happen." Niall Quinn's a big fellow too, but how often do you see him caught up in this sort of stuff? Fashanu caught me and I wasn't happy about it. I was in real agony on the ground. You can say sorry as much as you like, but when you're flat on the ground in pain, you don't always hear it.'

There is no love lost between Viv Anderson and John Fashanu. The two black players clashed seriously in their careers – once in the tunnel. But Anderson was moved to give, if not a defence of Fashanu following the Mabbutt incident, then a warning to the powers that be.

'The elbow is a deadly weapon,' the former Arsenal and Manchester United star said in the *Sunday Mirror*. 'It's creeping into the game more and more – and unless someone stamps it out, then a player is going to get very seriously hurt. Though the direct style of teams like Wimbledon, for example, lends itself to more physical contact, this problem goes deeper than that.'

Faced with a general outcry over the clash and a strong complaint from Spurs, the FA summoned Fashanu and Mabbutt to a specially appointed Commission of Inquiry, where both sides watched a video of the incident. Fashanu was infuriated by the FA summons since he hadn't even been given a booking for the incident by the referee. He insisted that it was 'a complete and genuine accident'. The FA inquiry, he told the *News of the World* in June 1994, was like being in a courtroom: 'Spurs had two lawyers in there spouting legal jargon, showing lots of videos from hundreds of angles and piling on the pressure. I took one look at that and thought, if this is what football is coming to, then I want no part of it. Yet all that was hanging over my head was a suspension – not even a fine.'

Fashanu was exonerated by the FA. 'I was cleared of any intent by an FA jury. But I still get opposition fans screaming for the ref to send me off every time I go up for a challenge with my arms remotely raised. Reputations stick and, if you are not careful, destroy you.'

Asian reporter Mihir Bose, writing in the *Sunday Times* in December 1993, accused Fashanu of not being 'above using the race card' when the player defended himself against his critics by pointing out: 'If this incident had happened to a white player it would not have been blown up. It's character assassination.' 'Fashanu,' said Bose, 'claims he has been able to ride out the storm because he's different from other black players and because of the backing of Hammam.' According to Fashanu: '[Hammam] is Lebanese and a very strong man. Had he been an English chairman, no way would I have had such support as a black person. I always feel that there is this veil over me. Somebody somewhere is wanting to pull you down.'

Mabbutt's injury wasn't the 'normal' kind you are exposed to on the field, and the Spurs captain revealed that he received consolation letters and cards from people who had been in road accidents or had been beaten up. He warned: 'Civil action is not what you want in the game, but I think you have to remember that when you go on the field you're playing football. It does not make you above or outside the law, and every player must remember that.'

In October 1994, Fashanu found that out for himself when events from nearly seven years earlier came back to haunt him. He was taken to court. The former Norwich and Northern Ireland international, John O'Neill, demanded £150,000 in a High Court suit against Fashanu and Wimbledon FC.

O'Neil's defence said that Fashanu was 'under a legal duty of care to him and all opposing players to play the game without causing foreseeable injury, without playing in a reckless, danger-ous or excitable manner, and without showing a reckless disregard for O'Neill's safety'.

It was December 1987, O'Neill told the Court, and he was 30 minutes into his debut game with Norwich, against Wimbledon, when his right leg was smashed by a challenge from Fashanu.

'I was aware of John Fashanu coming into the picture. Every-thing happened so quickly. I knew from the manner of his approach I was in trouble. Then he did me. He certainly was not going to play the ball and in all probability he was going to land on top of me. At the split second I played the ball I felt a severe blow to my knee, heard a loud crack, and thought I had broken my leg.

'When the physio came on, he told me he thought it was my ligaments. I was carried off. I have not been able to kick a football since. It is a serious thing to say about a fellow professional, but it was his intention to go for me and not for the ball.'

The ligament damage wrecked O'Neill's career and his chances of becoming a coach. Before Fashanu had a chance to put his side of the story in the witness box, Wimbledon's insurers paid, out of court, £70,000–£80,000 less than O'Neill had wanted. He went back to Northern Ireland to continue running his wine and spirits business.

Fashanu's lawyer said in the *Daily Telegraph* that whilst the insurers had been involved in the decision to settle, 'it was a commercial decision by my client'. Although, as part of the settlement, O'Neill had had to withdraw his allegation of assault against Fashanu, he said he still stood by everything he had said in the courtroom.

Fashanu said the case should never have gone to court and, in what was to become a familiar, if sinister, refrain during the following months, he blurted out: 'I think the Establishment is after me.'

It was all too much, he insisted. He got more slaps, bangs and wallops than he ever gave. 'People have tried to nobble me many times,' he complained, 'and I've been fortunate, I've survived serious injury.' His luck ran out in February 1995 when, ironically, a ligament injury received when he collided with Ryan Giggs ended his playing days. It was to give him even more freedom to concentrate on his arrest and subsequent successful defence of later match-fixing allegations.

In spite of Fashanu's over-hyped reputation for dangerous play, he wasn't, as expected to be, the first player sued by another. The first ever court case between two players over dangerous play involved a black player laying charges against a white one. Just a few months before Fashanu v O'Neill, Paul Elliott, the former Chelsea player, took Dean Saunders, the former Liverpool player and Welsh international, to the High Court. Elliott was seeking a million pounds in damages for an alleged reckless challenge by Saunders during a game between the two clubs in September 1992. Elliott lost his case.

Thank God he wasn't black. Eric Cantona thinks *he*'s had a hard time at the hands of the media (I think they used the Selhurst Park incident to give him the hard time they've always wanted to give him). But thank goodness that on that infamous January night in 1995 Paul Ince got there a tad too late to get stuck in defending his teammate. Ian Wright sent Cantona a 'there but for the grace of God go I' message after Cantona kung-fu kicked the foul-mouthed male spectator.

Eric is French, but so far as many white English are concerned, he may as well be black: he's foreign; he's been violent when seriously provoked (indicative of an uncontrollably violent nature); and he speaks his mind, not giving a damn what other people think (he's irrational and hot-tempered). And he's a great dresser, a little bit of a showman, dressed to kill. I make him an honourary black man for the duration of his stay in this country.

Black people say it quite often as they watch television news, listen to the radio, or read the papers. If we find out about some horrendously violent crime, the usual response is: 'I hope he's not black.' As the photofit pops up, or the man being hunted is described, we often think: Thank God he wasn't black. It's a ridiculous ritual. But then again we suspect many whites think: I bet he's black. After all, we live in a country where it is assumed that being a violent criminal is the favourite hobby of black males. Do prison beds lie?

The Penal Affairs Consortium, a group representing the views of thirty-one prison organizations, including probation officers and prison governors, published a report in 1996 entitled *Race and Criminal Justice*. It revealed that 17 per cent of the male prison population came from ethnic minority groups along with 24 per cent of the female prisoners – an overall figure of 18 per cent of all inmates. Britain's ethnic minorities make up only 5.5 per cent of the entire population.

The research showed that 'from street searches to prosecutions, bail and sentencing there is discrimination against ethnic minorities'. Home Office figures illustrated that young blacks and young whites have similar rates of offending but that black defendants are 16 per cent more likely to be refused bail, and that black people entering prison have, on average, fewer previous convictions than their white roommates.

Frances Crook of the Howard League for Penal Reform said in the *Voice*: 'The only possible explanation for the disproportionate numbers of young black people who are sent to prison is racism. There is no other explanation for it and it is a serious problem throughout the system. We have been concerned with the problem of racism within the penal system for some time, and the number of young black men, especially, that are put on remand.'

I daren't think what would have been done to Cantona if he had been black. Hanged, drawn and quartered would have been the soft option; and as for a probation order – dream on in your prison cell, baby. No black would, sixteen months after such an assault, go on to be judged Footballer of the Year.

Eagle-eyed Authoritarians

A Leeds fan once came on the radio to rant about Shearer's ability to whinge, whine and yap. He was particularly incensed that during a Leeds versus Newcastle game, Carlton Palmer had fouled Shearer, and the referee had given a free-kick. But then Shearer went up to the ref, a conversation was had, and Palmer was sent off.

'The sending off couldn't have been more straightforward,' said Shearer. 'He came through the back of me and that's a yellow card. If Carlton isn't clever enough to realize he was on one card a minute earlier and is risking another by ploughing through the back of me, that's his problem, not mine. It's no use pointing at me. The ref's had a straightforward decision to make and it had nothing to do with anything I might have said. I hope nobody is suggesting I got him sent off. If there was a delay between the foul taking place and the card coming out, you will have to see the referee about that.'

But Shearer has been accused of manipulating referees. The accuser was the Everton boss, Joe Royle, following what he believed was a 'dive' at a Charity Shield game. QPR defender David Bardsley backed up the allegation after a penalty was given against him for 'pushing' Shearer in the box. 'He's great at manipulating refs,' said Bardsley in the *Mirror* in August 1995. 'Especially at Ewood. Alan's good at that. You come to grounds like this and expect it.'

Referees are the cops of the game. As a Football Association advert explained, they 'enforce the laws of the game. They punish the guilty. They also protect the innocent.' And I believe, like the police force in wider society, these white men in authority who police the pitch keep an eye out for black players with their supposed 'disruptive temperaments' and 'violent' and 'aggressive' ways of playing. Black footballers frequently say they get rounded up, picked on, and disciplined repeatedly for being nothing more than the usual suspects. The footballing equivalent of the Metropolitan Police force's Operation Eagle Eye – bringing you that cleaner, fresher, black-mugger-free look to London streets – is deployed.

The Chief Commissioner of the Metropolitan Police, Sir Paul Condon, warned in his July 1995 letter to black community leaders that Operation Eagle Eye would target 'young black people who have been excluded from school and/or are unemployed' (i.e., potential muggers). It would use tactics, he said in a letter to the *Voice*, '. . . which previously we had used only for very serious crime. The main ones are intelligence, targeting of suspects, and surveillance. We need to use sophisticated techniques because mugging is a crime that leaves very little evidence other than terrified victims, and the information we get from victims. We want to put the fear back where it belongs – with the criminals.'

Home Office police, local authority and lobby group surveys have shown that blacks can be up to ten times more likely to be stopped and searched in the street than whites. Even the police had to admit, in a Scotland Yard inquiry in early 1996, that one in seven black people are pulled up and questioned, compared to one in thirty-two whites. And if arrested, blacks are less likely to escape with a caution. More often than not they don't get bail and find themselves remanded in custody. The former Lord Chief Justice, Lord Taylor, was moved to say, in a speech made to Leeds Race Issues Advisory Council in July 1995, that the criminal justice system 'is failing those it should be protecting by tolerating racist attitudes, making racist assumptions, and allowing blacks to believe they are beyond the law's protection'.

Some white people may claim that they do not view every young black male they see as a potential mugger. Some white people may share this young white man's view, expressed in the *Sunday Telegraph* that month: 'I don't think I am a racist, but I have to admit that subconsciously I do think a black man is more capable of mugging someone than a white man.' But if they had to point out the man, black or white, who would lose his temper, lose his control, get uptight, start shouting and swearing, get violent and hit out before the other person, they would pick out the black man. And the referees would join them.

Worse, provocation is never accepted as an excuse from a black person. Dissent is disallowed. It reminds me of those blacks who get charged or locked up when they go into a police station to complain about an offence which has been committed *against* them.

What you have in football is a tense and explosive situation, where white men in positions of authority on the pitch and in the dressing room are faced with black players whom, on one level, they fail to see as individuals, and, on another, whose background and cultural make-up they care to know very little about.

To survive mentally and physically, black people have had to make themselves study and try to comprehend the behaviour and mental processes of white people. There is no equivalent necessity on the part of whites – therefore it is a task which is rarely undertaken.

Most Premiership referees have felt the full weight of the tongue of mouthy white stars. But it is black players who have the reputation for 'verbals' and rebelliousness, rudeness and outright dissent.

Ian Wright, Arsenal's superforward, is regarded as mouth almighty when it comes to arguing with referees about their decisions. He has a glowing reputation for giving anyone who gets in his way an earful. But any dissent stems from a perceived injustice. He says referees who should be looking after him, protecting him from unruly players, are taking *his* name down instead.

He was asked by the FA to explain what he'd meant when he called referee Robbie Hart a Muppet 'straight from *The Muppet Show* – and you can quote me on that. You don't need referees any more, just robots in the stand. Or maybe we could get some other Muppets in to do it.' (I'd have thought that was pretty clear, myself.) He was fined £1500. At the time, a fed-up Wright said: 'What is happening is on my mind. I'm walking a tightrope. I can't enjoy my football any more. It's getting me down. I'm just doing my job and getting booked for it. I'm not a dirty player. I've never hurt anyone in a tackle.'

But Ian's warrior image comes before him. Although everyone knows he's not a dirty player, I believe referees book him because he's Ian Wright: he's damned because they look at the statistics and see he's already had a series of brushes with authority, and they respond by thinking he's bound to be trouble. They cannot see that this man is just an extrovert, because they cannot look at him as an individual the way they would a white player. An extrovert with a heart pumping with passion. Less passionate people cannot understand his intense feelings for the game: everything is at stake (he cannot forget how late he started in the game and that the clock is ticking louder for him than for some others). Turning the other cheek at an injustice is not in his nature – which leaves him, and many other black players, marked men.

As a former Arsenal colleague, the black footballer Paul Davis, put it in the *Voice* in January 1995: 'Wrighty's just enthusiastic.

He wants to do well for himself and for the team and score goals. Sometimes that spills over a bit, but I think people – especially refs and linesmen – sometimes see it the wrong way, and then he gets into trouble.'

Another former colleague, white striker Alan Smith, often played upfront with Wright. 'All the Arsenal players try and take responsibility to get Ian away from referees. Sometimes, I'm closest to him, so it's up to me to bring him clear,' he told reporters a few days before the 1993 Coca-Cola Cup Final against Sheffield Wednesday. 'Ian's certainly different to any other foot-baller I've played alongside. He's at the other end of the scale. I don't get wound up in games like he does, but sometimes I do wish I had a bit of his devil in me. Occasionally, I'm too laid back, but what can you do if that's the way you are? I don't think Ian will ever be calm. But it's no good trying to change him any more than it would be to alter me. To take away that desire and determination would destroy him.'

When spectators spat at Wright at Boundary Park, Oldham, he spat back – and got fined £1500. He was fined £5000 for giving a linesman the V-sign during an FA Cup Final replay. When the Millwall player Alex Rae wanted to rub in matters like Millwall beating Arsenal in an FA Cup tie – minutes after the defeat – the two men had to be separated. But the press paid less attention to Rae's involvement.

At one point in the winter of the '94–95 season, Wright had collected more disciplinary points than Arsenal's League tally: 41 to 32. His reward from the FA was a four-match ban and a £1000 fine. But two white players, Darren Patterson at Crystal Palace and Steve Bruce at Manchester United, also reached the same number of points; Bruce got a two-match ban and a £750 fine.

There is nothing authority hates more than to be challenged. 'You can't even talk to them any more,' Wright said, exasperated, in September 1994. 'When I asked why I was booked, one said he'd send me off if I said anything else.'

The other player often in conflict with referees for having too many strong opinions for their liking is Paul Ince. In his last season in England before his controversial move to Inter Milan in the summer of '95, Ince was said to be the player most improved by the new, tough, Fifa directives. One writer said Ince was 'refreshingly' concentrating on playing and passing the ball instead of 'offering belligerence towards referees'. Ince is a bad boy as far as football writers are concerned. His 'volatile' temperament comes up time and time again in writing which concentrates on his 'lack of [self] control', 'hair-trigger temper' and his 'apparent liking for involvement in incidents that have nothing to do with him'. His supposed lack of discipline and his 'acerbic style' get plenty of mentions.

During the campaign to qualify for the World Cup, the England manager Graham Taylor complained of 'headless chickens', saying after a game with Poland: 'One or two of our players were more interested in making war than playing football.' Everybody knew he was talking about Paul Ince, and another black player, the defender Carlton Palmer.

Ince's retaliation to critics of his style is straight to the point: 'You have to have fire in your belly. If I lost that I wouldn't be half the player I am. Personally, I think I've been able to control it over the last two or three years. It's been hard but I think I'm getting there.

'Of course I moan – some players will always react when a decision goes against them, and I'm one. But I have matured – I don't act the goat these days. I've managed to curb my temper. The way referees are going, I think that says a lot for me.

'Tackling is one of my major assets. It's dissent that has been the problem. I've made a conscious effort to control that and although I can't say I've been 100 per cent successful, I'm still trying. I know there will be times when I react, but that's just because I love the heat of the battle.

'When I arrived at Old Trafford,' he said in the *News of the World* in November 1994, 'I had a reputation as a loudmouth. And, yes, there were times when I was out of order. But I have worked very, very hard at changing that image. I've tried to accept responsibility and followed in the path of Bryan Robson and Steve Bruce by making myself a leader. And I think my disciplinary record proves it.'

There were whoops of joy, wild clapping and cheers from fans when Paul Ince was cleared by magistrates of assaulting a spectator and using threatening behaviour towards the crowd. A convicted soccer hooligan had claimed that Ince had punched him when the player had rushed to see what was happening to Cantona after the French man's kung-fu kick. A referee in the crowd had testified that he'd heard Ince yell at the Crystal Palace supporters: 'Come on, we will take the fucking lot of you.'

The Manchester United manager, Alex Ferguson, told the magistrates that Ince had had a troubled start when he'd joined such a big club from West Ham as a young player, aged 21. 'It took him a while to settle in. There was a bit of turmoil for a little while, but until you settle into a family situation, you don't get the proper rewards. When he was married, things progressed very well, and he developed into a fantastic footballer for us and a big influence for the club.'

Player and manager disagreed on whether Ince had a 'short fuse' or not, but Ferguson confirmed that Ince had an 'outstanding' disciplinary record (one sending-off in about 300 games during six years with United), and he was club captain on many occasions. 'We don't give that job away very easily, it's got to be earned, and I think over the last few years Paul has earned it.' In fact, Ince was captain on the night of that match with Crystal Palace.

A few weeks later, during the close season, Ferguson appeared to have had a complete change of heart. Ince told close friends like Ian Wright and Andy Cole, and his supporters, that he was shocked and hurt at allegations made by his manager when the two fell out over his unexpected and disputed transfer to Milan. 'We got the distinct impression that Paul was very unhappy with the manager because he hadn't spoken to him properly,' said Richard Kurt, a spokesman for the Independent United Supporters Association, in the *Mirror* in June 1995.

'Paul was also hurt by suggestions about his temperament and supposed lack of commitment. It was claimed he wasn't doing the business in training and that his attitude was bad after defeats.'

Here's a chief sportswriter, Nigel Clarke in the *Mirror*, reminiscing about the good old days: 'What I love about Keegan is his passion, his involvement, his basic joy at playing football his way. Anybody watching television on Wednesday night won't need to be reminded of Keegan's heart for the heat of a battle, and his total commitment. There he was scuffling with Billy Bremner, then pulling off his Liverpool shirt and throwing it down in anger at being sent off in the Charity Shield against Leeds. He walked bare-chested off Wembley, outraged, indignant and inflamed. Keegan went missing for two days after that, his heart and head full of the injustices of an FA ban.' Despite very similar characteristics, I've yet to read anybody wax so lyrically about Wright or Ince or any other senior black player who would see fit to behave as badly as that. The white man's 'total commitment' versus what's regarded as the black man's dangerous rebellion and attitude.

Kevin Campbell was Stan Collymore's replacement at Nottingham Forest in the summer of 1995. In 31 games he scored 6 League and Cup goals. However, in his defence, he suffered a recurring back problem which kept him out of the side from

September to December, and also had a knee-ligament injury and fractured ribs. He had to get used to being jeered by his own fans when he played and cheered when he was subbed. He, alone, was blamed for Forest's lack of goals. Manager Frank Clark was said by the *Sun* to deserve 'tremendous credit' for standing by him. (For all of one season?)

Campbell started the '96–97 season with a hat-trick against Coventry, aided by his new strike partner, Dean Saunders. The *Sun* report said: 'Goal-hero Campbell cold be forgiven for tasting champagne on Saturday night. Sadly he would not share his joy with the rest of us – refusing to speak to *Match of the Day*, Clubcall and all newspapers. He would not even have his picture taken with the match ball. Astonishing!'

The *Daily Mail* said: 'Former Arsenal striker Campbell declined to talk to those who had criticized his poor form last season immediately following his £2.5m move to Forest, but Saunders, a far wiser and more experienced man, proved an admirable advocate. He said: "Kevin had a lean season and the only thing that will put that right is for him to get goals now. All strikers go through bad patches. It's happened to me more than once and the only thing that ever puts it right is to find the net."'

Black players are heavily criticized for refusing to submit themselves to news conferences or interviews with the same white reporters who manufacture the fertilizer which feeds and nourishes criticisms of their performances and their attitude. When a white player refuses interviews, it's seen as his right, a logical attitude. Here's the *Sun* on Duncan Ferguson: 'There is even a certain aura of mystery surrounding him because, since he moved from Rangers two years ago, he has uttered barely a word to the media. That is because he felt he was given a raw deal back home for a few lively moments off and on the pitch.' No criticism for no news conferences, just understanding for the reasons for his romantic 'aura of mystery'. He's even commended for having what, the *Sun* says, it takes to succeed in England: 'a special talent and a combination of arrogance and aloofness'. No black player is ever commended for his arrogance and aloofness.

The difference in the way in which we are regarded starts when we're children. When black children are seen as disruptive in class, with 'bad attitude', teachers sigh and wonder what will become of us – like the man who told Andy Cole that he was destined for a life of drugs and crime. When I was growing up, too many black youngsters spent their school years in 'sin bins', places where bad (as in bad; not as in good) children went. Now with school league tables to maintain, these black youngsters whom the teachers can't control are simply expelled. Given the ultimate red card. A 1996 report by the Office for Standards in Education (Ofsted), the school inspection agency, confirmed what many African-Caribbean parents had known for years – more of their children were being thrown out of education than white children. The report said that black boys and girls are up to six times more likely to be excluded than white children: approximately 150 African-Caribbean pupils in every 1000 are kicked out compared to 30 in every 1000 for whites.

For lively black children whom teachers fear may not be too young to retaliate violently or verbally, there are other methods of control. In a Birmingham nursery unit, a white female teacher bound and gagged an asthmatic four-year-old black boy with sticky tape because she said he had disrupted a story-telling session. Ironically, it was a study of 6000 five-year-olds by Birmingham education authority in 1994 which revealed that black children outperformed pupils of all other races of that age 'in the most important skills of reading, writing and arithmetic'.

The report says similar results are revealed in national curriculum tests for 7-year-olds in English and maths. An Ofsted report found that the worst readers of English in the inspectors' own test were white pupils from disadvantaged backgrounds, and the best performance at both 7 and 11 was by black Africans.

But, by 16, it's another story for the majority of black students – we're then the least successful. What happens inbetween is the education system and its low expectations and practically zero motivation from bad teachers lacking in inspiration.

In December 1994, in the *Weekly Journal*, the author and columnist, Mike Phillips, told this story: 'As it happens, when I first went to school in Britain racist explanations for black boys' poor performances didn't have to be sophisticated. We weren't as clever as white boys or girls, they told us, and when we said we wanted to go to university or have a career they wrote on our reports that we were "unrealistic" or "over-ambitious". Later on, when I became a postgraduate education student, the explanations had changed. Linguistic incompetence was now the answer. Black parents couldn't speak the language well enough, so their children couldn't compete with white children. By the time I found myself teaching in south London, the accepted wisdom was that black parents didn't encourage their children to read or play with the right toys. And so it went on. Every time one explanation became redundant, another one emerged to take its place . . . The funny thing is how you can be lulled into a feeling of complacency and misplaced trust by all this bullshit, even when you know better. The rudest shock I've had in a long while was when I went to a parents' evening at my own child's school and a young teacher, a couple of years out of college, sat down and told me, with a kindly and patronizing air, that I ought to make sure that there were books in my home. There I was, a teacher with twenty years' experience, a writer of flaming books, living in a house where I couldn't *move* without stumbling over a book, and this young idiot was handing me a lecture about the importance of books. But, of course, he didn't need to know who I was. All he needed was to see a black face and he had his explanations ready. My problem was that, at that point, I had been so taken by the school's rhetoric of liberal anti-racism that it hadn't occurred to me that I'd find exactly the same attitudes from which I'd suffered in my own school experience.'

Descriptions of his early life paint a picture of Andy Cole as a boy whose 'combative, confrontational manner towards teachers got him suspended from school'. Can all the suspended black children be sullen, arrogant trouble-makers, whose crime is to answer teachers back? One of the main causes of disruptive behaviour is boredom, when intelligent minds are left untaxed. White teachers, like whites generally, also frequently misunderstand black people's body language: they see arrogance, defiance and aggression everywhere.

Cole's suspensions, his 'contempt for less gifted players', his 'rudeness' and his 'aggressiveness' were noted by his teachers. He's never been able to shake off these labels. The teacher who thought Cole had a good chance of becoming a pimp should have thrown caution to the winds. Why a pimp? Why not give young Andy some motivation, don't worry about him becoming big-headed: why not suggest that he could become a drug dealer? Or a drug dealer and a pimp. I'm sure this teacher's high regard for young Andrew and his future career options came through to the child loud and clear. Very rarely do teachers like that need to say anything at all.

Black children, especially boys, come up against these nil- (or virtually nil-) expectations all the time, and then these same teachers wonder why the children have what teachers describe as an 'attitude problem' or, that old and beloved workhorse, a 'chip on the shoulder'. One day, I would love to meet a black person who has never been told by a white person that they have an attitude problem, or in today's street lingo, simply that they have 'attitude'. It is probably the phrase used most widely by white people to describe the very few black people they've ever had to interact with. Especially the kind of black person who refuses to acknowledge the kind of white person who believes that, because he or she is white and he or she is in charge, he or she is therefore infallible.

Andy Cole is the kind of strong-minded person with lots of self-esteem who, if he thinks he's right about something, will tell you straight out irrespective of who you are. This is not how black boys and black girls are supposed to behave if they want to survive, prosper and be popular in a white setting. He says it was Ian Wright who, when Andy was disappointed and upset at being let go by Arsenal when he was still in the reserves, taught him to have confidence in his own ability and to hold on to his ambition to be not just one of the best, but *the* best.

But, according to the way it's now told, the 'surly young rebel' was put on the straight and narrow not by giving himself a good talking to, or listening to advice from his loving and supportive family and friends, but thanks to the white football Establishment. Salvation came courtesy of two years at the FA's School of Excellence at Lilleshall in deepest Shropshire. He had to, naturally, get out of his inner-city environment, Nottingham's Lenton area, and leave those no-good friends behind in order to be saved.

Cole blossomed at Lilleshall – much to the surprise of white writers, one of whom said: 'Lilleshall should have been like a red rag to a bull to Cole. It was rules, rules, rules.' Black youngsters are supposed to hate discipline of any kind, aren't they? What they actually hate is discipline without respect.

It's the lack of discipline in British schools added to the low expectations many teachers have for black children which has led an increasing number of parents of African and Caribbean descent to send their children 'back home' to learn some manners and get a proper education. Like any highly gifted youngster,

Cole needed an outlet for his incredible talent; he needed respect, and peers to compete with who provided a challenge. Lilleshall gave him all of that in abundance. Teachers there remember him as quiet and well-behaved. But, later, he was to come up against white authority again in the form of strict disciplinarians in the club system.

As far as I'm concerned, the charges made against black players for being 'ill-disciplined', 'lazy', 'unruly', 'uncontrollable' and 'unnecessarily rebellious' with 'severe attitude problems', are far more serious than allegations of violence on the pitch. You can dismiss the alleged violence because it can be proved that we're no more violent on the pitch than anybody else. The sport's most recent high-profile court cases involved black and white players in almost identical scenarios. A black victim, white perpetrator in one; a white victim, black perpetrator in the other. But the black player, Paul Elliott, was the one who didn't get a penny in damages although his career was, just like that of the white player, John O'Neill, also finished.

But allegations of a 'lack of discipline', 'laziness' or a 'bad attitude', etc., are much harder to dismiss because they are so subjective, and most of the time only one side of the story is heard: the side of the person who is making the allegation, normally a white individual in authority. Or the charges are levied without any attribution made. Football is a very closed world. How the hell do we know what's going on?

'Arrogant', 'sullen', 'trouble-maker', 'combative', 'confrontational', 'aggressive', 'attitude problem', 'surly', 'stubborn', 'bad timekeepers', 'lazy', are keywords. Tap them, in any order, into any database for footballers and most of the time the names that will come up will belong to black footballers. These are the words which are most commonly used to describe their personalities.

We, the public, aren't there in training to see if black players really do turn up late all the time, or even don't turn up; to witness that they don't work hard and are as lazy as many managers and coaches say. We're not there in the dressing rooms, offices, training grounds, club bars and wherever else managers and coaches interact with players to observe incidences of rudeness, dissent, bad attitude, volatility, insolence, surliness and shouting matches. What is clear is that when black players have behaved badly, it is rooted in their deep unhappiness about their situation, and to 'button it' is not a viable option for them at that moment.

A white man or woman can have a strong personality, not suffer fools around them, speak their mind, be tough and single-minded over what they want out of life, and people clap him or her on the back, saying things like: 'That's what the country needs, more determined people like them.' 'Aggressive' becomes a compliment; confidence isn't redefined as arrogance. A black man or woman with the same characteristics is regarded as a threat, a misfit and a potential danger to society. 'Aggressive' is no longer a compliment.

It seems that white minds can cope only with black personalities that fit extremes. Blacks are either passive, submissive and a bit dozy, or rebellious, surly and aggressive, with an attitude problem; they may be laid-back, smiley, happy people; or ferociously violent and aggressive. There's nothing allowed in between: it's far too complicated and difficult to expect and understand that black people can have personalities equally as complex and multilayered as any white. Are black people still too dangerous to be allowed to be individuals with the same personal freedoms of speech and action as whites?

Black people know that 'insubordination' (disagreeing with a white person in charge) only has to happen once with a black player for the alarm bells to start clanging in white minds, for it to go down on a 'conduct' record and be blown out of all proportion, splashed across the papers and be attached to a character for ever. Complain and you've got a 'chip on the shoulder'. We know, because it happens to us and our friends all the time in our working lives.

Ian Wright was so infuriated and unhappy by the constant clashes with Bruce Rioch, the new manager officially in charge of Arsenal after George Graham, that he did the unthinkable and put in a transfer request, although it was well-known that he saw himself as an Arsenal man and hoped to finish his playing days at Highbury. The omens for the two men hadn't been good from the start. Although Graham was renowned for his attention to discipline, he understood what made Wright tick and was on record as accepting him 'warts and all'.

When he arrived in the summer of 1995, Rioch had a need to impose his own disciplinary methods on the man who symbolized Arsenal. At the start, Wright seemed up for it: 'The boss and I had a long talk before the season started and he told me that I was not applying myself properly in training. Now I know that as long as I apply myself right in training, it will come right on Saturday. I am happier for it. I cannot wait for the next game. I love training now. We have no matches this week, but our five-a-side competition in training is just as important to us.' It didn't have far to go downhill from there.

Soon it was clear that the two men were having major bust-ups. Wright's 'bad attitude' was called into question several times by Rioch, who also accused him of having a chip on the shoulder (!), and of being arrogant. After Arsenal were knocked out of the FA Cup it was reported that Rioch laid the blame at Wright's feet.

Arsenal fans weren't having a transfer request, and made their feelings known: if there was a choice, Rioch would have to go, even if he hadn't completed his first season with the club. A truce was declared. But Rioch did have to go – dumped by the Arsenal board at the beginning of the '96–97 season. When

Wright went into print with his backing for the directors' decision, acting manager Stewart Houston and some players turned against him, apparently even refusing to speak to him. As Wright said pointedly, how comes everyone else is allowed to speak their mind, and nothing happens, but when he opens his mouth, the attitude is that he's got no right to voice his opinions. The attitude is: don't think, just put the ball in the net.

'Bad attitude' has to be the most common charge directed at black players by the white football management structure. What makes me suspicious about the truth in this charge is that it is also the most common accusation thrown at black people who aren't footballers. The rest of us.

Many black footballers are supposed to be lazy, idle creatures who abhor training sessions. A lie put about by managers who were reluctant to hire black players in the early days was that they were 'too laid-back'. One of the greatest stigmas attached to black people in general is that they are slow, lazy, idle people. We're supposed to be too busy being cool, laid-back and chilled out to get a day's work done. Yet, paradoxically, isn't 'to work hard' supposed to be 'to work like a nigger'? (In March 1997, the Lord Chancellor, Lord Mackay, publicly reprimanded Judge William Crawford QC for telling a woman in Newcastle Crown Court, who handed him a sick note; 'I often wonder why doctors sign sick notes with such ready alacrity . . . Why, I know many people with duodenal ulcers who work like niggers.' A complaint was lodged by an Asian social worker with court staff. In published extracts from his letter, Lord Mackay said he found the remarks 'particularly surprising, given that I understand you have attended the course organized by the Judicial Studies Board on ethnic awareness. I trust you now recognize that use of such expressions is likely to give offence and did, in fact, give offence to members of the ethnic minorities. I should be dismayed to hear that you had again, in your public position and judicial capacity, given any cause for offence in this or any similar way, and I expect you to make a greater effort to guard against doing so in the future.') But at the same time, a black person who is efficient, hardworking and likes to get the job done is seen as a creature from outer space. The lazy image is easier on the brain – even some black people buy it.

John Fashanu, with his fingers in many business pies, was severely criticized for being too busy with his outside interests to grace Wimbledon's training ground. Looking back at his time at Wimbledon, former manager Bobby Gould had some words of advice for Ron Atkinson when he bought Fashanu: 'He must watch the lad's training habits, which have dropped away,' he said in *Today* in August 1994. 'I know from my Wimbledon days how Fash would phone in saying he's stuck in traffic on Hammersmith Bridge while we were hard at it. I called him in one day to talk about his lateness and, thinking of club fines, he said: "Here you are, boss – there's my chequebook and gold card. Give them back after training."'

Fashanu may have been able to exchange banter with his manager, but his fellow Wimbledon players were so annoyed by his training habits that they called an emergency meeting. No one had anything to say to Fashanu's question: 'Do I ever not turn it on when it comes to Saturday?'

Derby defender Paul McGrath has a 'God knows whether he'll turn up' image because of the occasions he's been absent without leave. Other breaches of club discipline brought heavy financial penalties, like the time he was fined £5000 by Villa for missing the team coach to an FA Cup tie.

'Wayward' should be his middle name, it's used so often about him. His reputation as a boozer hasn't helped either. He's had bust-ups with managers Alex Ferguson (the final one so bad that he was fined £8000 and kicked out of Manchester United), Jack

Charlton and Ron Atkinson. And Villa had him on a pay-as-you-play contract.

Yet this man is an awesome defender. Why is he knocked for his heavy drinking? It wasn't any worse than his fellow Irishman, George Best, who's a national hero (and playing master-class football is only one of the reasons why). Best's bad-boy image has helped only to make him a lovable, idiosyncratic personality. Volatility with respect to Best now means 'expect exciting and entertaining experiences'. It doesn't mean disruption. Today, people pay money to see Best at some event or other in the hope that he'll live up to his reputation. That is if he turns up.

When McGrath went on drunken binges during his time at Old Trafford – the club he arrived at as a youngster – he wasn't propping up the bars alone: players like Bryan Robson and Norman Whiteside were also part of the Manchester United 'wild bunch' that infuriated Ferguson. McGrath came to United with more excess baggage than the usual teenage recruit: he was recovering from depression and getting used to having a mother whom he had not seen since he was a baby suddenly reappearing in his life – all while adapting to life under the spotlight at the country's biggest football club.

McGrath was the backbone of the defence for both his club and his national team, the Republic of Ireland, despite having the training schedule of a 5-year-old because of all his knee operations. Both McGrath and Fashanu gave more than 100 per cent on the pitch. Deep down the managers know this. Maybe the black players who supposedly don't work as hard as the white players don't need to.

Or maybe, as the Liverpool defender and Republic of Ireland international, Phil Babb, put it in the *Daily Telegraph* in March 1995: 'People say I'm lazy, but there's a streak in me that says this isn't the most important thing in the world. It's a game and there are other things I could be doing that could mean more to me. I give 100 per cent, but off the pitch, I just wonder about it sometimes.'

Stan Collymore was supposed to be 'idle as the day is long', yet he spent an entire season as the country's most expensive player, so he probably does have something going for him. When he was at Nottingham Forest his manager, Frank Clark, publicly attacked him and the black Dutchman, Bryan Roy, for not trying hard enough during a 2–2 draw with Tottenham in March 1995, claiming: 'Their performances were unacceptable to the other players and the fans. I had nine players battling and trying to turn the game around. Two others were just waiting for things to happen. I have a real problem. Poor performances I can accept. Deliberate poor performances, I cannot. The team is set up to get the best out of those two. But when they just stand up there waiting for another player to produce a super pass for them to score, then you wonder.'

The *Daily Mirror* said Collymore 'didn't do himself any favours, and looked nothing like a star. Uninterested and lazy, he wanted everything on a plate. And a knife and fork handed to him.'

Collymore never really forgave Clark for that attack. As he saw it, when things didn't go well for Forest, 'the buck seemed to stop with myself and Bryan Roy. While I don't complain when somebody suggests my play was poor, being told I didn't try properly is totally out of order. I always try. I want to score in every match. I'm in a position now where I don't need to be continually dug at like that. I like to feel wanted and appreciated by my gaffer, rather than come in every day for training on tenterhooks.'

In the *Sun* he said: 'I feel I've more than played my part for this club, both last season and for most of this one. I know I didn't do too well against Spurs, but it wasn't for the want of trying. The manager doesn't seem to realize how many runs I make, yet the ball never seems to reach me. Forest are known as a passing team, but I have got the pace and I don't think we use it.

'I watch when Alan Shearer is found with a 40-yard pass at Blackburn. When one of our players gets the ball I make a run, and he just passes it to another player, so I have to make another run. I have told the manager these things before. And I have made my point when I have been playing well, so it doesn't look as though I am moaning or making excuses.'

But his manager's outburst only proved that Collymore's 'lazy' tag was proving difficult for the player to shake off. In 1993, after a match between Forest and Notts County, the *Sunday Times* reported that: 'Much of the the local pre-match hype surrounding a showdown between two neighbours, who are hardly rivals, involved Mick Walker, the County manager. He had apparently cast grave doubts on the attitude of Forest's £2 million striker Stan Collymore, after the former Southend player had spent a mere day in training at Meadow Lane three years ago.' After the match, Frank Clark described the Collymore goal as, 'a classic. We know his attitude isn't always right in training, but if he gets the goals then he'll continue to grab the glory.' A 1994 match preview in the *Sunday Times*, of QPR v Nottingham Forest, said: 'Collymore also struggles to apply himself on occasions. His workrate, particularly when he loses the ball, does not always match that of his teammates.'

Collymore departed at the end of the '94–95 season to Liverpool for a British record fee. But his 'difficult' tag also followed him to Merseyside.

It started so well with a wonderful goal at Anfield in August 1995 against Sheffield Wednesday – 'the sort of goal that men on their debut would kill for' – and with his new manager's assessment ringing in his ears: 'He has a lot of things in his armoury I didn't think he had,' said Roy Evans, who'd interrupted a Caribbean holiday to sign Collymore. 'He has a really good awareness of what everybody else is doing. I thought he would be more of an individualist. He can play within the team. He puts people in and he puts good crosses in.'

The newspaper writers were more mindful. Colin Wood, writing in the *Daily Mail*, warned Evans: 'It doesn't exactly fit the picture painted of Collymore earlier in his career – a young man who would not conform, rejected by Walsall and Wolves, the club he supported and still has a soft spot for, picked up by Crystal Palace from non-League Stafford Rangers but quickly passed on to Southend. Even at Forest he had the reputation of being a rebel.' But Evans had already spent his £8.5 million.

Liverpool are renowned for their easy-does-it, pass-and-move build-up game; Collymore for his great runs. Could the two styles mesh? 'There will be modifications,' said Collymore, 'because my trademark is to get in behind people and get in early. Sometimes we keep the ball, looking for openings, and maybe as the season goes on there will be compromises between the two to get the best out of both.'

In October, *Sun* journalist, Mike Ellis, reviewing a Coventry–Liverpool game, wrote: 'It is going horribly wrong for the most expensive player in the country. Right now, that £8.5 million price tag fits like a noose around the neck of Stan Collymore. And when manager Roy Evans ended his misery with a 76th minute substitution, it smacked of an act of mercy.' Collymore had scored twice – including his debut goal – in 8 games.

Collymore said: 'Sometimes I get the feeling I am watching a great side and I am not involved, even though I am out there with them. Before the match the gaffer told me just to relax and play my normal game. But it was just not happening for me. It is very difficult right now. I know I must adapt to the Liverpool style but it is not what I was used to at Forest. We used to defend deep and hit teams on the counter attack, which suited me. But here many of the lads have been in the side for a long time and they are all comfortable on the ball. I am not getting into games the way I did at Forest and it is very frustrating. Whatever happens I will never lose my self belief. I have had a lot of ups and downs in my career. But I know the boss would not have spent all that money if he did not know my capabilities.' Things were getting so bad at Liverpool that he'd forgotten how he'd also criticized Forest for not bringing him into the game more.

Then the rumours started that he was missing training, even going AWOL. And there was supposedly resentment from the other players that, instead of living near the club, Collymore was commuting from Cannock, his home town in Staffordshire, where his family and close friends still lived. A 150-mile round trip. To sit on the bench, as he was being forced to do more frequently, or play in the reserves. (Or not, as the case was. In November 1996 he was fined £20,000 for refusing to play in the reserves.)

Collymore went public with his frustrations. In an interview with the magazine *Four Four Two*, he criticized the Liverpool management and threatened to quit if his future remained uncertain. 'If I felt now that I'd be stuck at Liverpool for the next two years and just be average, just go through the motions, I would give up football tomorrow without a doubt.'

'I don't feel that by leaving me out of the team the manager is taking the pressure off me. I don't know of any other industry that would lay out £8.5 million and then not have some plan of how they are going to use it or pre-plan to think: Is it worth buying this anyway? You would think people would think it through even if it is a £20,000 transfer.

'I thought I was going to a club with better players who would give me even better service. But I never sat down with Roy Evans to discuss the plan.' They were highly intelligent points to make, but Collymore – who was later to admit that he was shocked when he saw his words in print – forgot one important fact: black men are not supposed to criticize white men in authority, to analyse and question the rationality of their actions, to challenge them.

The Sun, featuring a large, ugly photo of Collymore, entitled 'Service With A Snarl', wanted Liverpool to force the striker to 'grovel', and to 'get on his knees'. After a two-hour disciplinary meeting with Evans, Collymore issued a statement saying: 'I'd like to apologize to everybody connected with Liverpool FC, including the supporters, for what, on reflection, has proved to be a damaging article. In the summer I was delighted to sign for Liverpool and my feelings remain the same. I joined for football reasons and I still remain confident, and committed, to those ideals and my future with Liverpool.'

The *Daily Mirror* said it was a 'Kop Out' that he hadn't been fined heavily and 'booted on to the transfer-list for remarks which undermined the authority and questioned the judgement of his manager'.

George Graham let Andy Cole leave Arsenal because he felt Cole was lazy and rebellious. As Cole remembered: 'My time there was so miserable, I nearly turned my back on the game. George drove me to the depths of despair. I was going nowhere and was desperate to get away. I was headstrong, disruptive and used to mess about. George pulled me aside many times and told me to work harder. "You're not helping yourself," was his phrase. Arsenal didn't think I could score goals,' he told the *Sun* in January 1995.

Cole's strike partner at Newcastle, Peter Beardsley, revealed in the same paper, after Cole left for Manchester United, that: 'If Andy had a fault, it was in his approach to training. He would be the first to admit he was hardly the most dedicated in the world. Maybe he could have worked harder, but he never tried to hide the fact that the only time he was really happy was when the sessions were over.'

A picture of Cole in the *Sun* was captioned: 'Shrug 'n' Shuffle Style . . . that's the laid-back action you can expect to come from Andy Cole.' Cole left Newcastle after shattering their goalscoring records and as the country's (then) most expensive player. But, naturally, none of that seemed to count; what was important, apparently, was that he didn't perform like they wanted him to in training. The record was ignored for the sake of an argument.

Cole was criticized when he was scoring at Newcastle for 'only' being able to do that, and then when he went to Manchester United and the goals dried up, they really got stuck into him – for not being able to score.

Nearly a year after his transfer, David Miller said in *The Times*: 'Alex Ferguson, for all his dexterity in winning earlier titles, is now faced with the reality of a mammoth blunder. Cole, bought for £7 million, is a failure.'

John Sadler wrote in the *Sun*: 'In twelve baffling, bewildering months, the irresistible force of Andy Cole has blown itself out. The free-scoring phenomenon, the devastating tornado that swept him towards the promise of a glittering, record-breaking career is over. Reluctantly and sadly, I fear that the career of Andy Cole as we once knew him is all but finished. Nor do I seek to justify writing at the time of his astonishing £7 million transfer to Old Trafford that it could mark the beginning of the end. The intimidating expectancy generated by his arrival and fee has engulfed him [in] a fog of uncertainty and doubt – no longer able to do what used to come naturally.'

Michael Henderson wrote in a match report in *The Times*: 'Cole is good at one thing – scoring goals. This season, having found the net once in seven matches, he is not even doing that.

111

He headed wide from an unmarked position in front of goal, allowed Immel to smother a poor shot and screwed another effort, a better one, past the far post. The supporters are right to expect rather more from a player who cost £7 million.'

And even if, elsewhere, there was grudging acceptance that Cole was an improved all-round player than he had been at Newcastle, this was dismissed because, as *Times* writer Andrew Longmore put it, 'in the process of conversion, Cole has lost his basic instinct for goal. He might be a better player, but the goal charts say he is not a better striker. Cole rarely talks to the press, but those close to him say his self-belief is still intact and that, like Ipswich Town, who last year conceded five to Cole and nine altogether, some team somewhere is going to pay dearly for the bad run. In his own defence, Cole can legitimately point to a lack of service from the wings, caused by the departure of Kanchelskis and the more roving role adopted by Giggs.'

Neither did Cole manage to forge the same on-pitch relationship with Cantona as he had done so effectively with Peter Beardsley.

The FA Cup Final 1996: Liverpool versus Manchester United. Both of England's most expensive players – both black – were playing. Both Collymore and Cole were substituted: Collymore by Ian Rush; Cole by Paul Scholes. A depressed Cole kept his head down and away from the camera lenses. He didn't want anyone to see his face.

Once he was substituted, the television commentators' barbed comments about his performance ceased; they agreed that Cole had to regain his confidence. But they failed to recognize that the media had sabotaged it in the first place.

At the end of the first season in which three black players were the three most expensive signings, two had huge question marks over their form and their duration at the clubs which had bought them, and the third, Ferdinand, whose superb form no one could question, couldn't even get into the national line-up. Was three blacks at the top of the hierarchy too unpalatable a proposition? An achievement too far?

Banana Skins Shouldn't Put You Off Your Game

'I want them here, and I want them here now – right now. Do you understand? Do you understand me. I want them here, *now*.' I was screaming so loudly down the phone at her, I didn't hear a word the poor telephonist managed to get in through my gasps for air. Whether she understood or not, I slammed down the phone, ran into the kitchen, and threw open the top drawer of the nearest unit. I took out an old carving knife and went to my front door.

He'd gone. But what did it matter, at that moment, that he wasn't there? I could feel the physical presence of his ugly voice hanging in the air. Ugly, harsh, slurred and loud, very loud. I don't know why I thought he couldn't be shouting at me, the male voice was coming from right outside my front window. Maybe it was because at first I couldn't understand what he was saying – all you could hear was this growling sound. Then he built up to his crescendo, and it was crystal clear.

'N-ee-g-g-a. N-ee-g-g-a . . . I'm gonna burn ya out. You fuck . . . fuckin n-ee-g-ga . . . yah gonna burn. Fuckin . . . just yer wait.'

I was now at the window. It was dark and he wasn't near a street lamp. I could see that he was tallish and thin, with short, stubby hair and a small moustache. He was wearing a shabby anorak and dark trousers. He looked very much like the next-door neighbour.

He was very unsteady. He was practically bent in half, and then suddenly raised himself upright, let out another 'N-ee-g-g-a' and kicked my car twice. He knew it was my car; he knew I lived in my house. It wasn't the man next door, but this white man lived very close.

In the main hall of my sixth-form college, a close friend of mine got into a fight. I was passing by on the balcony that overlooked the hall. People told me I flew down the stairs and jumped on to the small group of bodies and started punching and kicking. I don't remember how I joined him and his mates, I only knew I had to get down there because I was angered by what I'd seen.

Now I was angered that this white man thought he could say what he was saying outside my front door. I was angry that the police weren't there the minute I picked up the phone. I was too angry to wait for them. I was angry, and in the forty seconds it took to dial 999, give my address, have a one-sided exchange with a telephonist and get a knife, he had gone. I wanted that man to feel pain.

The fact that he'd disappeared that quickly confirmed my feeling that he lived nearby. The horror of that. I banged on the next-door neighbours' house. They are white. 'No,' the wife said, 'we haven't heard a thing.' The man had been shouting at the top of his voice in a deserted street.

I'd be hard pushed to find somebody who'll call me 'nigger bitch' or 'wog' to my face during the course of an average day (unless his name's Bernard Manning and I've been led blindfolded into one of his side-splitting comedy turns in a Northern working-man's club). Most people I come across aren't as overt as that man that night, because, of course, we now live at a time when racism is more refined, its expression quite subtle and sophisticated. Often you're not aware that you are the target of a racist until after the peeling of layers of other possible reasons leaves the only one which fits.

Many times I've ended up at home wondering: Well, what the hell did he or she mean by that; or why did they do that; or just what was all that about . . . why, why, why? You try hard not to put your finger on it because, despite our communal black bravado, it's still painful to have to put the final jigsaw piece in place. Especially when you're looking at people you thought had broken through the colour barrier. People like friends, colleagues and neighbours; people who are not anonymous strangers. Like summer pollen, racist behaviour, assumptions and comments are everywhere in our not-very-multicultural society. But you don't have to wait for a hot summer's day when tempers are high for it to explode in your face.

The sad and depressing fact is that so many white people believe that racism has been virtually eradicated in many parts of England. They want to believe that the majority of people are above such feelings. They cannot take in or understand the new racism because they can't see it for themselves. The new racism is not as easily digestible as a house daubed in racist slogans, or a beaten-up Asian shopkeeper. The nineties situation isn't as comfortably black and white as that any more.

I live on a white working-class street in north London. Over the years it has appeared that some of the neighbours have been deeply unsettled by blacks moving in. If I'd caught that racist bully, I would have had him arrested. I would have had a far more difficult time trying to get him arrested if I'd been at a match. A football stadium is a public place. But a football stadium is probably the only public place where that man would fancy his chances of legally getting away with shouting those words. Many men like him go to matches to air bottled-up racist sentiments they cannot legally express in public any more. They've paid their money and they'll say what they like . . .

'You fucking, cheating French cunt. Fuck off back to France, you motherfucker. You are a fucking animal. You are a fucking French bastard. Fuck off back to France. You don't deserve to be on a football pitch. You are a fucking animal.'

And then, to a man, the sportswriters wondered why he did it. They wonder because they've never had to put up with that shit themselves, but cannot believe that anybody else could possibly have difficulty in tolerating it.

It had to happen to a white person first, and the white person had to react with violence, before the extent of the horrors inflicted on black footballers by white racists were understood properly. Until it's happened to whites, until *they* feel it, it doesn't really exist. Everybody else – blacks – is overreacting.

You 'idle black bastard'. A white man from the Midlands won compensation of more than £16,000 because his boss called him that, and made other similar abusive racial remarks. The man, a crane driver at British Steel, was white, with swarthy skin. The tribunal ruled that he'd endured mental trauma, been left 'badly scarred', and was forced to leave his job.

The man said he was as English as fish and chips or Yorkshire pudding. 'I like sunbathing and do go a nice dark colour. But that's as black as I get. This guy knew I was as white as he was, but he kept calling me a black bastard almost every day until he made my life a misery.' He'd sued under the Race Relations Act saying, 'It is not a pleasant thing to be racially abused, as I now know.'

If black players applied for compensation for every time they had been called 'black bastards' in their working lives by whites, the football clubs would need more than an astronomical pay-day from BSkyB to cover the costs.

When the Cantona kung-fu story broke, I was working with a group of white colleagues, and the odd one out in more ways than one. At first, nobody knew what the Crystal Palace 'fan' had done or said. I had a cold feeling in the pit of my stomach.

'That man, whoever it was, in the stand, I just know that man shouted something awful,' I said.

I thought their heads would fall off as they shook them violently in protest.

One girl shouted at me: '*Nothing, noth-thing*, should provoke him into kicking a fan.'

'He probably got what he deserved. Bastard,' I muttered tightly.

'Do you know how much they get paid? He's a *fan*.' She was furious with me.

When the newspapers published pictures of the holier-than-thou 'victim', I said to myself: 'He's a racist.'

Somehow the man's version of his words – 'Off, off, off. Go on, Cantona, have an early shower' – didn't quite tally with what Cantona and other members of the crowd heard. And then came the 'revelations' of how the 'fan' had been convicted of having attacked a Sri Lankan-born petrol station attendant with a three-foot-long spanner during his attempt to rob him, and how he supported racist organizations.

A couple of days later, the same girl, subdued, said: 'But black players put up with it.'

'So that's OK, then,' I replied, and turned away. This time, I was maddened at the audacity. Nobody had taken a blind bit of notice when we'd suffered it. But when it's time to preach (or retreat) it's usually time to bring on the noble blacks.

The only important legacy of Cantona's kick is that white people now know that a white man would not tolerate racial abuse of the kind that blacks 'put up with'. It's a crime that black players have had to put up with it, and have had to manufacture excuses to themselves for having to do so, to prevent them from losing their sanity.

'I know what must have been going through his head,' said Ian Wright, sympathetically, in the *News of the World*, 'because

I've been so close to losing it with a supporter. You cannot defend the indefensible, but there have been times when I've just wanted to get in there and sort them out because of the disgusting, degrading things they've said about me or my family.

'I've been there on the edge, but I've pulled myself back purely because I could not allow them to pull me down to their level. Now I look at what Eric is facing, and thank God that I kept my self-control, thank God that I didn't put my livelihood at risk and shame my wife and kids.'

Cantona had kung-fu kicked racism in football on to the agenda for everybody to discuss, including those not interested in the game. One single white man's trauma experienced in a single night equalled the pain and psychological damage endured individually and collectively by dozens of black players over decades. Players who had bananas thrown at them, were spat at, sworn at, heard monkey impersonations directed at them, and were called racist names by fans and players alike. As a test for their characters, you understand.

'There's much more pressure on black players to maintain a level head,' says Paul Elliott, who once played for Celtic. 'And that's why a black player has not been involved in a Cantona-like incident. You have to commend black players for this. What happened to Cantona is something that black players have had to put up with for many years. I put up with it for the best part of my fourteen years in the game,' he told the *Guardian* in March 1995. Nearly eighteen months earlier in *The Times*, he'd revealed: 'In Scotland there were monkey chants and bananas thrown on to the pitch. Every time I came into possession of the ball, they would boo and shout: "You black bastard."'

Elliott told the *Guardian*: 'The problem has been there in some areas for twenty years, particularly when you travelled north, but immense progress has been made in the last twelve months. I can remember playing against my own club, Chelsea, some years ago and I had to suffer banana throwing – the club had a terrible reputation at the time. I have taken great pleasure in the improvement.'

'Between 1981 and 1985,' an article in the *Observer* pointed out in March 1994, 'a section of The Shed would check the Chelsea team sheet before attending a match. If the name of Paul Canoville appeared they would find some other means of entertainment that afternoon. Canoville was Chelsea's first black player, and at a time when the racism there was at its most virulent ... The Shed, once a notorious breeding ground for bigots, was now a recruiting office for white supremacists and not a welcoming place for black football supporters.'

Brendon Batson, deputy chief executive of the Professional Footballers' Association, can't even bear to think about it. 'During my playing days, the abuse was horrific. There were some grounds I played at when I was pleased there were fences to keep me away from the fans.'

Chris Kamara, current manager of Bradford City, looked back at his playing days in *Four Four Two*: 'There's no comparison between the state of racism now and when I started playing in the mid-1970s. To be honest it's few and far between now but when I was at Portsmouth I was booed the whole time by a section of our own supporters, the NF element, which seems to have gone now. Newcastle was bad too, you'd get bananas thrown at you and all that. It was hard to keep playing in those conditions, but to be honest what hurt most of all was when you'd walk into a room and your own team-mates would go quiet because they'd been telling jokes that would offend you.'

And hurt it did, and does – however much some players, notably John Barnes, like to deny it in public. Ces Podd was at Kamara's club for fourteen years as a player. 'When I began playing, it was a nightmare,' he remembered, 'grimacing' in a May 1993 *Voice* profile. 'I was spat at and I was called names by supporters and players alike. I used to become very upset and emotional – I even cried at times. I don't know how many times I came home and told my mum I was going to pack it in. But she told me if I wanted to be successful in everything I do, I had to be strong enough. She also told me about the hardships she and my dad had experienced in bringing us up, and I found it very consoling. I was also fortunate enough to have Brian Edwards as the manager at Bradford City at the time, who understood the problems. He encouraged me to carry on and he appealed to supporters to get behind me instead of knocking me all the time.'

'Barnes, when asked, has claimed that in the thick of the fray, it is not possible to pick out individual comments or even songs from the crowd,' wrote Dave Hill in his 1989 biography of the Liverpool midfielder, *Out Of His Skin*. 'Batson of the PFA expresses a different view, a cautiously dissenting one: "We *are* conscious of it. Because if any person is going to be subjected to ninety minutes of abuse, you'd have to have a hide thicker than a rhinoceros to say it didn't affect you. I always remember going to places like Leeds and West Ham where they used to hurl bananas at us and what have you . . . and it is so insulting. But what do you do? Do you react to it, then maybe throw your game completely, and then be subjected to more of it? You've literally got to grin and bear it. And I think that is one of the problems in itself. If you grin and bear it, everyone thinks, 'Oh, well, you're accepting it.' But I can assure you that black players *don't* accept it." Maybe Barnes was telling the whole truth as he saw it or maybe he was being the practical diplomat, his father's son. What seems certain, though, is that to have said anything different, to confess to being wounded, would have amounted to an invitation to further attack – the black footballer's Catch 22.'

The poisonous cocktail of pain and suppressed anger is debilitating, dehumanizing and potentially deadly for the black person who has to experience racism but is forced by circumstances to turn a blind eye and pretend to be deaf. (We suffer more high blood pressure, heart and stress-related illnesses because of prejudice.) Perhaps it is in recognition that this situation is no longer acceptable that a new generation of black stars have started to stop grinning and bearing it.

I'LL NEVER PLAY FOR 'RACIST' GOULD AGAIN was the *Sun*'s backpage splash in April 1997. The Wales and former Wimbledon manager, Bobby Gould, had to explain the remarks he'd made which had led the talented Cardiff-born Bolton striker, Nathan Blake, aged 25, to make his vow. Gould told the *Guardian*: 'All I said was, in a situation where we've conceded three goals against Holland, "Why didn't somebody pick the big black bastard up?" Something like that, something that has been said many times in many dressing rooms.' The 'big black bastard' was Nottingham Forest's Pierre Van Hooijdonk. But it was the bib incident six months after that Holland game which sparked the public row. Gould told the *Sun*: 'In training I picked four teams – yellow, green, white. I said to them, "The rest of you stay in black, and that's you Nathan" . . . Am I a racist? Go and ask Cyrille Regis. Ring up Sam Hamman and ask him how many black players I wanted to buy. Perhaps Nathan has finer feelings than other people. In future I will take that on board.'

'I still want to play for Wales but I don't want to play for him. I have a total lack of respect for him,' Blake told reporters. 'I could not believe what I heard. I am an established striker. I should not have to listen to it from my own people, especially from my manager.' The bib row happened just before a World Cup qualifier against Belgium; Blake refused to play in the game. He also refused to accept an apology saying it meant nothing because, as he revealed in the *Daily Mail*, 'he could also recall an incident when he was playing for Cardiff City six years ago when Gould made a racist comment about him and black teammate Ray Daniel.' The *Mirror* said that 'reference [was] to "banana boats"'. Gould kept his job.

It seems that too many white people still feel that calling a black person a 'black bastard' is acceptable. They don't have a problem with it. It seems that black people will have to wait until white people have a problem with hearing and seeing them being called 'black bastards', and any other form of verbal abuse to do with their colour, before fuss and bother turns into action and results. Until then, protestations from young and older black players will continue to fall on deaf ears. In February 1997 the BBC's *Six O'Clock News* showed pictures from a November 1996 game between Arsenal and Manchester United during which Peter Schmeichel could clearly be lip-read calling Ian Wright a 'fucking black bastard'. (The news report had arisen because of a second confrontation between Schmeichel and Wright at Highbury in February 1997.) My blood went cold when I realized what Schmeichel was saying.

Chelsea's manager, Ruud Gullit, told the press: 'If someone calls me a black B, I don't take it as a racist insult. Why? Because I *am* black.' Silly fucker, I thought (and I used to like him). Funnily enough, when the then Conservative Foreign Secretary Malcolm Rifkind was called a Jew ('*der Jude* Rifkind') by the quality German newspaper, *Frankfurter Allgemeine Zeitung*, that same February, there was national outrage in the House of Commons and in the newspapers. The Labour MP, Gerald Kaufman, told the *Guardian*: 'I think this is absolutely disgusting. It is something I think the Prime Minister should take up urgently.' A Tory MEP said he would bring the matter up in the European Parliament. The German journalist and her paper apologized within three days and promised not to use the phrase in future. But Rifkind *is* a Jew. If, using Gullit's analysis, Jews shouldn't get upset at being called Jews or Jewish because they *are* Jews, why was there such a palaver?

The Crown Prosecution Service had a little look into the Wright and Schmeichel affair. The result: no charges were brought against Schmeichel. The chairman of the Commission for Racial Equality, Sir Herman Ouseley, was quoted in the *Mirror*: 'If the FA thought there was any evidence of racist remarks between these two players, they should have resolved it themselves. It's just a cop out to hide behind the police. I don't know of any charges brought by the police in Great Britain against anybody for making a racist remark. So they are not going to do anything in this case, are they? Unless they bring in an army of lip readers! No, it is not a case for the police. It's a case for the FA.' Well, in that case, the result: Schmeichel was not punished by the FA. There was no apology from Schmeichel, Alex Ferguson or Manchester United's board. Instead, all the headlines and articles focused on Wright's 'temper' and 'behaviour'. So blacks are the cause of the racism they come across? Why didn't the powers-that-be *independently* find what Schmeichel mouthed offensive? Didn't it, in the late 1990s, definitely bring the game into disrepute? Wasn't it misconduct? Maybe not. Maybe that incident and the way it was handled merely reflects the prevailing climate. In the era of the New Racists, attitudes which came to the fore in earlier decades are merely disguised to suit the hypocrisy of the 1990s: there will be a lot of hot air and pious statements, but there will be no action and no results. Therefore, although more younger black players now refuse to grin and bear it, the end result, courtesy of officialdom, is the same as that faced by black players in the seventies and eighties. Nothing happens.

Some supporters of Southern clubs may feel awkward at throwing bananas at black players when their own teams may now contain several blacks, and *their* performances may be disrupted, not the opposition's. But the inner emotions remain the same, so it's a case of our blacks are different, better than the other side's niggers. And woe betide the 'our blackie' who signs for another side. His conversion to niggerhood status is instant, as Manchester United's Paul Ince found out. Hammer fans even went shopping in February 1994 to commemorate the first return-visit by Ince to Upton Park.

'When they start throwing banana skins at a player it's a sad reflection on life,' said Alex Ferguson, Ince's manager. 'What can I say? Ince was wonderful [he'd scored a goal], showing a lot of character against that treatment. After four-and-a-half years I thought that would have blown away.'

The *Mail on Sunday* match report in which Ferguson's quote appeared said: 'From the moment Ince emerged from the tunnel he was the target of sustained and vicious abuse.' However, nowhere in the article does the reporter name the sport the West Ham fans are taking part in as racism. The fans aren't racists; the article calls them 'the hooligan element', 'the louts', 'bully boys', 'critics' and, of course, 'boo-boys'. Critics with a bunch of bananas handy.

In the land of opera they sing their racism. When Ince became Inter Milan's first black player in June 1995, he also became a special target – as Paul Elliott, who'd played for Pisa in Serie A, warned him in the *News of the World* at the time.

'He's a foreigner, he's black, he's playing for a Northern club and he has cost seriously big money. The fans at clubs like Naples, Bari and Lecce will not like that at all. They are jealous of Northern clubs. Milan is very affluent. There are a lot of social and economic problems in the South. I had a lot of grief there. The crowds were always booing and taunting. In one game against Napoli, I came into contact with Maradona. The crowd were so incensed they tried to get at me. I had to be escorted off at the end of the game. Another black defender, Julio Cesar, broke his leg at Naples. As he was stretchered off, the crowd were throwing bottles from the stand.' Ince arrived in Milan to be greeted by racist graffiti on the walls of the San Siro stadium.

Although reluctant to even name the thing otherwise known as racism when it manifests itself in Britain, our press mount their anti-racism high horses when the crime takes place in another country. Under the heading: PREJUDICE AND HATE ITALIAN-STYLE: THE FIRST BIG CHALLENGE FOR INCE, the *Independent* wrote: 'Go to an Italian club game these days and there is a good chance you'll see plastic blow-up bananas being waved around in the stands as soon as a black player comes in contact with the ball. On a bad day there will also be jeering, abusive banners and the odd swastika. If the fans from the opposing team are in a really ugly mood, then they might even start chanting '*negro di merda, sei solo un negro di merda*' (shitty nigger, you're just a shitty nigger) to the salsa beat of Guantanamera. For black, Jewish and Third World players hoping to make their mark in Europe's most prestigious football arena, it is hardly the welcome they dream of. The laid-back, non-alarmist explanation touted by many Italian commentators is that fans are a loutish lot by nature but not particularly racist; they merely use any excuse, including ethnic origin, to give players from the opposing team a hard time.'

Where have we heard these excuses before? It's quite amazingly hypocritical that the writer can condemn the Italians for being 'laid-back' and 'non-alarmist' on football racists when white journalists in the United Kingdom share the same appalling attitude towards the 'loutish'. Obliviously, the article even claimed: 'It would be wrong to dismiss the treatment of Ince and others as a simple piece of laddish fun. Racism is without doubt on the increase in Italy as the number of African and East European immigrants rises noticeably, and resentment wells up in young Italians suffering the ill effects of economic crisis.'

*   *   *

London's Queens Park Rangers not only has several black players, but also has, proportionately, the largest black fan-base in the Premiership: about 3 per cent, according to the Leicester Centre for Football Research. But it was at Loftus Road in February 1995 that Ian Wright tried to spit at fans who were racially abusing him. He hit a female security guard instead. She started a private prosecution for criminal assault, but the star paid her £750 as an out-of-court settlement.

In a letter of apology to her, Wright wrote: 'I would like to make it clear from the outset that during the first half of that game I was subjected to a torrent of racial abuse and foul language from QPR supporters. This continued as I came off the field at half-time. I have no recollection – but I accept that there is evidence to this effect – that as I left the field I spat in your direction. I honestly have no recollection of this incident which would have taken place in a highly charged atmosphere, and if what is said is correct, then I say categorically that I was not motivated by any malice to you personally.'

The woman responded in the *Sun*: 'There was a lot of shouting and a few home fans were yelling abuse. But I don't remember anything racist directed at Ian Wright.' The FA fined the player £750.

They're more upfront up North. Barnsley were reported to the Commission for Racial Equality in October 1995 after Ian Wright was forced to suffer monkey chants and vitriolic abuse from their racist fans when Arsenal played them in a Coca-Cola Cup tie. A radio commentator said Barnsley stewards stood around doing nothing, some were even laughing, while the abuse was taking place.

John Fashanu said at the 1993 launch of the Let's Kick Racism out of Football Campaign that there were matches where he would avoid covering the whole of the pitch, going instead, 'from penalty-box to penalty-box and staying away from the touchlines to avoid the abuse'.

But it took a game against Everton during the 1992–93 season to shock him. 'I was coming off the pitch,' Fashanu recalled, 'when I got a lot of abuse. When I turned round I saw they were only about seven or eight years old. It was the first time in many, many years that I reacted to abuse they were shouting at me.'

The boys were screaming: 'You black bastard.' Where did those children pick that up from? Fashanu reported them to the police, not, he says, because he wanted to press charges, but to make sure that the youngsters, and their parents, were spoken to. He had been particularly upset because there had been a black child standing, silently, with the white children who were shouting their heads off.

Everton insist that they do not have a problem. They continued to do so even after reports that, following their 3–2 exit from the FA Cup at the hands of Division One's Bradford City (who have a black manager, Chris Kamara) in January 1997, white Everton fans spat at a black Everton supporter and racially taunted black Bradford players, Andy Kiwomya and Des Hamilton, as well as Everton's sole black player, Earl Barrett.

'We don't have a problem here,' an Everton official told me. 'We work a lot with minority groups in the community and we don't have a problem. It all stems back to a Liverpool match when John Barnes was playing, when he first joined Liverpool, and there were chants shouted at Barnes from the Everton crowd. The Barnes thing wasn't very nice; even as a supporter watching at the time, I didn't find it pleasant. But that was back in the eighties.'

The bananas, 'black bastard's and monkey chants may have been directed at Barnes during that game, but Everton fans also taunted their local opponents. 'Niggerpool,' they cried.

That may have been the eighties version; in the late nineties, that black Everton supporter didn't even bother to complain after the match. And a witness said nothing was done to help him at the time of the attack by his fellow supporters.

'Let's be honest,' the Everton official insisted, 'you can never stop anyone shouting anything. But you may be able to do something after the event.'

Maybe black people being able to do something 'after the event' is the only real change since the early sixties when the black South African, Albert Johanneson, came to England to play for Leeds. As the former Leeds coach, Syd Owen, recalled in a BBC television profile *Remember Albert?*: 'Albert was one of the first coloured players to play in English football and it was a big occasion for him. And I knew some of the problems that Albert would have to adjust to, life in this country, especially him being a coloured person.'

According to Peter Lorimer there were 'taunts from the crowd, you know, and they used to do jungle sounds to try and put him off. I think it was one of the things he didn't adapt to.'

'They talked about the working-class North when I was in middle-class London,' rugby star, Martin Offiah, told the *News of the World* in 1995, 'but I still had no idea people would vent their feelings so vociferously. Among the crowds you do get there is far too much prejudice. It doesn't seem to matter that over the years rugby league has enjoyed its black heroes from Billy Boston onwards. Certain places, such as Hull, St Helens and Warrington, have always been notorious, and elsewhere the prejudice remains.

'I've had the lot over the years. You know, I'm talking about bananas being thrown at me, the ignorant shouting, coming off the field covered in spittle. Why should my mum see things like that? My folks are from Hackney and have hardly modelled their lives on some of the experiences to be had at Northern rugby league grounds. And, remember, I'm on the wing, nearest the crowd.

'It's actually the individuals who are the worst. I had every sympathy for Manchester United's Eric Cantona at Crystal Palace. OK, he shouldn't have kicked someone in the crowd – that was totally unacceptable – but I know the feeling. I have been driven close to the edge many times. You take 80 minutes of constant abuse, sometimes just because you've begun the game by falling over, and it's very hard to maintain your composure. Yes, I've often felt like leaping into the crowd and kicking someone myself.'

But woe betide the black player who retaliates against the racist white opponent. World Player of the Year, AC Milan's George Weah, headbutted Porto's Jorge Costa in the tunnel during a Champion's League match in November 1996 and broke his nose. Weah said Costa had called him a 'nigger'. UEFA called up the Liberian for a disciplinary hearing. He got a six-match European ban. UEFA's statement said: 'The committee took into consideration George Weah's particularly gentlemanly conduct on the pitch. He has received only three yellow cards in UEFA competitions during the last five years, and was also granted a Fair Play Award by FIFA.' Well, what a lucky boy Weah was that they took all that into account and let him off with just a six-match ban. The committee probably didn't give a monkey's about what would make a player with that kind of record lose his temper.

At Inter, Paul Ince shoved opponent Giampietro Piovani for calling him a 'dirty black bastard'. The referee sent Ince off. Southend striker, Dave Regis (brother of veteran Cyrille), elbowed Derby's Croatian defender, Igor Stimac, after Regis claimed he was racially abused throughout the match. Regis was sent off – his first red card in more than 160 League games. Stimac said: 'If Regis has trouble with his culture that's up to him, but I didn't make any racist remarks.' Ronnie Whelan, Southend's manager, said: 'Dave told me that Stimac was abusing him for most of the game and he just snapped. He shouldn't have done it but it was under severe provocation. There's a big campaign urging fans to kick racism out of football, but it has to start with the players.'

Even the FA had to admit, post-Cantona of course, that there was still a major problem with racism in the game. 'We are concerned,' said Graham Kelly, 'about the increasing level of abuse which footballers seem to have to suffer. We don't feel it is acceptable, we don't think it is part of the game and we hope to talk to leading politicians about an initiative to deal with it.' Yes, let's sit down and 'talk' about an 'initiative'.

Black pain, debilitating trauma and psychological damage is heavily diluted by the football industry. As discussed, the activity of racists is variously described as: 'booing', 'jeering', 'barracking', 'needling' or 'giving stick'. In another avoidance of naming the thing, the racists are called 'fascists' (giving them a worldliness and a pseudo-intellectualism racism doesn't possess). And, of course, there's the favoured, rather childlike, 'boo-boys'. Being a 'boo-boy' even sounds quite jolly. Nothing as nasty and as evil as it actually is in reality.

A player like Barnes, who's been on some jolly England outings with his personal following of boo-boys, cloaks the personal damage to himself by trying to shrug it off, and by calling it 'nationalistic' chanting: 'You have to accept being booed as part and parcel of the game,' he says. 'You need to take it with a pinch of salt,' Barnes told the *Guardian* in 1995. A nice, logical, rational statement, except that Barnes was the only England player who had to pack the Saxa in with his kit.

But even Barnes, as dignified as he is, doesn't possess the ability to deny the effect on him when he remembers how England fans abused him at that Wembley game against San Marino. 'It was a terrible night, and I will never, ever forget it.' San Marino was a very low point, but things didn't improve much. They hated him and they wanted him out of the game – whether he played well or badly for England was irrelevant. The result of the game was also irrelevant: England had beaten San Marino 6–0.

Time passed but nothing changed. Talking to the *Observer*'s Gary Lineker in April 1995, a few days after another display by the 'boo-boys' at the England–Uruguay game at Wembley, Barnes blamed the start of the abuse on the *Daily Mirror*. 'They did a piece saying that because I wasn't born here I didn't have the necessary commitment to play for England. So when the performance didn't go well the crowd looked at the lack of commitment thing and I became a prime target.'

Lineker commented: 'The fact that the Jamaican-born Barnes has persevered for his adopted country despite the boo-boys is evidence of his devotion to the national team. Barnes has handled what he admits has been a very hurtful situation with great dignity and diplomacy. Not for him a two-fingered salute or a two-footed foray into the front row, but a certain temperance and a determination to prove them wrong on the field.'

But it didn't even have to be an England game – Barnes was abused at the Liverpool versus Bolton Coca-Cola Cup Final in 1995.

'I reckon,' said Barnes in the *News of the World*, on the day of the Final, 'the people doing this are not so much racists as nationalists. I've been made a target because I was born in Jamaica and because I once admitted that in cricket matches I support the West Indies. Bryan Robson and I used to have jokes about it. I would always rib him about English cricket. The people who have a go at me at Wembley have latched on to that. They are the same kind of people who would give Eric Cantona a hard time because he is French. They just hate anything or anyone that is foreign. And when England are perhaps struggling I always get it in the neck, I'm always to blame.'

White fans' racist behaviour is often legitimized by white

sportswriters because the spotlight falls not on their racism but on how the player's performance may have provoked it. And if the player's game hasn't provoked it, then the focus is on how the player reacted to the racist chanting. Time and time again it's the player's form and character which are called into question, not the fans' behaviour.

England managers felt that the 'boo-boys' were reacting to Barnes' tactical roles on the pitch. It was never racism. Reporters felt the 'boo-boys' were merely lamenting the fact that he has 'never done it for England and he's had his fair share of chances'.

The *Daily Mail*'s Neil Harman considered Graham Taylor's options before the England–Holland game at Wembley in April 1993. 'Taylor confirmed Barnes' selection in the left-sided midfield role he discussed over the weekend and was not put off by a critic's reminder that the player used to insist under Bobby Robson's regime that he was never intended to play in midfield. "I'm looking for him to fulfil a specific task, as one of three out-and-out midfield players rather than as a flank player tucking in," said Taylor. "We aren't suggesting he's going to be a dashing outside-left. The crowd's reaction? John knows that if it happens, it happens, and he's got to come through it. He isn't turning away from the challenge."'

'I'm told John Barnes got some stick from the crowd,' said Terry Venables after the England–Uruguay game. 'I didn't hear that myself, but I would say he did quite well. There are different definitions of bravery and John Barnes didn't shirk from taking the ball or asking for it.'

'On the left, the experience of John Barnes and Peter Beardsley was appealing, but its age showed,' wrote Ian Ridley in the *Independent on Sunday* about the match. 'Barnes played too deep, drawn to his new Liverpool role. He performed competently when assigned the task, as had Barry Venison earlier, but one would expect as much without a pressing opposition. The jeers for Barnes were from those wrongly expecting something more.'

'The crowd's baiting of Barnes puzzled player and coach alike,' observed Joe Lovejoy in the *Sunday Times*. He asked: 'Might not spectators expect more from the player immortalized by *that* goal than the mere retention of possession? "You may have a good point," Venables conceded, "but he can't play the game he used to play. He plays the game in the centre of the field now. His skills are still there."'

'Venables,' said the *News of the World*, 'clearly determined to make Barnes a permanent part of his set-up, is baffled by the hostility from the terraces. He said: "I don't know what it is about Barnes. I don't know whether people see what I see. If we are going to play a passing game, we need people who can pass, work and not panic under pressure. He always wanted the ball when it could have been easier for him to disappear. I think he showed a lot of character." Barnes has been given a holding role in midfield by club and country and is a vital member of Venables' squad for next year's European Championships.' In the event, he wasn't – he was a member of a TV panel.

I have no record of an England manager coming out and attacking the England fans who've verbally lynched Barnes, and ordering them to stop. Just as British society has anti-racist legislation, the football world has the 1991 Football Offences Act, which makes racial abuse an arrestable offence if chanted 'in concert with one or more others' – a loophole for racist individuals. But in the same way that general anti-racist laws are underused or ignored altogether, so the football authorities have been reluctant to implement the laws at their disposal, saying they have to receive a complaint first. Just a handful of fans – 26 – had been convicted under the Act by 1995.

The racial insults and abuse are also legitimized in the industry by the widespread attitude that the 'fans' only do it to put black players off their game. As if this was a great tactical and psychological ploy, an additional bonus for the manager. In reality they do it because they want to do it, they get a kick out of doing it, and because they can generally get away with it.

'If,' said Wright in the *News of the World*, a few days after Cantona's kick, 'a player turns round and gives fans a mouthful after taking stick throughout the match, he's reported to the police and they're duty bound to investigate. But what would happen if I stopped a match, went over to a policeman and pointed out a fan who had been swearing and giving me abuse? Would I get the same hearing as a fan? I don't think so. I can't defend Eric, but I know where he was coming from.'

The industry isn't really interested in booting racism out of football because it is too busy with its own racist practices. We have white-run clubs, white management, the white Football Association, white referees and white sportswriters. One all-dominating colour, one dominant perspective: white. Softly-does-it criticism of 'hooligan' [i.e., racist] fan behaviour is an excellent smokescreen to divert attention away from examination of working practices which indirectly encourage fans to believe they can get away with their racism. It doesn't have to be overt to have an effect. The aim is still to protect the interests of white people, not to encourage the participation of blacks, or to have regard to black interests. But very few white people say that outright in our new era; most go through the correct motions expected of them in a 'multicultural' society, but the end result is the same.

As Ian Wright pointed out in the *Mirror* in August 1994: 'At the start of every season, soccer authorities come out and say, "Let's kick racism out of football". But halfway through the season, everybody forgets about it.'

The football authorities don't take racism seriously because it doesn't affect them or the bulk of their players and supporters. 'The Football League,' said Herman Ouseley, the first black person to chair the Commission for Racial Equality, 'still do not recognize that this is a problem. They want it dressed up as something else, as a problem of hooliganism or something like that, but the targeting of black fans and black players for abuse has been a specific problem.' He was speaking at the 1996 launch of the CRE's anti-racism campaign – its fourth.

The Football League is more than happy to turn up every year for what's turning into the annual launch of the Let's Kick Racism Out of Football campaign and hand out posters to the clubs, or make sure there's a couple of 'anti-racist' sentences in club magazines. 'We give the CRE,' the League has said, 'an unparalled platform to promote this initiative. We have 72 clubs who all offer help in some capacity, from programme adverts to billboards, to specific anti-racist campaigns. We have promoted this campaign to all our clubs.'

But it's rare to see a physical or verbal racist incident between white and black players and supporters acted upon publicly and swiftly by the authorities. If the black target of the racism doesn't complain to the authorities, that, it seems, is that. The end of the matter.

Sport is the only arena where black men and white men can compete as true equals. Man to man. As masculine as each other. They are in the closest proximity to what challenges them most: the other man, the other colour. You could take on the white man legally and whup him – wasn't that the great attraction of boxing? The American comedian and actor, Eddie Murphy, said soccer would not be successful in the States: 'The game will never take over from baseball. Baseball's the only chance we blacks get to wave a bat at the white man without starting a riot!' the Sunday Mirror reported during the 1994 World Cup.

Paul Ince added: 'All the black idols are in basketball, baseball or boxing. They make phenomenal money compared to American soccer pros. Kids want to grow up like them. It's natural.

There are a couple of good coloured lads in the United States team. But they'll hardly be around long enough to become role models.'

Role model or not, blacks in American sports are an ordinary feature of normal life. As American goalkeeper Kasey Keller, who played for Millwall (and was perfectly situated in the New Den to research his study of racism in sport as part of a sociology degree he was taking), put it in the *Observer*: 'When an opposing black player fouls one of our players you hear cries such as "spook" and black this and that, but whenever Etienne Verveer [black, former Millwall midfielder] is in possession, he is hailed as a hero. In America I couldn't imagine Michael Jordan going up to slam dunk the ball and the crowd racially abusing him.'

Sport plays such an vital role in the black man's psyche because it's the quickest way to say: 'I'm better than you, white boy – and I'm going to make more money than you.'

Unlike, for example, in the music and fashion industries, black sporting talent cannot be ripped off, left uncredited; white duplicates and cover versions cannot be made and celebrated. If you want a particular black talent, you can't white-clone him, there is no alternative but to get the real thing. In the sports world, the black supertalent is on equal terms with white in the economic driving seat. You can't white-out a black face in the publicity brochures because that will drive the public away – instead of putting bums on seats or increasing sales. In television and film, you can't confine him to the sidelines or make him a wallflower in group gatherings, because white people want to see HIM. And they'll pay for that privilege. So, he gets paid, and he demands and gets full exposure. The fashion world may claim that a black model on the cover reduces magazine sales, but the golfer Tiger Woods not only has his choice of golf magazines, he gets on the cover of *Fortune* too.

Only recently, in the eighties and especially now in the nineties, have white men had to realize how much their own sense of masculinity is wrapped up with employment, money and responsibility. With huge numbers of them now unemployed, many of those seeking work have had to settle for low-paid, unskilled, perhaps even part-time jobs, mainly in the service industries. Like too many black men have done since time immemorial.

That's why for black men it has always been different. They have been forced to create a masculinity that needn't depend on having a job and money to be functional; for black men there has never been a guarantee they would have the jobs, the money or the economic power needed to support their families and their communities. And yet, to change the gender in the title of former American slave Sojourner Truth's speech: 'Ain't I a man?' A resounding yes, if you are in sports and you are taking on the white man directly.

If you can't do better than a black person in life, you're nothing, aren't you? For whites who feel that way, the sight of a well-off, confident black person is a deeply destabilizing one.

Linford Christie said that the racial hatred directed at him was based on people feeling that he had 'too much power, too much wealth. It's like you should know your place and you don't,' he confided to TV psychiatrist Anthony Clare.

It's hard for a black sports star to have to recognize what amounts to almost a dual black masculinity. First he has the masculinity he literally sports in his arena; then there's the masculinity he's forced to wear once he leaves his sportsworld behind.

Guy McKenzie, a black friend of Albert Johanneson, remembered (in the BBC tribute) bolstering the man he was to outlive. 'We used to tell him that you're a man and you must live as a man. The only difference with the white man and you: the pigmentation of our skin is different. You're black and he's white. No man is better than you.'

A generation later and the stand-off continues. Christie would get stopped by the police when he was out driving in one of his three Mercedes. They didn't know it was Linford. They thought it was just another flash black who'd got above himself by driving a flash car – which he'd probably stolen or bought with illegal money.

'I was stopped four times in 1986 after collecting a car a sponsor bought for me,' said Christie in a *Today* campaign against racism in sport. ' "What's a nigger like you doing in an England tracksuit?" the policeman asked. Another time I was pulled over and asked to produce my driving documents at a police station as soon as possible. But I had already been ordered to do that earlier the same day. It seems to be accepted policy to stop a black man who is driving a new car. It would be nice to think that these incidents were isolated, but they're not.'

Christie told how he and fellow track star, John Regis, were walking home with a few friends when they were attacked by some drunken white men. 'Some police stood by and did nothing until John started to gain the upper hand. Then they intervened, slamming John up against the wall. It was John's first experience of blatant prejudice and it came as a big shock. And like me, John has been stopped many times driving expensive cars and quizzed for no reason ... most black members of the British athletics team can tell similar stories.'

The stand-off can even come down to remarking on how someone is dressed. I overheard a white man call a black male journalist 'arrogant' for wearing what was obviously an expensive new suit to an industry function. Anyone who feels that comments about a man's style can't be racially motivated, needs to look no further than the case of Jason and the comedians.

Jason Lee of Nottingham Forest had a head of long dreadlocks which he tied up in a ponytail during games to stop the locks from flying in his face. Two white, middle-class comedians, Frank

Skinner and David Baddiel, decided that the player's hairstyle was a huge joke and it became a running theme during their nationally televised football comedy show. They tormented the player. Baddiel even blacked-up on his show, stuck a pineapple on his head, while material supposed to resemble dreadlocks cascaded down. He had no shame.

As any white person who lives in an area where black people live (or interacts with or observes black people) could have informed the comedians, Jason Lee's hairdo is a common one in Britain's black communities.

The player became so distressed at the constant references to his 'pineapple' head, that it began to affect his performances. The terraces taunted him about his dreads; there were stupid cartoons and hurtful references in the tabloids which led to stories in other newspapers. His family got upset. His manager became involved; the player accused Skinner and Baddiel of wrecking his career; and he was transfer-listed. In the end, Jason fell on his sword, and cut his locks. He went bald.

'I looked in the mirror,' said Lee in the *Sun*, 'got my clippers and thought: Why not? Two minutes later it was all gone.' He had brought himself down to the comedians' size.

To cut your locks is a very significant step. Even if there are no religious or cultural reasons for your dreads (today, many young blacks just want 'funky' dreads because they look good), to grow them to shoulder length and longer can take years: they are then an investment of your time, care and attention.

It was appalling. I was in the hairdresser's when I read about Lee's new haircut. A man grabbed the newspaper out of my hands, shouting: 'Nah, it's not true.' But there was the picture of a grinning Lee holding the top of a pineapple above his head, and the headline: HE'S GOT THE PINEAPPLE OFF HIS HEAD. The salon shook its collective head.

'Soccer star Jason Lee has shaved off his notorious "pineapple head" dreadlocks,' said the *Daily Mirror*, 'after TV jokes about his bizarre hairstyle turned the fans against him. Yesterday as the Nottingham Forest striker proudly showed off his new bald look, he quipped: "They can't make a joke out of this."'

We, in that Camberwell (south-east-London) hair salon, knew their 'joke' was nothing short of racial harassment – even without Baddiel's get-up to make sure viewers got it. And the silly player let them get away with it. Funny, though, the comedians never touched Ruud Gullit. But, then again, bullies are always careful about who they pick on. Gullit would have cut them down to size. Indeed, it was said in *The Times* that one of Gullit's advertising contracts (for Mars M & Ms) has a clause which prevents him from cutting his locks.

White males love to accuse black men of being arrogant and cocky. A black man who carries himself well is a direct challenge to a white man – something in his stomach tightens, and he has to look into the black man's eyes or turn away. Both are options he wishes he didn't have. A black male American writer described how, whenever he was in an enclosed space with white men (a lift, for example), they would suddenly start to puff out their chests. One white male writer said of Paul Ince: 'Even the way he swaggers on to the pitch suggests a rather inflated ego.'

When blacks swagger off the pitch and into the outside world, a lot of white men want to bring those inflated egos down a peg or two, to remind black men that society still sees them as lower than white men. A friend of mine told me she'd witnessed an exchange between a white dustman and a black barrister outside the barrister's expensive house in West London. From his patronizing and challenging tone, she said the dustman clearly believed he was talking to an inferior being. It went past ordinary rudeness.

One of the luxuries we don't have as black people is being able to consider people as simply rude. It would be relaxing to think that someone is merely a rude so-and-so, but we let bad behaviour go more than once or twice at our peril. So often racist assumptions are fuelling the rudeness. How do we answer the question: would they have been more polite if I'd been white? It hangs in the air until the repetition of asking erases the benefit of doubt. And, frequently, observation of how the same 'rude' person changes his or her manner when dealing with whites confirms all.

A punch in the face following a racial insult doesn't leave much room for doubt. When Stan Collymore was called 'Chalkie' and punched outside a nightclub in Cannock, he set about the two men. But he was the one who ended up in court. The name-caller said he knew that 'Chalkie' meant a black man, but didn't know that it was a racist insult. They never do. Inside the nightclub, the man's woman friend had called Collymore 'a black bastard and said [he] should go back to Ethiopia'. He called her 'fat'.

Although Collymore was cleared of assault, he still feels the case hangs over him and adds to his 'problem boy' image. Incredibly, the fact that he had defended himself against racist louts made those in charge of the football industry ask even more questions about his character. 'That didn't help,' says Collymore referring to the case. 'And it added more fuel to the fire of those who want to have a go. I resent the problem tag because I don't see myself as causing any problems.'

Off the pitch there's no let up for many black players. All 5ft 6in of Mark Stein took on a 6ft 2in white man who had been taunting him with racial abuse after a match between Stoke City and Stockport County. Stein was found guilty of assault.

Striker Chris Kiwomya was drinking with other Ipswich players at a nightclub in the town in November 1994 when he was called a 'useless black bastard' by a 'fan'. The fan was punched in the eye. One of his neighbours said: 'There are a lot of people in the town who are upset because Ipswich are bottom of the

League and it looked like someone decided to vent their frustration on [Kiwomya].' When times are good, we can be one of them; when times are bad, we're black bastards.

There still appears to be an unease (and fear?) among white people inside and outside the sports industries that when blacks 'enter' a sport, they will progressively 'take it over'. It's happened in certain track events like sprinting; then there's boxing, basketball, and now even golf, the sport long regarded by black people as the last bastion of white privilege and racial prejudice, has a half-black half-Asian young man, Tiger Woods, as its acknowledged champion. He received death threats after winning the 1997 Masters tournament in multiple record-breaking style. In boxing, before the Detroit Brown Bomber, Joe Louis, heavyweight champions were all white. It was 'their' sport, with their Dempseys and Marcianos. Louis was the first black heavyweight – we loved him, and still love him, for that. And now we dominate. Ali will always be a black god. And, yes, the vast majority of us do love Tyson, jailbird or no jailbird. In Britain, black footballers have gone from just a handful twenty years ago, to approximately 15 per cent of registered players, whilst black people are just 1.6 per cent of the general population. What is the poor white man to do in the face of what amounts to be a black male virus going from sport to sport? Will he attempt to reclaim the white male ego? And how will he do it if he does?

What happens to the white man's sense of superiority, of masculinity, if the best man is the black man? Initially, it is outrageously churlish to do anything but acknowledge the result – even grudgingly. (Mind you, that didn't stop some English fans refusing to cheer goals scored by black England footballers.) If a white star appears, over a period of time – it could be weeks, months, or years – the black man's achievement will be demeaned and dismissed. If no white star appears, the black man's race will become the reason for his success. The black man has some innate ability, 'inborn superiority'. He wins without having to exert discipline or train himself mentally and physically because black people are built for sports. That's why all they're good at is sports.

The man who ran the first four-minute mile, and later became a consultant neurologist, Sir Roger Bannister, has this to say on the subject: 'It's certainly obvious when you see an all-black sprint final that there must be something rather special about their anatomy or physiology which produces these outstanding successes, and indeed there may be, but we don't know quite what it is.' In his speech to the British Association Conference in September 1995, Sir Roger speculated: 'It may be that their heel bone is a bit longer or maybe it is because of their adaptation to a warm climate. Or it may be their lower subcutaneous fat which means their power-to-weight ratio is better. Maybe they have an elasticity or a capacity innately of muscle fibres to contract quickly, which is some adaptation to a warmer environment because this would increase the speed of chemical reactions.'

'When I was a young athlete I was once told: "You're the wrong shape and the wrong colour to make it to the top." These words were next to a picture of Sally Gunnell holding the Union Jack outstretched after she'd won the Olympic 400m hurdles final in Barcelona the year before. 'That encouraging piece of advice,' she told *Today* in August 1993, 'came from Andy Norman, now the promotions officer for British athletics and one of the most powerful people in the sport. His remarks startled me – but they also stirred me. I thought to myself: "Right, I'll show you, I'll get there." Andy's jibe came during the era of the Grace Jackson type, when all the top women seemed to be black and 6ft tall. I didn't quite fit that description, but what Andy didn't realize was how determined I was to make it to the top.'

When white goalkeeper, John Burridge, asked himself why African runners were so successful, the answers made him change his lifestyle. In addition to not drinking or smoking, he had plenty of early nights and ate mainly porridge, rice, dried fruit, steamed fish and vegetables. This was on top of extremely high motivation – sparked by his poverty-stricken childhood as a miner's son – to make a lot of money. He had his own version of that black will to win. Plus high self-confidence and an inability to live without the game. He was still being employed as a non-contract Premiership goalkeeper when he was 43, one of Britain's oldest active professional footballers.

In an editorial entitled: 'Black power on the track', which I think is worth quoting from at length, the *Independent* discussed Sir Roger's speech. 'Sir Roger Bannister must have made a lot of people uncomfortable yesterday ... Discussions about human performance, whether physical or intellectual, based upon racial generalizations, are easier to make than they are to prove. Put in the wrong way, such theses can do great damage. Once you start saying black people are genetically inclined to athleticism, what next? Is Sir Roger also inadvertently backing *The Bell Curve*'s case that black people are also genetically predisposed to being less intelligent than white people? His argument also touches upon the legacy of slavery. In explaining black superiority on the track, Sir Roger suggests that adaptation of muscles to hot climates may have enhanced performance, along with a relative lack of fatty tissue. What if, as some experts in America argue, these characteristics, at least among Afro-Caribbeans, spring from the selective breeding that took place during several hundred years of slavery? In that time, twenty million people were shipped across the Atlantic from West Africa: size and strength in men, and breeding capacity in women, determined their price. All of this is an awkward reminder of the past. It should be set alongside some equally awkward thoughts about the present. The success of black stars in sports speaks of inadequate opportunities in other walks of life. In the United States, for example, a sporting scholarship may be the best chance that a black teenager has of gaining a proper education. Here in Britain, sport has always been, and still is, one of the few ways out of poverty for members of some minority communities. Sir Roger was frank enough yesterday to admit that his comments were made with the benefit of medical rather than sociological expertise, and so ignored the evidence that social and economic pressures have, throughout history, been a factor in propelling human beings to exceptional physical and mental feats.'

In his book, *The Race Gallery: The Return Of Racial Science*, Marek Kohn concludes: 'It is true that the only certain race is the human race. Perhaps, however, the time has come to explore how biological variation and social constructions are related. Dealing with difference may be easier said than done. But denial no longer appears to be an option.' I couldn't agree more (putting rigorous training – and even colour – to one side, why do East Africans do better at distance events than other black Africans, e.g. West Africans?), so long, as the *Independent* put it: '. . . the debate is conducted with care and attention to accurate data'. Earlier, after a review of some of the research done on the impact of physical differences between the races in sports, Kohn wrote: '. . . it seems reasonable to suppose that human groups do vary in some physiological traits that are implicated in athletic ability, and that some of this variation is genetic in origin. But that does not warrant jumping to conclusions about the relationship between physiology and performance, since sport is a cultural phenomenon, not a biological one, and since the physiological evidence itself is more complicated than it at first appears. To make it possible to talk about physical differences, without reiterating the old racist subtext, physiology needs to be uncoupled from psychology. Black people need to feel that discussion of African physical traits does not reinforce the stereotype that associates blacks with the body and whites with the brain. Sportspeople may enjoy great wealth, social status, fame and personal satisfaction, but they do not control countries, financial systems, or the development of technology. If praise of black athletic achievement inhibits the development of black intellectual potential, the leading lights of black communities may be enormously popular, but they will lack real power.'

If black and white men are equal sportsmen on the pitch, there is only one way you can attack that equality: bring in white society's interpretation of that black man's standing. Remind him he's a nigger. That outside, in the real world, he's behind you. A minute ago, he thought he was another player, now he's cut down to size: he's a black bastard.

It's truly amazing to see and experience how many whites will resort to colour at the slightest provocation or disagreement. Often, even among those who would consider themselves 'civilized' whites, this knee-jerk reaction to a black person who has annoyed them lies just beneath the surface.

They had both been England captains; and both had high profiles in their Premiership sides. But when Manchester United's Paul Ince went down in the box in the first half of a game at Old Trafford and tried to claim a penalty, Nottingham Forest's Stuart Pearce didn't see a fellow footballer.

'It's been years,' a furious Ince said in the *Sun* in December 1994, 'since a rival player started calling me black this and black that. I don't mind anything else but when they refer to blackness, that's out of order. It surprised me that it came from Pearcey.

It's very disappointing that a senior professional like him should say such things. There is no excuse for it. The stuff that was said to me was completely out of line.'

'When it does happen in a game,' he told the *Daily Mail*, 'it really upsets you. You do react. People are old enough and mature enough to know that we are trying to stamp this sort of thing out of football. So when a player says something to another player, you are bound to be angered by it. If someone comes out with the normal industrial language, or an insult or two, you don't bat an eyelid. When it's a question of colour, it's different.'

Cantona had had to pull the two men apart in the scuffle which followed Pearce's racial abuse. What was telling about this bust-up was the depressed look on Bryan Roy's face during the confrontation, as he stood next to Ince. Ince's form was affected for the rest of the match; but Pearce went on to score.

John Barnes has a little mantra: 'Racism is a problem in society, not just in football . . . As long as there is racism in society, it will be in football, too.' Which seems to suggest that until society gets its act together there's nothing the football industry can really do. However, if the game doesn't tackle racism on the pitch, it legitimizes it both there and in wider society. The football industry is a part of society.

The referee did not include any references to the Pearce incident in his match report to the FA. And Alex Ferguson left it to Forest's Frank Clark to deal with the matter. He didn't do anything either: 'I've spoken to Stuart and as far as I'm concerned the matter is over, I won't be taking it any further.' The PFA did nothing because neither United nor Ince complained to them. Black players in lower divisions suffer incidents like that on an almost weekly basis. It is not remarked upon, and so it continues.

White players often defend their racist abuse on the pitch by saying it was done in 'the heat of the moment'. Everybody suffers heats of the moment, but it seems only whites react by noticing black people's colour. Commentators defend them by saying the remarks were 'off the cuff', as if the player concerned was merely remarking on the weather. But are these white individuals so lacking in critical faculties that they restrict themselves to the first thing they notice about somebody? If you believe that someone is trying something on, or is no good at his job, why not accuse him of that, why not call him a 'fucking cheat', or a crap player, as you would do if he were white? Why is calling him a 'black bastard' or a 'black' this or 'black' that preferable to anything else? Because the aim is to demean him as a human being.

This lessening of status can be expressed in many forms.

Infamously, Ron Noades, chairman at Crystal Palace, said in a Channel Four television programme made in 1991: 'When you're getting into midwinter in England, you need the hard white men to carry the artistic black players.'

When Millwall fans invaded the pitch in May 1994 in an attempt to get their hands on Derby County's two black players, their chairman at the time, Reg Burr, accused the black players, Paul Williams and Gary Charles, of provoking the display of racism. Derby had to substitute the players for their own safety, leaving them in the dressing room as an extra precaution. Paul Williams was singled out by the Millwall chairman: 'Mr Williams,' said Mr Burr in the *Mirror*, 'is physically aggressive and an unpleasant player. He provokes [the crowd]. If he wasn't black they'd be saying something else about him.'

Non-Premiership side, Millwall FC, has a special place in the hearts of Britain's black footballers. In a survey for a 1994 BBC current affairs programme, *All Black*, they voted the Old Den the ground they most hate to play in because of the abuse they come under. Abuse legitimized by racist comments like the above from the club's authorities. Nothing was done by the FA.

Mr Burr, however, didn't waste much time in writing to Graham Kelly at the FA, enclosing a stack of newspaper clippings, after Ian Wright summed up how black footballers felt about Millwall on Arsenal's clubcall, just before Arsenal faced Millwall in a FA Cup tie in January 1995. Millwall club officials had the nerve to be angry and warn about filing FA and police complaints, despite the appalling factual evidence black players could testify to.

'At Millwall they try to intimidate you and the atmosphere is hostile. You always get racial abuse down there. Millwall is the one place which makes you think: Let's show this lot I can play,' said Wright. 'When you play at great grounds around Europe there is an atmosphere about them that makes you want to show what you can do. At Millwall the atmosphere makes you want to stuff it up them.'

First it was the Derby players' faults, now it was Ian Wright's. Despite not receiving any complaints from the police or match referee, Burr had written to Kelly, and that was enough for the FA to write to Arsenal and describe Wright's comments as 'foolish' and 'ill-timed'. There was a strong hint that they would have liked to charge him with bringing the game into disrepute. It's a shame club managers and the FA aren't as quick off the mark when they have aural and visual evidence of what black players have to go through.

During the game the Millwall crowd at Highbury put on an excellent show of what Wright had accurately described. He received his twelfth booking of the season – in very debatable circumstances, before the baying visitors in the stands – which led to a ban. He was spat at, a Millwall supporter tried to attack him, he was tripped by a Millwall player just as the game ended and, in the incident mentioned previously, got involved in a scuffle at the bar with Alex Rae. A police officer had had to escort him down the tunnel after Arsenal's physiotherapist rushed on to the pitch to protect him from a man who'd run on to 'do' him. The next day, Wright woke to read one tabloid had labelled him A WRIGHT NUTTER. It was all Ian Wright's fault, of course. Arsenal also lost 2–0 and were out of the Cup.

The Old Den has an extra special place in Wright's memory. It was where he made his England debut in a B international against Yugoslavia in 1989. As he wrote later: 'The first time I pulled on an England shirt should have been one of the proudest days of my life. Instead it was spoilt for me in a terrible way by racism. I can generally handle racial abuse, but this time it hit me hard. I was playing for England and getting slaughtered because I was black – no other reason. I left the Den feeling kicked in the teeth when really I should have walked away from there feeling sky high.'

Everton actually give Millwall a run for their money: in a study by the John Moores University in Liverpool, Everton came top of the league of clubs black players hated visiting because of racist abuse.

If the industry wanted to stop racist nonsense, they could remove it from the grounds, stop play when black players are abused, remove racist fans from the grounds and withdraw season tickets from offenders who hold them.

Clubs are culpable. Games should be stopped when players are subjected to racist abuse, and supporters who've been warned continue with their taunts. Black players shouldn't have to 'put up with it' as a test of character or bravery. Why should they be the only ones subjected to those tests on the field? Stop the game and arrest the racists. If there are too many racists per police, just stop the game. As Cantona and Ferdinand said in their Nike ad: 'What do you see? A black man, a Frenchman or a footballer? Is it OK to shout racial abuse at me just because I am on a football pitch? Some people say we have to accept abuse as part of the game. Why? I know that violence is not acceptable in sport, so why should we accept hatred?'

Once again, the root of the problem is found within the ranks of the white footballing Establishment, with the people who run the game and who claim to have a higher moral authority. If you have an all-white team run by all-white management, why should your fans welcome the sight of black players in opposing teams? If you have a problem employing blacks why shouldn't your followers have a problem seeing them on the pitch?

Blackburn Rovers, it seems, manage to keep a nice, clean, all-white team-sheet. Although the club's most recent managers, Kenny Dalglish and Ray Harford, managed to prise white footballers from their existing clubs – Dalglish often being referred to as a 'magnet' for British players – they couldn't seem to prise away any black players.

Blackburn officials say if they don't have any black players it's not their fault. One told me: 'It's actually getting hold of one. The other Premiership clubs don't want to sell. We've got other nationalities in the team – nobody talks about them. If the players aren't available that we want, well . . .'

And it's certainly not to do with the 'racism thing'. It's the form thing. As Blackburn put it: 'If we haven't played a player [black], it's because the player isn't up to scratch. It doesn't matter . . . wouldn't matter what colour their skin was.'

As the *Guardian* reported in December 1996: 'Since 1991, when the club's multi-millionaire owner, Jack Walker, took charge, a black player has only turned out for Blackburn in two games, both away from home.' Much to the satisfaction of neo-Nazis, who have inundated Blackburn's supporters' site on the Internet with congratulatory messages. One read: 'Home team should mean home team. Blackburn should mean Blackburn. Not Rainbow Warriors.'

The only blacks at the club in early 1997 were two teenagers in the youth teams – Junior Obeng and Marlon Broomes – who came through the ranks. Their first-team careers will be interesting to monitor. Black people on training schemes in other industries (e.g., the media) are often used to ward off 'delicate' questions about black representation on staff. As mentioned, it's what happens to blacks after training, that's important.

The biggest economic, social and political crime this century is the suppression, underuse and misuse of black talent and ability. In the football industry, it is a positive encouragement to racist fans to see football clubs with all-white teams on the pitches. What clearer image do they need to validate their prejudices?

It never fails to rankle that, in the wealth of material produced by the press each August to launch the new season, the Subbuteo-type graphics of male models wearing the new kits are virtually always white. What kind of myopic representation is that? Deliberately not seeing what you don't want to see. As long as the clubs, the institutions and the football media remain racist, why should the fans change their attitudes? The *Sun*'s August 1995 two-page spread of men sporting new strips was accompanied by a panel showing the faces of the paper's soccer reporters. Not a black face – real or imagined – in sight.

In 1994, aided and abetted by John Fashanu, Nigerian international Daniel Amokachi became Everton's first black player in nearly twenty years. Before him, a winger called Cliff Marshall was with the club for a short period in the 1970s. Many people believed the club's management had a policy of not signing black players. It's difficult to see what else could have kept the club all-white for all those years when there was a plethora of good black players around.

As Fashanu remembered in his weekly 'Bash' in the Sun in August 1994: 'Everton were, without doubt, the worst club for racism in the Premiership. When the crowd chant in unison, "We're white, we're white," you know they have problems.' However, he believed that under manager Mike Walker Everton's racist image was beginning to change.

When he arrived at Everton, Amokachi said: 'I've heard about the fans' reputation as being racist. But I'm not worried about that. My only concern is to do well and make Everton great again.'

The club denies its record on employing black players could easily lead to charges of racism. 'It depends what you mean by black' was the answer. Er . . . ? 'We don't take on board the accusation,' stated the Everton official during our phone conversation, whilst admitting that they had come under some criticism. 'It may be a fact, but it's not to do with race. We're not the only team like that, it's just the way it happens.'

In July 1994, the following piece appeared in the *Guardian's* 'Why I hate . . .' sports column, written on this occasion by a Mike Owen: 'We were about to sign a real World Cup star. He even knew how to score a goal. But suddenly Sweden's Martin Dahlin changed his mind. He was staying at his German club, even though it reportedly couldn't match the wages offered by nouveau riche Everton Football Club, in Liverpool 4.

'His about-turn was hard to understand. But then it was suggested in the press that he had been advised to give Everton a miss. It's our reputation, you see. Everton FC is seen as having the same relationship to blacks as Yorkshire County Cricket Club to Asians, and Glasgow Rangers to Catholics. We've heard a lot about them, but have very little to do with them.

'Dahlin would have been virtually our first black player. Back in the mid-1970s, we did have Cliff Marshall, a winger from Toxteth. He looked promising, but was shown the door after seven appearances.

'Over the years, people began to talk about us. Every club, it seemed, had a black player, but not Everton. Conspiracy or cock-up? I opt for the latter and, as a lifelong Everton supporter, it makes me cringe.

'Season after season, the Everton board ignored the monkey noises from the terraces directed at the growing number of visiting black footballers. It was only after years of a chant straight out of the KKK song-book – 'Shoot, shoot . . . shoot that nigger!' – that the club, after many complaints, clamped down. But the damage was done. Fascist groups saw Goodison Park as a place to sell their rags. Black players linked with the club were likely to get hate mail.

'Now mega-rich Peter Johnson, formerly chairman at Tranmere Rovers, has taken over the reins at Goodison, promising to pump into the club at least £10 million of his fortune from a Christmas-hamper empire. I don't really care if we never have a black player, or if we pack the side out with them. But Johnson has to dispel this festering idea that Everton is a bastion of racism.'

Amokachi had a miserable and depressing time at Everton. He was brought in by one manager – Walker – who soon departed, and then had to prove himself constantly to another, but never really got the chance to do so because Joe Royle repeatedly refused to play him.

Everton say Amokachi was a well-liked player. 'The shirt sales were huge,' said the official, 'for a man who didn't play as much as he could because he didn't reach his peak form. [Amokachi] felt he could have done better. There was nothing racial about it, he just didn't reach his form. When a new manager comes in, players don't always fit in. Daniel was flamboyant, a flair player. That's not quite Joe's style of player. His sale was a mutual thing. I really don't think we have a problem here.'

The highlight of Amokachi's time with the Merseyside team was when he came on as a sub by mistake in the second half of the 1995 FA Cup semi-final against Spurs. Royle hadn't wanted him to go on. But the Nigerian didn't know that. He scored two goals, catapulting his team into the Final, which they won. That didn't stop people calling him 'Amataxi': big, black and carries a load of passengers.

'I came to Everton at the wrong time,' recalled a depressed Amokachi. 'If I had arrived when things were going fine, it might have been different. But there were a lot of pressures. Everyone expected me to turn things around playing up front, which is not where I play.' In the summer of 1996 Everton sold Amokachi to the Turkish club, Beşiktaş. That left Rochdale-born Earl Barrett, an old player of Royle's from the manager's Oldham days, as the only black in the squad. Apart from Barrett, Everton has a youngster, Danny Cadamateri – 'looks like Trevor Sinclair, same knotted [dreadlocked] hair' – in their youth team who, like the two Blackburn boys, came up through the ranks.

Amokachi was a misfit, a 'free spirit' who wasn't one of them. It didn't help matters that this Nigerian, used to capital life in cities like Lagos and London, and those on the Continent, had to live an isolated life in Liverpool.

The isolation of being the only black in a Northern club can be compounded by having to live in the area. Both Les Ferdinand and Andy Cole kept homes in London while at Newcastle. The black Brazilian, Emerson, didn't find Middlesbrough to his liking (nor did his wife). Cole found the more cosmopolitan Manchester better suited to his taste when he transferred from Tyneside.

The UK is frequently described as a 'multicultural country'. And England does have some cities in which African-English, Caribbean-English, Asians and people from other cultures live in enough numbers to be noticeable. However, even in these cities, there are only a few areas – mainly working class or recently gentrified – where black and white live in close proximity. Apart from certain quarters, English cities have clearly defined black and white areas. We don't call it segregation because this is England and people don't like naming the thing which makes them feel uncomfortable. But residential segregation it is, with both sides preferring it that way.

There have been some deep, honest friendships and hatreds formed between the black and white working classes. Decent relationships, unknown in the other class brackets, because of their grounding in honesty and shared lifestyle and tastes. But, for the vast majority of the country, it is, as I like to say when attending media events, 'all white on the night'. I have to say this at daytime events too. A large percentage of white English people can spend their entire lives not having to interact with a single black person.

In cities, white contact is often limited to superficialities and light banter with the few black colleagues in the work place; or polite remarks when making purchases at the shop counter, the staff canteen, or the railway station, etc. We, as black people, have to know them; they don't need to know us. In such an insular world, jokes about dreadlocks resembling pineapples become hilarious, no doubt, to a white person.

If you're black, there's no escaping with a nice house in the country. A survey in 1994 said that 'virtually everyone from ethnic minorities living in rural Norfolk has experienced racial harassment, taunts, discrimination or violence'. The study by the Norwich and Norfolk Racial Equality Council was said to confirm 'earlier research in the West Country that revealed extreme racism suffered by ethnic minorities, which make up less than 1 per cent of the rural population.'

Despite their greater white numbers, the appearance of just one black face can cause unbelievable trauma among whites, which they then vent on the black concerned.

Black footballers also find it difficult to settle down up north. 'There is no problem with my knee and I passed the medical,' Crystal Palace's John Salako said in the *Mirror*, as he turned down a £2 million offer to join Newcastle in June 1995. 'I'm not prepared to discuss the details of the deal, but Newcastle put an offer on the table and I decided it wasn't right for me. People will think I'm off my tree to turn down a club like Newcastle, but I took a look around the place and didn't think I could settle there. It's a different world.' Salako signed eventually for Coventry. His Crystal Palace team-mate Chris Armstrong had just completed a £4.5 million move to Spurs after having rejected Everton. He told the *Daily Mail*: 'The chance to carry on living in London appealed to me but the choice was down to football reasons.'

'Southern players have had notorious difficulties settling in the north-east,' reported *Today* in June 1995, 'but Ferdinand is ready for the change of air. "I've got a few phrase books and intend to learn the language," he smiled. "I played in Turkey for a year and loved it so much I wanted to stay another year. But QPR wouldn't let me. If I can enjoy Turkey there won't be a problem moving 250 miles up here."'

The West African striker Tony Yeboah's goalscoring immediately rejuvenated the Yorkshire club Leeds after he signed for them in January 1995. But a few months later there were rumours that he might return to the German side Eintracht Frankfurt. The *Guardian* in April 1995 reported that he planned lengthy discussions with the club at the end of the season regarding his future '. . . once he has completed lengthy discussions with his wife, who has not settled as easily. "If it was down to me I would stay here for 10 years, but it has not been so easy for my wife and daughter," he said. [Bill] Fotherby [Leeds' managing director] envisages that a luxurious new home will ease that problem.'

Even if the northern club is willing, it cannot protect its black star full-time against racist white fans. Neither can it protect its black star against white racists who aren't football fans and only see 'a nigger'. And nobody can protect the star's family as they attempt to live an ordinary life and do ordinary mundane things like walking down the street, or popping into the shops.

'I'm not going to talk about Andy Cole. Let's talk about players who want to play for this club week in, week out, in the right manner. If you want to talk to him, go and find him somewhere in London,' exploded the Newcastle manager in the *Sunday Times* in October 1993. Kevin Keegan was furious. Seven months after signing 'Goal King Cole', Golden Boots had walked. Seven months after moving to Geordieland, Andy Cole couldn't stand being the only black face he ever saw on the streets. He missed his family in Nottingham and his friends in London. And as the team were in London for two games within a few days against the same club, Wimbledon, why couldn't he stay over in between the games?

'I didn't walk out on the club,' explained Cole. 'I just told the gaffer I was homesick.'

When you are the 'only black', isolation is the horrible weight you have to bear. Some people are the 'only black' because of where they live, the profession they are in, or the level reached in their profession. A few black people like the feeling of being set apart from the rest of their race; others hate it. All suffer.

When Cole signed a contract with Newcastle, he signed away contact with black people – the first time this had happened to him. After Nottingham, he lived in London, where Arsenal had taken him on as trainee; then it was on loan to Fulham, and from there it was Bristol. London is more than 20 per cent black; Nottingham and Bristol have healthy black populations.

To make matters worse, he was sent to live in Crook, a County Durham mining village, where many white people did a double take on seeing a black man – before they recognized him as the 'coloured' lad, the first one, to wear the worshipped no.9 shirt, that was. When he'd made his first appearance for the club there were still audible gasps – in 1993 – that he was black. 'It had started quietly a couple of months earlier when he had signed for £1.75m – most people had not heard of him before the speculation started,' wrote a Newcastle fan in the *Independent* in January 1995, 'and those of us who saw his debut as a substitute at Swindon remember more than one voice say, "Jeezas – he's black!" as he stood to strip off his tracksuit. Racism, a blight that affected us more than most clubs, was already on its way out – but Coley sped it on its way.'

Ensuring his new club was promoted from the First Division to the Premiership by scoring 12 goals in as many games helped that bitter pill go down. As did 41 goals in the next season. Being so successful in the no.9 shirt made Cole an honorary white Geordie. After the 'homesickness' bust-up with Keegan, Cole moved into an upmarket part of Newcastle proper. But off the pitch, he was still ill at ease. Going so far north, he said, made him feel as if he'd travelled to the end of the earth. He flew back and forth from London regularly.

'There's always something to do there. I want to succeed and do well, but I've had trouble coming to terms with living up north. This place could hardly be further from London. I'm finding it hard being away. I've lived in London a long time. When I left school, I went straight there and enjoyed every minute of it. I've still got a lot of mates there,' he explained in the *Sunday Mirror* in October 1993.

As long as he kept putting the balls in the back of the net – 68 in 84 games in less than two years, smashing a record which had stood for nearly 60 years – Cole was lauded in Newcastle. 'He gets the ball and scores a goal – Andy, Andy Cole!' sang the Toon Army.

But Cole's special status didn't mean some Geordies had suddenly gone colour-blind. His family weren't famous footballers, though, they were just black folk in a white land. The racial abuse they suffered affected Cole, reminding him of the kind of treatment he could have expected had he not been Andy Cole the footballer, 'Wor Blackie'.

In the *Sun*, in December 1994, he made a simple request: 'I just wish the people responsible would remember my family have the same skin colour as me. When they hurt my family, they hurt me. These things are bound to upset me but life goes on. I won't have problems because of who I am. Personally, everyone has treated me well.' His family stopped going to games at St James' Park. And, of course, when the Goal King failed to score in nine games, it ended with his sale to Manchester United, a city where he settled in quickly. 'Cole should have little problem settling in the team,' outlined Henry Winter in the *Daily Telegraph* in January 1995. 'Or the North-West. Manchester is a more multi-racial city than Newcastle and the ebullient presence of players like Paul Ince will accelerate Cole's ability to put down roots. Besides, his home town of Nottingham is little more than an hour away in Cole's BMW.'

Les Ferdinand replaced Cole in the no.9 shirt, until he was forced to give it up to the real thing, the white Geordie, Alan Shearer. Cole and Ferdinand have been Newcastle stars, but neither was, or is, likely to attain the cult status of the white gods, Jackie Milburn and Malcolm Macdonald. Twenty thousand people turned out to welcome Shearer home to the club.

'Quick and stealthy, Cole did not fit the stereotype of Newcastle No.9s who were built on the same awesome lines of Milburn and Malcolm Macdonald. At 5ft 11in and 11st 21b he cuts a lean figure, although he possesses a strength that neither his frame nor his shy off-field persona would imply,' wrote Guy Hodgson in the *Independent* when Cole transferred to Manchester United. 'The most obvious difference, however, was his being black. Geordies, like Liverpudlians, were not noted for their racial tolerance, but Cole conquered any prejudice by his sheer weight of talent. He was, simply, *the* cult figure at Newcastle, someone who has altered deeply ingrained and ugly attitudes. "If you had said 10 years ago," an editorial in a Newcastle fanzine, *The Mag*, read last season, "that the hero of the Toon Army would be a black lad you would probably have got some pretty strange looks. However, the impact that Andy Cole has had on Newcastle is startling. He's educated anybody who is still living in the past ... anybody who now thinks we would be better off without black players ... with his devastating pace and his eye for goal."'

In May 1997, the organization Human Rights Watch Helsinki reported that 'racially motivated violence and harassment in the United Kingdom is an extremely serious problem that is getting worse'. They revealed that the UK's figure of 12,199 reported racist incidents in 1995–96 meant we were higher up the racial attacks league that year than Germany and France. But many blacks do not bother to report racial attacks and incidents of harassment. Human Rights Watch Helsinki noted that: 'Estimates of the real figures based on the official British Crime Survey of 1991 indicate that approximately 32,500 violent assaults and an additional 26,000 acts of vandalism were racially motivated.'

There are a few more blacks on my street now. One family moved in next door to the racist thug who attacked my car. Yes, I found out where he lives. If I move, I shall do the best I can to make sure my house is sold to a black family.

Your Cheating Hearts

I see them every day. A group of nine or ten very black young men who emerge around midday. Some with penis haircuts, others with funky dreads; the rest haven't been to a barber for months, if not years. During the course of the day, they regroup in threes and fours around the Lock. Mixing and matching. They are drug dealers. The degree of separation between the British ones and the ones who clearly left Africa very recently is marked not by their accent, but their dress sense. There is something about an African, newly arrived in Europe and wearing his finest, that makes you wish you were blind; whilst you can't beat a black Londoner in the fashion stakes.

These young black men do nothing all day but accost white girls who are passing by, loosely dressed, in the summer, in their skimpy little bits of cloth. The white girls want drugs or sex, or sex, or drugs and sex – they get what they want. The young black men trade with young, skinny white men (who can't keep still and need a good wash), as they lounge under the two large willow trees or sit and stand by the canal's hump-back bridge and the towpath.

When they hang out by the Tube station, the place resembles a makeshift African bazaar right in the middle of little ol' London town. There is drumming for the white folks, loud tapes blaring disgusting music, damn smelly incense and revolting beads and other peculiar oddities for sale to deserving tourists.

Coming back with my lunch one spring day, I watched a young white office girl (knee-length navy skirt, navy tights and fetching white M&S blouse) visibly beef herself up to walk past these black men sitting on the bridge, who were watching and willing her to approach. She clearly wasn't one of their usual white girls, but it didn't matter, she was white, wasn't she? She's a target, and available. The office girl was so scared you would hardly know she was in the middle of her capital city at a quarter past one on a very sunny day with dozens of people, cars, offices, shops and traffic wardens around her.

I smiled to myself grimly because it reminded me of being fourteen or fifteen and having to gear myself up to enter record shops in north-east London on my way home from school. I would be desperate to buy the records I'd set my soul on that week, but equally desperate not to have to face the crowd of silent, head-nodding young black guys outside and inside the shops.

After a cursory glance at your face to make sure they didn't know you or your immediate family, they would look your body up and down, inside out, as if they had just started at medical school. A fate worse than death, only just tolerable, because to go without those records would have killed me anyway.

Looking at that poor white girl, with her eyes focused on the ground, handbag clutched to her side (aha! being mugged is the least of your worries, dearie), I thought: Twenty years ago, they weren't dealing drugs openly on a main street in the middle of London in fucking broad daylight.

The most you'll see these drug dealers take in public is a whiff of their own weed which, naturally, they'll pass around the group. On the bridge, one of the ugliest-looking stared into my face and drawled: 'Waant sahm wid?' He's never had to ask again.

Monday is a day off or an evening start – due to stocktaking, perhaps. The rest of the week, from midday to midnight, they sit and stand, get tired, drink and fight each other. Where do they go to the toilet? They piss by the wall separating the Lock from the garbage company. They're always careful to wipe their hands on their trousers. Most days, they'll take the trouble to turn their backs on the passing public.

Everybody knows what these black men do and how they make their money. Why shouldn't they know? Too many of the young men and women who make up the trendy let-it-all-hang-out crowd overcrowding this part of the borough at the weekend are these men's happy, satisfied customers. The clients come down to seek them out during the weekdays now. I watch them dealing. Everybody knows what they do, it seems, apart from the police. They do know, but they don't care.

Why should the police bother? It's only those blacks and their drug culture again. It's the only thing they're good for. It's OK, isn't it? These men are black, and black people have a natural tendency to all things druggy: from dealing to taking. Let's get those parking tickets distributed, the council needs the money. A few yards away from the drug dealers, a bobby tut-tuts at the legitimate shopkeeper who's parked on the double yellow.

Drug dealing, drug taking, drug abuse, drug crimes, drug money, are all seen by many whites as synonymous with being a black person. I remember being in a pub in the centre of London with a group of white friends from work. As I was going to the loo, a stranger, white, who'd walked past my friends, asked me where he could get some 'stuff'. The 'inner cities' was a useful euphemism for black people in the 1980s; it's now been updated to 'drug-torn inner cities'.

Drug taking is seen as being prevalent among black communities, with a starring role for areas like Manchester's Moss Side or Hackney's Front Line. So if the drugs spotlight is going to fall on a sports personality (overtly or covertly), isn't it natural that it should fall on the black ones? Don't they, because of their drug-culture backgrounds in those inner cities, know more about harmful substances than their white colleagues? Isn't it in their blood?

Too many of the sports personalities whose names are linked to drug tests have been black. The mutha of all sporting drug cheats is still Canada's Ben Johnson. Or Jamaican-born Ben Johnson as he soon came to be known in his disgrace. As noted, in glorious victory, colour and original nation status are irrelevant; in failure or disgrace, colour and original nation status are the defining characteristics. Locating Ben Johnson's blood relationship to a country the white world thinks is well-positioned for honours in the drug trade was important. It still is. As a consequence, black sports people get singled out by the authorities because of the mythical relationship between blackness and drugs.

Who could blame themselves for thinking there's a lot of it going on in athletics, especially when the athletes themselves say so? According to a Sports Council survey conducted in 1995 (*Drug Testing Awareness of Elite Competitors*), one in four of Britain's Olympic athletes believed that the use of performance-enhancing drugs had increased in the year previous within their industry. Half of the competitors who replied to the survey wanted anyone found using steroids to be banned for life – and the athletes knew which other athletes were doing it. They wanted more random and out-of-competition testing.

Positive images versus positive samples. Linford Christie sued a black-owned humorous magazine, *Skank* (minute circulation), for a cartoon which implied that he was on drugs. He won. I thought he went over the top: it was supposed to be a joke. But I also understand why he did it. Christie knows that all eyes are on him. Always. And he's not taking any chances, not even with silly cartoons that a handful of people will see. He feels his achievements, even as he wraps the Union Jack around him, have been damned by faint praise by white Britain, and loud, unspoken insinuations about how he broke all those records in the first place.

In December 1994 the *Guardian* reported that a Home Office Advisory Council on the misuse of drugs recommended that ethnic monitoring of police stop-and-search operations for drugs should be carried out. 'Effectively this would mean that each force would publish the number of stop-and-searches conducted, the ethnic origin of those searched and which searches had resulted in seizures or prosecutions. Open and consistent ethnic monitoring would help to establish greater confidence in police among ethnic communities.' *The Times*, commenting on the report, said that the police 'recorded 351,700 stop and searches in 1992, an increase of 16 per cent on 1991. Drug searches increased by 14 per cent and represented 35 per cent of the overall figure recorded in 1992. But the report says that the increase was not translated into arrests, which increased by only 3 per cent for drug offences.' By 1995, more than 690,300 people were being stopped and searched in England and Wales, nearly half of them (46 per cent) in the Metropolitan Police area. In 231,900 cases the reason for the stop and search was drugs, and from that number, 30,700 were subsequently arrested. 'Police are empowered to stop and search anyone provided they have "reasonable suspicion",' said the *Daily Telegraph*, 'that he or she may be carrying drugs. The procedure has been seen by some as an excuse to harass young blacks.' As stated, black men are up to ten times more likely to be stopped and searched. Figures for the ethnic breakdown of drugs searches are still not published, so we can't see the number of black people on whom drugs are *actually* found. The Home Office says it has accepted the Advisory Council's recommendations and hopes to start breaking the figures down ethnically by the end of 1997.

Although Christie has been tested repeatedly, there have also been allegations that he and other senior British athletes haven't been tested enough by athletics officials, because of who they are.

'Gunnell, the world and Olympic 400 metres hurdles champion, retained her European and Commonwealth titles this summer,' wrote Neil Allen in the *Evening Standard* in September 1994 (following the positive dope tests on athletes Solomon Wariso, Diane Modahl and Paul Edwards), 'but found her post-Commonwealth Games mood turning sour only minutes after she got off the flight home from Canada. "No sooner was I in the car than BBC radio came on with a discussion about drugs-taking and there was the ex-swimmer David Wilkie claiming that those who were recently caught in British athletics were just the scapegoats for much bigger names. I was so furious. When I thought what Linford, Colin [Jackson] and I had done this season, I felt like getting on breakfast TV and blasting back at the way we were getting smeared so unfairly. You can only take so much of this . . ."'

The next month in the *Observer*, the distance runner Liz McColgan announced: 'There are a lot of people on the British team who are doing it, and it is so blatant, yet everyone just turns a blind eye. I think it's about time not just for making an example of a little person, but for cleaning out the sport completely. It's very, very hard being a clean athlete, being totally against any drug use whatsoever, to sit back and to find that people are doubting even me. You know: "Was she on it, because she was world champion?" It's definitely not right. And yet there's people that you know are doing it and they never get caught. They must have friends in high places.'

An angry British Athletic Federation riposted that Linford Christie, Colin Jackson and Sally Gunnell had given a combined total of forty-one negative drugs tests that year. The *Observer* reported that Christie had been tested sixteen times, Roger Black ten, and Du'aine Ladejo twelve. That November in the *Voice*,

Du'aine Ladejo took us through a recent weekend: 'When I'm training, I wake up at 8 a.m. on a Sunday because I drive up to Birmingham to train with my coach, Tony Hadley. But when I'm not, I sleep in because I normally go out on Saturday nights. This Sunday was different because I was woken up at 9.23 a.m. for a drugs test. The Sports Council called and said they would be around in five minutes and they turned up in three. Taking a drugs test is not a problem for me. Waking me up at that time of the morning is. I didn't give them any attitude but this guy wanted to get into serious conversation and I just wanted to return to my bed. To make matters worse, he was a Roger Black fan.'

At the 1988 Seoul Olympics, Linford tested positive for a banned substance, pseudoephedrine, but was cleared because he had taken it unknowingly in ginseng tea. But he's never forgotten the way he was treated by the authorities, re-lived in his autobiography, *To Be Honest With You*:

'I went into a room at the athletes' apartment block with members of the British team management. They started a serious cross-examination. I suppose they thought they had to but I knew I hadn't done anything. They made me begin to believe that I had. To this day, I don't know if I've forgiven them. They came into my room and took away all of my vitamins. I had to tell them everything – what I had eaten for breakfast, and so on. Everything I had worked hard for had just gone down the drain. I just wanted to die. I wanted to kill myself. I've never cried so much. I felt those people took away a lot of my self-respect; everything I had.'

The most disturbing recent example was the case of the athlete Diane Modahl. Because she was pretty, young, slim and was good at what she did, the shock and feeling of betrayal at alleged drug-taking was intense for the rest of us too. But not quite as intense as her own misery. I remember standing transfixed in a newsagent's, staring at this huge picture of her splashed across the front page of *The Times* during the official hearing of her case in December 1994. I felt very sorry for Diane.

Samples taken from Diane, Britain's 800 metres star, in Lisbon in June 1994, tested positive for high levels of a banned substance, testosterone. Actually, 42 times higher than in a non-athlete; 7 times higher than the levels expected in a female athlete. You'd never have guessed, would you, to look at her? After a long legal struggle, Diane's innocence was vindicated.

I knew a woman whose doctor told her that for some reason she had higher than normal levels of testosterone in her. 'Well,' a man friend said to me, 'that explains a lot about her, doesn't it.' He thought this woman was aggressive, bad-tempered and domineering, but conceded that she was good at her job. She was just like a man, really.

The first defence is usually 'I didn't know', or 'It was in my cold and flu remedy'. The latter can be true because some of the substances banned by the authorities are genuine components of over-the-counter medicines. But confusion, uncertainty and fear now reign. One of our top sprint coaches, Mike Smith, said in *Today* in September 1994: 'It is getting to the stage where little kids are terrified to take the mildest cold-cure remedy because they are frightened they might get banned. We have no way of differentiating between innocent accidents and wilful cheating, and the young kids who are just taking up the sport are totally confused. We need to punish the guilty, not the innocent, and restore confidence.'

Until recently football lovers could say smugly that their stars' noses, arms, lungs and hearts were clean. Although world football had that druggie Maradona – it was a cocktail of ephedrine-linked substances that finally did it for Diego at the '94 World Cup in America – he was foreign, wasn't he? And he was a bloody cheat on the pitch anyway, let alone off it.

But footballers are exactly the kind of prey whom the most common kind of drug dealer is after. They have money and they socialize a lot. With the adrenalin still pumping after highly charged games, or in an attempt to relieve the general pressures of their work, where do the majority go to wind down and relax? To a pub, drinking club, a party or a nightclub, their pockets filled with cash. Enter the drug pusher, his pockets filled with 'social' drugs. If it's a young player, there's the additional pressure of being with friends from outside the football world who may be taking 'recreational' drugs.

Black south Londoner Tony Finnigan played in defence for Fulham and Crystal Palace before being sold to Blackburn Rovers in July 1988 for £45,000. He left in 1990 in what the papers called a 'storm over race-hate taunts' and described his last year there as a 'season of hell'. While at Fulham he was fined for possessing heroin. He revealed that drug dealers had tried to use him to get to his ex-Crystal Palace teammates and friends, Ian Wright and Mark Bright.

'I am regarded as a man about town and people tried to use me to get close to my high-profile friends,' said Finnigan in the *Sunday Mirror* in December 1995. 'Dealers try to give players drugs in return for money or tickets, but I was not prepared to be their go-between because my friends do not take drugs.'

Liverpool's young striker Robbie Fowler said, in the *News of the World*, that he'd been offered drugs in a nightclub. 'It happened once and I don't know what I was offered. I was out having a quiet drink with my mates. A guy came up to me and said: "Do you want some drugs?" I said: "No, I'm not interested." And I walked away. People know you are a footballer and that you've got money. They think you are going to spend it on drugs. But it's wrong and I don't want to know. I've never touched a drug, but you know they are about.'

Hardly any player is interested in taking performance-enhancing drugs like some athletes do. A 17-year-old YTS Tranmere trainee, Jamie Hughes, used speed and became the first British footballer to be charged with using a performance-enhancing substance. Amphetamines can be classed as performance-enhancing because they can act as stimulants to increase energy and awareness. He was banned for two years. Hughes said his drink had been spiked in a nightclub.

Graham Kelly, the FA's chief executive, admitted there was a drug problem in football – but caused by the youngest players: 'There have been concerns that the very young players, the 16-year-olds, may be into the so-called recreational drugs.'

The FA brought in random testing for 'social drugs' during the '94–95 season. They were after those naughty unknown teenagers, whilst, unknown to the august body, at least one of their big household-names was getting up to far more dangerous pastimes. They launched a million-pound campaign with a 'Fit For Football', 'Don't Be A Dummy' message, threatening children as young as nine with random tests.

'On each occasion,' Kelly said, 'we will be looking to test at least three players at random – and that will also include those from the youth teams. We don't think there is a problem as such. But we must be seen to be vigilant as part of the attempt to improve the image of the game.'

The football community could sleep safely in their beds at last, with only nightmares to worry the thin-skinned about how Carling, one of the top brewers, sponsored our Premier League. Serious athletes avoid alcohol because it's a drug which impairs their performances. Yet the drunken Jack-the-lad footballer and his fans are two of the industry's most enduring characters.

It's a tale of two players, one white, one black; and a tale of two drugs, one white, one black, which reveals that British football's attitude towards drug-taking depends on who gets caught doing it. And, of course, racial assumptions are made regarding their reasons for taking drugs.

The white player is the (then) Arsenal and England midfielder Paul Merson; the black player is Spurs' Chris Armstrong (then at Crystal Palace). Both players are strikers; both, at the time, were in their mid-twenties and were married with young children. They were worth roughly the same amount on the transfer market (£4–5 million); and were busted in the same season, 1994–95. Merson's drug was cocaine, the white stuff for white, affluent people. Armstrong's drug was cannabis, the dark weed synonymous with darkies, rich or poor.

'I'm hooked on cocaine,' he confessed, solemn-eyed, with set lips and neatly brushed hair. The *Daily Mirror* must have felt they had got their rumoured £100,000 worth when Merson sold them the story of his addiction, and became the first Premier League player to admit to taking drugs.

Apparently he'd spent up to £150 a night sniffing coke in the loos of pubs and nightclubs. It was sparked off, he said, by depression at being left out of the team, and by huge gambling debts. The coke-taking first happened during an evening out with friends and Arsenal fans at a Hertfordshire pub. That night he had already downed eight or nine pints of lager when he was offered his first 'line', which he sniffed in a rolled-up five-pound note.

'It had started off as an experiment – but it got to the stage where I just HAD to have the stuff. In all, I must have gone through £2000. And that was just what I spent. There must have been much more coke I was given by people which I didn't pay for.

'It's almost ruined my life. I've jeopardized my career and my marriage. At the time I just thought it was one of those things which I would never try again.'

But he felt the drug gave him confidence, more energy and

allowed him to keep up with his drinking. 'After that first experiment, I thought, This is great. I can go out drinking all night and be as right as rain the next day.'

Merson put his hand up for all three of sport's main vices: drink, drugs and gambling. He 'blew' more than a £100,000 gambling. Of all three, drink probably dominates in football, where the sober are regarded as spoilsports at best, and criminals at worst, and where some of our best-known ex-players – George Best, Jimmy Greaves – have lead lives seriously marred by drink. Merson is the first to reveal his cocaine addiction; twenty years earlier, Greaves made headlines around the world when he admitted he was an alcoholic.

Merson hadn't even realized there was anything odd about the amount of drink he was putting away. In fact, he was a bit of a cheer(s) leader for the fans: television reports of his descent from grace were marked by repeated use of Merson's unique pitch celebrations, where he liked to pretend he was downing pint after pint, head thrown back, tongue hanging out like a cow's. The fans had loved that – it had showed he was one of them.

At a tearful news conference, he said those pictures now made him cringe. 'I am an alcoholic. This disease will be with me all my life and I have been told I must take it one day at a time. Alcoholics will understand that. I have a choice in life. I can get back to the drink, the drugs and the gambling or I can change and do something with my life. My life was going nowhere, but it is getting better already. Now my nights out will be at Gamblers' Anonymous and Alcoholics' Anonymous – no more in pubs.'

Merson's soul-baring – he even said he'd been close to suicide – astounded the football world. He claimed that he knew of no other players who got high on coke, but rumours persisted that players were indeed using drugs to help them deal with the pressures of the game. A former Crystal Palace player, Mark

Dennis, described cocaine as: '. . . the footballer's drug. It is expensive and glamorous, with that champagne image, and its use is widespread at a lot of top clubs.' Dennis claimed he had an addiction to coke.

Arsenal came through for Merson, giving him time off to sort himself out. The club said: 'Paul has given outstanding service over recent years and helped us to win a number of major trophies. Although we do not condone what Paul has done, we intend to give him all the support that we can in order to help him through this difficult period.'

Peter Hill-Wood, Arsenal's chairman, added at a news conference that it would be pointless to 'throw the book at him. Merson has gone beyond that kind of punishment. What is the point in us fining him or suspending him? Somewhere inside Paul is a smashing boy. He is just the latest in a line of players who are unable to cope with what football gives them. I can think back to the thirties when players with talent wasted it. He is the latest. Nothing changes. He does not have a particularly high intelligence and is unable to cope with the fame and fortune that football has brought him.'

Merson was sent on a six-week course of counselling and treatment for his cocaine habit at a Hampshire clinic chosen by the Football Association. 'There is no question of discipline,' Graham Kelly said. 'That would only come if we confirmed that Merson had a serious problem, and he refused to co-operate with our rehabilitation.' The FA didn't charge Merson with bringing the game into disrepute by using an illegal Class A drug, didn't fine or ban him.

A grateful Merson, acknowledging his 'phenomenal support', said: 'The FA have been brilliant, and the club and my family have been really understanding.'

He wasn't allowed to play during his rehabilitation for his own good. By February 1995, just over two months after his public admission, Merson was back on the pitch at Highbury, leaner, fitter, loved and forgiven by the fans and the football Establishment.

Monday January 23rd 1995. The players were limbering up for the usual light training session following the weekend. Nobody heard the mobile drug testing unit drawing up in front of the Mitcham training ground belonging to the Premiership club. Nobody was expecting its arrival – and that was how the supervisor working for the Sports Council wanted it. Three players were asked to give a sample. The drug squad left as quietly as they had arrived. Nine days later the FA had the urine test results. They contacted the club. It was urgent.

The rumours started a couple of months later. Why, the sports press wanted to know, had Chris Armstrong not appeared in a vital FA Cup replay against Watford? Crystal Palace's manager, Alan Smith, with his pinched-faced star sitting next to him, tried to tell the journalists that Armstrong had been rested on medical advice because of an injury – but he refused to name the injury. Armstrong didn't say a word.

'I've been asked not to say any more at this stage,' Smith implored, 'and I have given my word. There is nothing sinister in this. But I must be guided by the club's surgeon.' Armstrong told his foster dad that he had 'a mild hamstring injury'.

Someone leaked, and the next day it made the front pages. Chris Armstrong's urine sample had contained traces of cannabis. A top Premiership striker had failed a drug test.

Chris Armstrong was born in Newcastle of a Nigerian mother and an Irish father. By the time he was four, his father had disappeared, and he and his older brother were in local authority care in south London. He was fostered out and, from the age of eleven, was brought up by Roy and Pam Ashfield, who lived near Wrexham.

'I had a nice life,' Armstrong remembered fondly in the *Daily Mirror*. 'It certainly wasn't hard, and I wasn't deprived.' He keeps in close touch with the Ashfields, and with his natural mother, but refuses to see the father, who abandoned him.

'I don't want him to come and watch me play,' he says firmly. 'I've no desire to be reunited with him.'

Chris Armstrong was not, and is not, an addict of any kind. Certainly not a drug addict. But who would have known that from the reaction of the Football Association and Crystal Palace. What Armstrong does possess is an element of that black, broken-home background, which many whites believe gives rise to drug taking.

However, Armstrong was brought up in a stable, loving environment created by his foster parents. Colour is the only factor which truly differentiates Armstrong's and Merson's working-class backgrounds. Merson had said that he'd smoked dope when he was a teenager because everybody he knew did it.

Cannabis is a grade B, non-performance-enhancing, recreational drug. It is much less harmful than any category A drug; it's not a 'hard' drug like the cocaine Merson used. Millions of people around the world use it to help them relax – including, increasingly, more 'respectable' people. The moves to legalize it have been well-documented.

Merson had given his reasons for snorting cocaine. An equally pressurized Armstrong, carrying a heavy £5 million price tag, worried about his lack of goals in recent games. Knowing he was expected to save his club unilaterally from relegation, he'd had a few spliffs to help him relax. He knew his manager doubted him and thought he was 'lackadaisical'. Alan Smith had said in the *News of the World* in March 1995: 'Off the pitch he seems just to drift by and, unfortunately, that can carry over into games.' He even accused the player of 'letting himself and the club down' by 'not trying'.

'It is totally wrong to accuse me of not trying or caring,' Armstrong had replied in the *Sun*. 'The finger is being pointed at me because of Palace's position. If we go down, the blame will be heaped on me.'

This shy young man still couldn't believe that what had started off with him appearing in goal a few times to help out his mates, before playing for a local Welsh miners Sunday league side, had led to a life of luxury for doing the work he loved. The downside was the huge burden of great expectation. It had all happened so quickly.

'When I left school at 16, I just stopped playing. I still loved the game, but I just didn't have time to play,' a June 1995 *Sun* profile reported. 'I needed the money so I started work in this burger factory. Anyway, I never really felt I was good enough to play at the highest level.'

He spent the week packing boxes, but the Sunday knockabouts had resulted in him being signed by Wrexham; then by Millwall, and then to his amazement, for a million pounds, by Crystal Palace. Now Palace were having to keep away the big kickers like Everton and Newcastle. Both the Irish Republic and Nigeria wanted Armstrong for their national team squads. He wanted to play for England.

Armstrong and Merson were men who didn't have the confidence or self-esteem to understand why anyone should be interested in them. 'I never dreamed of playing football for a living,' Armstrong said in wonder. 'A professional career never crossed my mind.'

The FA banned Armstrong from playing. No one knew how long this would last – he was dubbed Chris 'Bannabis' – and the authorities weren't saying. Alan Smith fumed; Armstrong sat out vital games in the FA and Coca-Cola Cups. It was two weeks of hell for the striker. But even worse, it came on top of nearly two months of monitoring, undergone once his club had been informed of the sample's results. At least seven more dope tests had been conducted on Armstrong during that period: all had been negative. Crystal Palace, like its fellow south-London club, Wimbledon, always has a healthy number of black players signed up. Smith sprung drug tests on his entire squad and declared in the *Mirror*: 'This club is clean, clean, clean.'

The FA knew about the measures taken by the club. But when the case became public knowledge, they decided to impose the ban. Alan Smith said: 'The way it has been handled has made it appear worse than it is. I'm very disappointed. We couldn't have done any more as a club and I couldn't have done any more as a manager.'

The FA ruled that Armstrong had to go for 'treatment' as an outpatient at a rehabilitation clinic. He saw the same specialist whom Merson had seen. It was supposed to last a month, but the doctor said it was a waste of his time. The FA insisted that the player they clearly saw as a problem boy stick to the full course.

For Armstrong, it must have been like being abandoned all over again, twenty years on. Unlike Merson, he was given no chance to put his side of the story publicly because the FA threatened him with even more disciplinary action if he did. Unlike at Arsenal, there were no board officials who rounded to support him in public. At the height of the crisis Ron Noades left for a Portuguese holiday. Armstrong asked himself why the chairman didn't stay behind to help him through the storm. The *Sun* said 'he has told friends he feels badly let down by Ron Noades'. Merson and his family were sent abroad just before the news broke of his crisis, so that he could be protected until it was deemed safe to return and face the press and the cameras.

When a paper claimed that his agent was trying to sell Armstrong's story to them, the FA, Crystal Palace and the PFA were aghast, and warned again of punishments if this was true and the player was involved. No paper bothered to take up the offer of an exclusive in-depth interview with the star. Armstrong said he knew nothing about the attempt to cash in on his troubles. No action was taken against Merson under FA–PFA code of conduct rules for pocketing the *Daily Mirror*'s money for his newspaper exposé.

Armstrong was unable to clear his name publicly but, furious, he got his agent, John Mac, to pose this: 'The Professional Footballers' Association Chief Executive, Gordon Taylor, has admitted on television that nine players have been caught by the new drug-testing procedure, and yet Chris has been the only player exposed.' Why had he been singled out? Ron Noades said he had wanted Armstrong to serve his punishment 'under the disguise of a bogus injury'.

Alan Smith defended his handling of the case in the *Sun*. 'I maintain I did what was right with Chris Armstrong. I have broken no confidences, I haven't revealed medical records and, from where I was sitting, I was the only one who could view the whole situation.

'I had the player's trust and I was in contact with the FA and the rehab people. I also knew of the rumours in the media. I could have lied and said Chris was dropped from the Watford game and people would have believed me. I could probably have got away with it against Chelsea. But once he wasn't playing against Liverpool, there would have been questions.

'There were rumours at the club about just who had failed a drug test. Maybe if this had not been publicized, the wrong message would have gone out to our teenagers. Maybe they would have thought it was OK to do it – I don't know. All I know is I did what I thought was best for Crystal Palace and a player who has to help me out of relegation trouble, and I stand by my actions.'

On his return to the pitch, Armstrong recovered the goal-scoring form he'd lost for most of the season. But his manager wasn't in a forgiving mood, as he revealed in the *Sunday Mirror*: 'Let's not beat about the bush,' Smith said. 'The facts are that he has still only got 4 League goals in 33 games and that's appalling. Any striker worth his salt should be getting at least 15 a season, but we all know the reason why Chris hasn't delivered.'

Snide remarks like that supported suspicions that Smith was more concerned about getting his goalscoring machine back into the team than sticking up for him as a non-addict during the club's fight with the FA. It was all a far cry from the total support given to Merson in public and in private by Arsenal's manager, George Graham, and the Highbury board.

Black left-back Roger Stanislaus started his football career as an apprentice with Arsenal in 1986. After spells with Brentford and then Bury, he returned to London in the 1995 close season to sign for Leyton Orient in Division Three. He'd only been with the club for a few months when the unlucky dip picked him out for a random drug test after a match. How he must have wished he was Paul Merson.

The test results showed that Stanislaus, like Merson, had taken cocaine. Barry Hearn, Leyton Orient's chairman, fired him two days after the results came out. 'There are no excuses,' the club said, 'footballers don't do that sort of thing.' In February 1996, the FA banned Stanislaus for a year.

While reflecting that the player had been in the wrong place at the wrong time, given the paucity of random drug testing, the *Independent on Sunday* commented: '. . . no sympathy should be spared a proven cheat'. In the official *Professional Footballers' Association Handbook* on players, Stanislaus is referred to as the man who 'brought disgrace on the game'. The same book admires the other self-confessed coke-sniffer, Merson, for being an exciting player who has put his 'well-publicized problems firmly behind him'.

The Football Association's one-year sentence on Stanislaus is the harshest yet to be handed down. As Stanislaus came to the end of his ban in February 1997, and considered the very limited openings for future employment in his profession, the FA were looking at the case of the white Ipswich midfielder, Adam Tanner, who had been caught in a random drug test at the club's training ground two months earlier. He'd also taken cocaine.

The FA commission decided to ban Tanner for three months – backdated to early January to coincide with the date Ipswich fined and suspended him. Even though the evidence of drug-taking at Portman Road was even more annoying for the club – chairman, David Sheepshanks, had just been elected chairman of the new Football League board – Ipswich didn't get rid of Tanner.

Why the difference in treatment between Stanislaus and Tanner (and, indeed, Merson)? Either all footballers who take cocaine are cheats or they are not. So why don't they get the same sentencing? Where's the justice in pretending that the time of day, or day of the week, a footballer takes what an FA official sweetly called 'Bolivian marching powder' is what really counts?

Apparently, Stanilaus' case shocked the FA more because he tested positive after a Saturday match; whilst Tanner and the others tested positive after training. Ludicrous. Either drug-taking footballers are punished severely or they are not. The FA said it wanted to send a 'message' with the one-year ban on Stanislaus. He certainly got it. A year later they gift-wrapped the 'message' in layers of tissue paper and cotton wool for Tanner, who clearly hadn't quite understood what the FA's problem was and what they were on about when they sentenced Stanislaus.

When Merson made his comeback, no less a person than England's coach, Terry Venables, boosted the forward's confidence by declaring to reporters that his international career was still alive and kicking. Venables said: 'I have great respect for Paul, who has brought these problems to the surface. I would welcome him back if he can put all of this in the past and get back to his best form. It is totally up to him.'

Stewart Houston, who took over at Highbury as caretaker manager from Graham, revealed that when he was still the assistant he'd worked with Merson down at the south-coast rehabilitation clinic. 'You have to give him full marks for the way he has applied himself,' Houston said in the *Evening Standard* in March 1995. 'He accepted he had a problem and knew he had to conquer it to save his career. He has worked as hard as I've known any player work and has shown a great attitude. In terms of weight, diet and fitness level, he is a different player.

'I now hope that he fulfils the potential we all know he has. I've told him his ambitions have to be high and if he continues to work at it, there is no reason why he shouldn't get back in the England team.'

The FA had classified his cocaine abuse as a 'minimal problem'. Even his return to the pitch was said to have been co-ordinated by the FA, Arsenal and 'specialists', who advised that it would be detrimental to keep Merson away from playing for too long. Clearly, in the FA's mind, Merson's 'confession' was evidence that he was having problems, whilst Armstrong being caught was evidence that he was a criminal.

Remember, Merson had been on coke, was an alcoholic, and a gambler. Armstrong had had a few spliffs. In September 1996 Merson was recalled into the England squad by the new England coach, Glenn Hoddle, who said, as he announced the squad to reporters: 'It's a great example for people, who, perhaps, are not in the public eye. All credit to the lad. All credit to people who stood by him, people who counselled him . . . it takes a lot to come out and say the things that Paul did. I'm not a counsellor, but I'm not sure that you ever do get over addictions. You can only deal with them, and Paul Merson is doing that.'

Eric Cantona claimed in his book, *Cantona – My Story*, that he'd seen players offered drugs in dressing rooms before matches by victory-driven club officials. 'I have been disappointed to discover that we players are only merchandise which passes from club to club. I have seen the deceit at work and I have seen the pills which you are advised to take in the dressing room in order to improve your performance.'

Cantona doesn't say what these pills are or, indeed, whether he has ever taken them, and he makes a clear distinction between performance-enhancing drugs and recreational ones. 'When you are not playing football, or running, or boxing, or when you leave the tennis courts, it's your right to live as you want to do.

'Maradona took cocaine far from the stadium of San Paolo where he was a god every Sunday afternoon. And I consider that a legal system, whether it's in Italy or Argentina, is not in a position to give lessons of virtue and morality to anybody. Maradona should never have been suspended from the game that he graced for so long.'

Crystal Palace were relegated from the Premiership at the end of that season. (A Palace fanzine said Chris Armstrong 'single-handedly' relegated the club.) Alan Smith resigned. Armstrong was sold to Spurs for £4.5 million as a potential replacement for Jürgen Klinsmann after Newcastle pulled their £5 million offer because of the 'dope problem'. Newspapers and many Spurs fans were less than enthusiastic about the purchase. Spurs manager, Gerry Francis, was forced to explain why, as the *Sunday Mirror* put it, he had 'splashed £4.5 million on [a] drug shame star'.

'Chris has assured me,' said Francis, 'that it will never happen again, and I am prepared to go along with that because he seems to me like a boy who really wants to work and learn.' The article was headlined: I'M NO DOPE! ARMSTRONG SWEARS IT.

Looking back, in the *Mirror* in August 1995, the badly treated player said: 'I went though a lot and a lot was said about me. I tried not to let things get on top of me, but it wasn't easy.'

'You Beige Bastard,' Doesn't Have Quite the Same Ring to it

In my early teens, I spent the hours between 9 a.m. and 4 p.m. with white people at school in Islington; after school my life was black. Teenage after-school hours in Hackney meant my life was blacker than black. Hackney black people were the kind of people who were very particular about who they hung out with and who they went out with as boyfriend or girlfriend. Your boyfriend or girlfriend could be a complete and utter shit, but it was taken for granted that they would be a black shit.

We did, kindly, allow one or two mixed-race youngsters into our sanctuary, but they had to be BLACK in their attitudes. (They were often more black than we were, as they felt, and we felt, they had something to prove. We made allowances for their strange mutterings about people called 'Aunty Lil', and mysterious disappearances on occasional Sundays to visit something called a 'Nan' who lived in odd places like Brighton. We had grandparents whom we dumped ourselves on at midnight on a Wednesday, if we felt like it, and they were only bus rides away.)

I was about 18 or 19 when a girlfriend broke ranks and started going out with a white guy she'd met at work. One Saturday night she lost her mind and brought him to a party. In Hackney. We all had a good look and a sly giggle. Nobody in the packed room talked to him; hardly anyone spoke to her. The two of them just stood there like exhibits A and B in a race-relations trial. They left early.

Everybody there had known her for years; we were supposed to be her friends. But we were all just waiting for them to dance, to see how they did it (they didn't oblige), and wondering if they'd fucked each other yet. She would have got the same treatment in Harlesden or Brixton or Peckham or any other similarly tight black community in London. She married her white man and they went to live in Sutton.

What made me date the two or three white men with whom I had brief encounters in my early thirties? Because I could, that's what. It was inconceivable at 20. Then, fascinated by the attention I was receiving from some white men at university, I confided in a close black girlfriend from Hackney. She looked at me sternly and said: 'Just think. Fancy waking up next to a flat pink bum!' Our legs gave way, we doubled over, then had to sit down, clutching at each other. It was the kind of laughter which says nothing further needs to be said.

Many white women don't just fancy but actually succeed in waking up next to the firm black buttocks of prominent sports names. And these black male personalities enjoy, it seems from the numbers who do it, waking up to naturally straight – not permed or weaved-on – hair.

Why do black men and white women seek each other out? Black folklore has it that white women are loose, aren't fussy who they screw, and are dying to get their hands down the pants of black men. Our men will supposedly go with anything, and can't wait to get their black mites on those white titties. The former Olympic swimming champion, Sharron Davies, banned a picture of the hands of her black husband, the athlete Derek Redmond, cupping her naked breasts, from being used in a 'sexy' calender featuring British sportswomen.

'We stole the idea from the picture of Janet Jackson,' she said. 'We've always liked the shot. The picture of me was lovely – nothing was showing – but at the end of the day, I thought it was too risqué.' This *Sun* front-page story was accompanied by the 'risqué' picture.

'It's sexy and I enjoyed doing it,' said Derek. 'A lot of people would say I'm a very lucky man.'

The author and journalist Julie Burchill once said of Davies and Redmond that they demonstrated how perfect the combination of white female and black male was. The white woman and the black man were made for each other.

The following letter appeared in the black *Weekly Journal* in November 1995, from a woman in south-east London: 'I read with interest Richard Liston's Sports Talk in the *Weekly Journal* recently, calling for more black footballers to stand up against racism. While I agree with the sentiments of the piece, I only have sympathy for Ian Wright because he is the only one with a black partner. For the others mentioned, and many more besides, standing up would represent a conflict of interest because they are married to the people who are their oppressors. These black men have no interest in tackling the problem of racist abuse of black players at football grounds. What is wrong with black men today? Racism at football grounds will continue because not one of the black players have the guts to stand up and be counted . . . by keeping silent they are perpetuating myths.' The 'others mentioned' were Chris Armstrong, Trevor Sinclair, John Barnes and Stan Collymore.

John Barnes is happy these days to be associated with football's anti-racist campaigns (even if one suspects he would prefer the term 'anti-nationalist', or some other euphemism), but he used to be criticized by blacks for not speaking out against the racists in the past. Would the letter writer be right in putting this down to the sexual and marital choice he has made?

There is no getting away from the fact that black people do ask themselves why blacks in and out of the public eye have white partners. It has always created enormous debate amongst us – it continues to do so especially if the black concerned is a 'successful one'. Many whites, never having considered the situation from a black point of view, are bemused by the antipathy expressed by a number of blacks to inter-racial relationships. Shock and upset is often disguised by calling the blacks concerned 'reverse racists' and accusing them of not being aware that a melting pot of coffee-coloured people is the ideal way forward for the human race.

Black people do not always have the benefit that whites have of being able to look at a mixed-race couple and just see two people together. We often think and argue about the social, cultural, historical and sexual reasons behind their relationship. It's not as simple as refusing, obstinately, to allow for individual choice and, indeed, love.

In a feature spread entitled: BLACK IN BRITAIN in March 1995 in the *Guardian*, writer Manuna Forna considered mixed-race couples. 'Neil Pinder, 36, is a teacher and black London's foremost organizer of social events among the glitterati. When he's told his marriage to Deborah, a white lecturer, is an act of betrayal against the black British community or a sign of his internalized racism, his reaction is concise and unprintable. He's been hearing a lot of this kind of thing and he's tired of it. "Our relationship is based on love, compatibility, shared interests, mutual respect – the reasons two people usually marry," he says. "We had a similar upbringing, went to the same school, have the same religion and we've been together for 22 years. That's more of a guarantee that our relationship will succeed than one that's based on race alone." His explanations are likely to be given short shrift in the black community. In a recent study, *Changing Ethnic Identities*, the Policy Studies Institute found: "Respondents felt strongly that some successful black people try to cut themselves off from other black people and feel that a black partner is a handicap to them . . . This was particularly resented because such individuals acted as role models for the black community. Marriage to whites was seen as a signal to others." We could see it as an illogical sort of racism. There is another interpretation. In the same way that British society as a whole expects its upper echelons to set standards, black British society expects a code of behaviour from its prominent people, and any well-known black person who marries outside his or her race is set down as yet another indication of the deteriorating relations between black men and women.'

The *Guardian* article quoted a professional black female: '"Today's black women have to go through a long hard struggle to get where they're going. En route they develop a level of inner strength that black men find intimidating. One reason is that black men are often brought up by a mother who's willing to do everything for them and has treated them as if they were something precious, and as a result black men come to believe that black women owe them something. Both parties end up looking for qualities in the white race that they don't find in each other." [She] believes that white society regards successful black couples with a degree of suspicion and discomfort. "Two black people together is seen as a threat. For example, if two or three black people in the office go out to lunch together the rest of the office wonders what they've gone to talk about. Similarly, at the predominantly white social gatherings you find at a certain professional level people will feel more comfortable with their one or two black colleagues if they have white partners. A white partner makes you more like one of them."'

A woman told the *Independent on Sunday* in April 1997 that she had 'friends who have purposely got pregnant by white men, so their children are mixed race, and hopefully have a better start in life, because they're coffee-coloured. I'd never go that far.'

In November 1994 the *Sunday Times* sought the opinions of mixed-raced adults on how society viewed them. A male barrister whose father was from Sierra Leone and who was brought up in a mainly white mining town in the North-East said: 'White people have never treated me any better because I am light-skinned. I went to a prep school and I was the only black kid there. At secondary school, I was called a wog on the first day. My experiences in my formative years were the same as any black person's would have been in the same situation. There was no special treatment just because one of my parents was white. I don't believe in any of this rainbow people rubbish. It's a product of confused political correctness. I can see all the negative sides of inter-racial relationships. The white establishment would like to see sub-groups and sub-divisions in the black community. It's divide and conquer – just as it was during slavery. Anybody who believes that so-called mixed-race people nowadays are separate from other black people is buying into that oppressive system of values.'

A model who had pale skin and blond hair was raised by her black father and white mother. She told the paper that at school she was called everything under the sun ('honkey, nigger, mulatto, zebra') and had to educate herself about black history and culture. She read *Malcolm X* when she was about 15. 'A lot of white people treat you as though you're not really black. They think "You're one of us". It's because of that that some black people think that light-skinned people get a better deal. We should not be fighting among ourselves. I don't see myself as less black. I know that a lot of the bookings I get as a model are because I'm light. Sometimes when you meet the clients, you can see the twinkle in their eye when they look at my portfolio. I hate that – but it's a superficial business. It was once suggested that I should have a nose job because it would make me more "commercial". What that really meant was that it would make me look almost completely white. I refused. I want the father of my children to be black. My mum believes that love sees no colour, but I don't want the black to be washed out of my family.'

In October 1994 the *Weekly Journal* ran an article entitled THE DARKER SIDE TO A SHADY COLOUR COMPLEX, which discussed the preferential treatment light-skinned blacks appeared to get within black communities. One woman encapsulated it like this: 'Light skin on a black woman is like blond hair on a white girl – she may look like the back end of a bus but she'll attract men like flies.' Another revealed: 'I grew up in Hertfordshire, which is a predominately white area. No one cared about what shade of black I was – I was black, full stop. When I moved to London [black] people would call me "redskin" and "browning". Many darker-skinned women look at me and assume I must be arrogant or vain, just because I'm fair."'

Brewer's *Dictionary of Phrase & Fable* defines the terms for 'Negro offspring' thus: 'White father and Negro mother = Mulatto; white father and mulatto mother = quadroon; white father and quadroon mother = quintero; white father and quintero mother = white; white parent and quadroon parent = octoroon.' Interestingly, the definitions assume that the person who is black is the woman – a throwback, no doubt, to slavery (as indeed the terms are) when black women were raped as a matter of routine by white slave owners and plantation workers, and black men – up to this century – were lynched for as much as looking at a white woman.

The *Journal's* article linked the apparent better treatment of lighter coloured blacks in some instances today to that period: 'As is well documented the roots of this phenomenon lie in slavery. In white society, the closer to white you were the higher your status, graduating from mulatto to full-blooded African. In slave societies where varying legal privileges depended on individuals being given classifications such as "quadroon" (one fourth white) and "octoroon" (one eighth white), a shade hierarchy observed by whites very quickly became entrenched in black minds . . . After the cultural revolution of the sixties, which gave birth to the slogan "black is beautiful", shadism went steadily out of fashion. The days when black beauty pageants offered separate prizes for Miss Mahogany, Miss Sandlewood and Miss Pine may be long gone, but one look at the black community, and more importantly, society at large, is a testament to its survival.'

Many black footballers, even those with a 'full black' upbringing, like John Barnes, are with white partners.

'He moved into the next house with his playing mate, Lee Terry. Tanya, the girl on the other side, went out with Lee, and I went out with John. We both married. Then Tan got divorced. But then she married Vinny Jones. It's nice. We've been each other's bridesmaids,' she told *Night & Day* in May 1995. Suzy Barnes was 20, and John 18, when they met after he joined Watford. They were together for nearly ten years, and had two children, before they got married in 1991.

Looking back at their Watford days, Suzy admits in *Today*: 'I'd started out thinking, frankly, he was lucky to get me.' But then came the transfer to Liverpool where John became a soccer hero. 'As I got pushed into the background, I ended up thinking I was lucky to get him. John didn't seem to need me.' There was a semi-separation when Suzy decided to move back down South. Eventually Barnes realized that a family was what he wanted, and she accepted that she couldn't have him all to herself.

For some people, Suzy represents the typical footballer's wife. The *Today* newspaper article began like this: 'Perhaps it's her pink varnished toes, digging daintily into the thick pink pile carpet. Or maybe the thigh-skimming skirt. Or the thrusting bosom. Or the pencilled lip liner, fashionably one shade darker than the pearlised lipstick.

'Whatever. The first impression you get from every picture ever taken of Suzy Barnes by herself is of [the] archetypal footballer's wife – the kind of tanned bleached blonde to be found in discos and nightclubs, draped on the arms of soccer stars while sipping Malibu and pineapple through a straw.'

However, the writer, Olga Craig, did go on to say that Suzy is 'actually bright, friendly, generous, and fun to be with. It's just that at the click of a camera she transforms. Goes through her well tried and tested routine and becomes a football blonde. Why? Sadly, because she believes that's what is expected of her.' She has to look the part.

Suzy Barnes spends her time looking after her immaculate children, her immaculate, if not to everybody's taste, image, and her immaculate luxury house. Her husband has plenty of space to do whatever he feels like doing. He loves going out clubbing; she has early nights. He's away playing at Christmas and Easter; she's at home. In the summer, she says he has one week that's not football and which corresponds with the children's school holidays. 'Then he'll go off to Jamaica alone. Whenever he gets back he just takes to his bed for hours and hours and says, "I love my bed, I love my bed. I'm never getting out of my bed again."

'The thing with footballers' wives is, at 20 you move to a house where your neighbours are far older – radiologists and GPs. Old friends get a chip on their shoulder. That's why it's good to team up with other soccer wives. You've got somebody of your own age, and you don't feel guilty buying expensive suits. They don't say, "Crikey!"'

John Barnes leads his black and white lives. Suzy doesn't crowd him; and she doesn't pretend to be keen on the game. 'If they're playing at home,' she said, 'I might take the children. It's a day out and a chance for a chat with the girls. But, to be honest, I've never been at all interested in football. All I ever know about John's game is from the papers.'

*   *   *

The East End of London used to pride itself on having generations of the same family living around the corner from each other for decade after decade. When you got hitched, you married a good East End girl or boy. Ideas above your station meant travelling to a home in the Essex countryside instead of getting off the Tube at Bethnal Green. Paul Ince thought he was the cat who'd got the cream when he succeeded in wooing East End girl, Clare. Clare, you see, was a posh white Eastender; and Ince definitely came from the wrong side of the tracks. As if that wasn't enough, he was black, and he was poor.

'We were at the same school in Ilford but we really hated each other,' Paul confided to the *Sunday Mirror* magazine in March 1993. 'I was one of the down-and-outs who struggled to have dinner money while her mum used to bring her special sandwiches to the gate every dinner time. Her friends used to stand in the corner with their flash clothes, jewellery and Barbour jackets. We would walk past in our old parkas and they'd hiss stuff like: "You scum – you don't belong in the school."' Guess who wasn't coming to dinner – yet.

Ince's father had walked out of his life before he was 2; his mother went to Germany when he was 10, saying she needed money to buy him a football kit, but she didn't return. By the time Ince was a football YTS trainee he had started going out with Clare. She worked as a well-paid secretary to one of the directors in the Bank of Credit and Commerce International; he was desperate for a strong, stabilizing presence in his life. She now provides it in buckets; and he has provided her with a lifestyle befitting that of a millionaire's wife, which her flash schoolfriends would never have thought him capable of.

When his transfer from West Ham to Manchester United was called off at the last minute because of what one doctor thought was a groin injury, it appeared that the threat to his football career wasn't uppermost on Ince's mind.

'Paul was in tears,' Clare recalled. 'I'd never seen him that upset. I just said to him: "It's not the end of the world, I'll stick by you." He said: "You're going to leave me." I told him: "Football isn't everything – we're going to prove there is nothing wrong with you."'

'You're going to leave me.' Naked fear. She was more important than football, even if football had provided him with everything he thought was necessary to keep her. There was no contest if it came to a choice between the two most important possessions in his life – as Inter Milan found out.

The Italian newspapers summed it up: 'These things happen when it's the wife who wears the trousers. They have such women in England, as we got to know through Mrs Thatcher.'

Ince was jeopardizing a £7 million transfer to Inter Milan because Clare wasn't over the moon about it. He didn't know what to do – despite the sums involved and the fact that Alex Ferguson and Manchester United had made it clear that Ince was free to leave. (This, in itself, was a massive shock for the player.)

At one stage he travelled to Milan to talk to Inter but left without committing himself to them. British sports pages screamed that the problem was that Clare couldn't find a decent house from among the choice of million-pound luxury villas shown to the couple by eager Inter officials.

'Mrs Ince to decide,' said the cartoon, underlining its message with the caption: 'Behind every successful footballer there's a woman – unfortunately.'

In the *Mirror* Clare's stepfather was reported as saying: 'She's terribly upset. They have a beautiful house in Bramhall, Cheshire, and are very happy; and the houses they were shown in Italy were no way up to the same standard. She told us she broke down in tears at Lake Como.'

Inter's vice-chairman, Gianmaria Visconti Modrone, tried to

make light of it all and find something positive: 'It is just a case of Paul and his wife finding the right place to live. It is a very big moment professionally and we are very happy to see Paul as a man who is concerned at the happiness of his family. This has demonstrated that we have the right man. We knew Paul the footballer. We didn't know Paul the man.'

The Italian press was outraged at this snub to two essential components of their culture: football and style. Both had their headquarters in Milan. Milan was being insulted. Our own columnists weren't having this display of petticoat power either. Here was a man who was a master on the pitch, but was incapable of laying down the law in his own home. Here was a man who was upsetting one of the world's most famous clubs and risked losing a multimillion-pound deal. Because of what? His wife. Who was in charge here?

In the *Sun*, Greavsie said: 'So now we know who the real Guv'nor is in the Ince household – and it's certainly not Manchester United and England star Paul. Paul might parade the car with the registration number GUV 8, but I bet his wife Claire drives it.

'The Guv'nor arrived in Milan this week, pen poised ready to sign. Except his missus wouldn't let him. First, Claire wasn't sure about the city. Then it was the houses that weren't up to scratch. Finally, in what can be perfectly described in either language as a fiasco, the whole deal collapsed at a Press conference, as the Guvnor returned home to consider his options.

'Or should that be *her* options? Maybe, Inter should have bought Claire instead. They've always liked someone who could stick the boot in and *I* certainly wouldn't fancy playing against her.'

'But why is it always the English players,' wrote Nigel Clarke in the *Mirror*, 'who embarrass us abroad? Why cannot our footballers act with the kind of sophistication that is normally the birthright of most European stars. The Inces, Paul and his wife Clare, have been offered a lifestyle that would be among the most enviable in Europe. He has only to ask David Platt about that.

'Ince would want for nothing. He would be secure for life, and live in the proverbial lap of luxury. That's if he still fancies the move to a different stratum of society.

'I happen to believe that Ince is a magnificent footballer. But he has shown something less than good manners and breeding by devaluing his Italian negotiations.'

He could be one of those black men whose personal, if not professional, self-esteem is such that they routinely cannot believe that they have been lucky enough to succeed in attracting a confident, well-turned out, independent white woman. A woman with 'class' who wouldn't normally 'go' with a black man. A woman to parade to your friends. And with his broken family background, a woman who had given him a family.

There are still plenty of black people who believe that black men target white women in the belief that white women will confer status on them. I've always found it rather depressing to think that people actually think that white people take black people up a notch in the world, as if we exist somewhere down below in a dark bottomless well to be dragged upwards by any and every culture other than our own, as if that job needed to be done in the first place.

Laura Bruno, claims the *Observer*, is up with the best of them – Mike Tyson's agent Don King – when it comes to negotiating deals: '. . . she did all right for a *Guardian*-reading middle-class girl from south London. She was in on nearly every deal Frank made in 14 years as a professional boxer, including the one that mattered most: it was Laura who haggled the hardest when Frank landed his fourth world title shot and then, when the new champion had to take the short end of the purse against Tyson in his one and only defence, Laura drove King to distraction with her hard-headedness. She was the best second in the business. Laura dangled her husband's comeback story in front of the tabloids – inevitably finding him a place in the *Sun* – and brilliantly milked interest by dragging it out over the summer.'

Historically, black footballers have dragged themselves to the top, or thereabouts, of their profession by themselves, before the women came along.

The question is: why are the women nearly always white girls? Especially now, when there are so many black girls from all kinds of backgrounds and classes, giving black footballers the opportunities a lot of their forebears say they didn't have. Black footballers today don't have the excuse that perhaps their dads, granddads or any other male relatives had: 'There weren't any black women around.'

One commonly held belief within black communities is that given that most men prefer the easy life at home, a white woman is less demanding and easier to please than a black woman.

And then there's sex. Doing it with you is taboo. Oh yes, it still is. All those who deny that the history of forbidden sex between black and white continues to have a tremendous impact on today's relationships are being wilfully myopic.

'I feel slightly uneasy walking down the street with him, or taking public transport,' said a white English woman married to a black Brazilian. They live in England. 'There is a flicker of uneasiness in white men's eyes, partly because black men with white women is one of the last great sexual taboos. The white male fear of black sexual prowess is very real and evident. On the other hand, at parties I've been ignored by black women. Often we leave such gatherings after just an hour,' reported the *Daily Mail* in August 1996.

In my experience it is middle-class black women with white

lovers, and middle-class white women with black lovers, who are most vehement in denying that the sexual-taboo element still exists, and cannot be ruled out as a factor in the attraction of their relationship.

One white professional woman demanded of me whether I realized how much she had 'given up' to be with a black man. She said that I had no right to say that sex with a black man was a factor. All of this woman's boyfriends had been black. I thought it was almost as if she felt I'd lessened the significance of her 'sacrifice' by introducing the sexual element.

A friend of a friend of mine lived in paralyzing fear of what her father would do if he ever found out she was seeing a black guy. She was a lovely girl, if a bit quiet, and we all used to hang out together now and then. I got to hear about the complicated plans she would have to lay (she lived at home) to enable her and her boyfriend to meet up, and the endless lies she would have to tell her parents. A survey of the thoughts of fathers of white girls who find out that their daughters are seeing black boys would make informative reading for the 'myths like that are dead' brigade.

But these female choices and domestic lives of the black footballers criticized by the *Weekly Journal* letter-writer merely mirror the extraordinary sexual regrouping black men are initiating in the world outside the football grounds.

In 1996 the Office of National Statistics published a report which said that one in three black men is married or living with a white woman. And, between the ages of 16 and 34, the likelihood that a black man is with a white woman rises to 40 per cent. Most of these men have black mothers and fathers. What can explain the high figures? Figures which keep growing: 50 per cent is the latest to emerge.

These men obviously don't give a damn about black opprobrium being heaped on their unions. Although there are very many blacks who hate the notion of black and white forming relationships (interestingly the loudest voices belong to black men who attack black females with white males), as a whole, black people, however much they disapprove, tend to have an attitude which says: live and let live as long as you don't dump your hang-ups in my face. They certainly wouldn't attempt to kill a white person for daring to have a black partner. Although an insult now and then doesn't go amiss.

The African-American world heavyweight boxing champion (WBC), Oliver McCall, came to London in August 1995 to defend his title against Britain's Frank Bruno. Here is part of a conversation they had, as reported in the *Sun*:

> 'McCALL: "I'm not your brother, I've heard word on the street you don't even respect your own people here."
> BRUNO: "I love my own people more than I love ice cream."
> McCALL: "Yeah, and we all know what your favourite ice cream flavour is."'

Black Bruno is married to white Laura and they have three children. The *Sun* was shocked and appalled that anyone could display such hateful prejudice.

'After the fight,' wrote the *Weekly Journal*, 'Bruno made much of the fact that McCall had called him an Uncle Tom at a prefight press conference. "I'm not an Uncle Tom, I'm not a sell-out, I love my people," said Bruno, who thought that the reason McCall had called him that had to do with the colour of his wife. It doesn't. Many black people have said similar things about Bruno. What they are referring to is the way in which he comes across on television, when he often seems culturally naive and almost never says anything in praise of black people. Rightly or wrongly, many black people see black celebrities as representing the whole community. It may well be the case that

Bruno does a lot for black people privately and out of the glare of the media. But he is hardly ever seen at black events or functions. So no matter what he is doing, people will always criticize him unless he is seen to be doing it. It will require more than just words for Frank to be as loved by the black community as he is by the white community.'

Perhaps McCall could afford to be smug. Among America's nineties black élite it appears that there is some revision going on. Couples like Whitney Houston and Bobby Brown; Denzel Washington and his wife; Michael Jordan and his wife; Spike Lee and his wife; Eddie Murphy and his wife; and Mike Tyson's girlfriends, all have the same thing in common: they are all black relationships (or at the very least black on mixed-race relationships). These stars, and many more in the current American entertainment, sports and music worlds, have business lives which are lived in mostly white circles, but they have clearly made conscious decisions to partner black women and men.

'Celebrity miscegenation is almost unheard of in America, where black consciousness mitigates against mixing the races,' wrote Lesley Thomas in the *Sunday Times* in March 1994. 'Many now feel black Britons should follow suit. A recent article in *Pride*, a magazine aimed at black women, asked: "Why are inter-racial marriages among the famous so prevalent in Britain?' Loanna Morrison, its author, said there were too few well-known black couples. "We need them as role models for the rest of the community. I don't think there's anything wrong with mixed marriages, but the sight of a famous black couple is a rarity in Britain."' The piece was accompanied by pictures of Frank and Laura Bruno; Lenny Henry and Dawn French; and U2's Adam Clayton and Naomi Campbell, who were then engaged.

But the forty- or fifty-per-centers in the UK are in a society where there are white people angry enough to want to kill to prevent black and white fucking. As a young man, originally from Barbados, found out when he followed three white men in their twenties as they drove their van into a London petrol station in the autumn of 1994. One of them glanced behind and noticed a car pulling up with the young black man and his white girlfriend inside. Furious, one of the men ran to the car, kicked the passenger door and punched the window. The Bajan got out of his car and asked him why he had done that. ''Cause you're black,' was the answer.

By now his mates from the van had joined the white attacker, and the three whites set about the black man with screwdrivers. Then one of the whites jumped into the Bajan's own car and drove it over his legs. He was badly injured, but survived this murder attempt. The judge sentenced two of the men to three years; the third got five. Shortly afterwards, in November 1994, the sentences were referred to appeal for being too lenient. The Court of Appeal increased them to five years each; and seven years.

A young, good-looking black guy who was in a long-standing relationship with a white girl told me that when he looked at black women he saw his mother. Don't get him wrong: he loved his mother, but he also knew what a tough life she had had. It wore her out. In his mind, black couples faced a hard life in front of them in a white country. Who needs that? Life's too short, mate. A black man and woman living in a majority white society are making a statement of defiance merely by showing a white world that they are together. This guy was aware of and prepared to confront the possibility of an attack by a white man because he had a white woman at his side, but he was unwilling to fight what could be death by a thousand racial injustices which black couples are likely to face. He had seen what it had done to his mother.

Some years ago I was in a nightspot in Manchester with a boyfriend. The vibes were strange, but I couldn't put my finger on it. I thought it was possible that in some mysterious Northern way, the clubbers could tell that we were from down South. It was a small place, after all, even if it was trendy. It was only when a slow record was put on and individuals became couples that it hit me: my boyfriend and I were the only black couple on the dancefloor. Every other couple was mixed: mostly black guys and white girls, but there was also a sprinkling of black girls and white guys. It was the oddest sensation. We were uncomfortable with them; they were uncomfortable with us.

'I couldn't believe it,' a mate of mine said, exasperated, on the phone. 'Every single one of them was with a white girl. Pushing a trolley. I just put the stuff back on the shelves and walked out. I couldn't bear it. It's just getting worse.'

Summer 1996. Sainsbury's on a Saturday afternoon in Birmingham, and every mixed-race couple she'd seen was black man – white woman. Enough to put a young, pretty, and single black female off her shopping any day of the week.

Surely 40-50 per cent of black males choosing white females as partners amounts to more than the personal preferences of a few people, and needs to be thought about? Surely, if you observe what amounts to a trend in society, you have to ask questions as to why that trend is happening?

Have black British men decided that the intermingling of genes is the best way to deal with a legacy of historical racism which continues to plague their existence – overtly with physical racial attacks and covertly with the coded racial attacks and harassment of the New Racists? Have they – and an increasing, but smaller, number of black women – decided that inter-racial relationships are the answer to racism because their half-white, half-black offspring will experience fewer racial problems than they did? Is the rapid increase in mixed relationships a sign that black people are creating an environment in which white people will feel more at ease with their presence here?

The forty-fifty-per-centers, I believe, have simply made a choice: if you are a black man living and intending to die in Britain, it makes good economic and cultural sense to spend your life with a white woman.

The forty-fifty-per-centers cannot claim in the 1990s that there are no black women for them to date, live with and marry. A Nigerian male journalist told me that he'd married his white European wife because when he came to England, as late as the 1970s, black female journalists were rare.

If the odds on a black male – black female relationship surviving successfully in England are too long, the easier option is to mix the races. At least that way you would be guaranteed a 50 per-cent stake in the future via your half-white children.

'There was always a feeling,' a black police officer who worked in southern England said in a May 1994 issue of the *Guardian*, describing the reaction of his white colleagues to his sole black presence, 'that if I was prepared to ditch my blackness, forget my culture, it would be easier, but I didn't want to do that. I'm proud of it – in fact, I don't know enough about my history and my culture so I'm certainly not going to abandon it just to be accepted.'

I've always found it ludicrous and pathetic, especially in the light of the history between the two races, that whites feel blacks have to make themselves acceptable to them. That it is blacks who have to make the effort to fit in.

That officer was articulating a feeling which many blacks who are in daily, isolated contact with white people sense strongly. The knowledge that if you act as if you were 'one of them', joked in their idioms, made social and cultural references which were also theirs, avoided all talk about anything remotely 'black', then the world would be a very comfortable place. For whites.

And won't it be even easier, if you have a white partner, to fit better into white surroundings? It would make it comfortable for everybody all round. There is nothing that sticks out more painfully at white gatherings than a black couple. I used to sometimes get the feeling that I was, if not quite causing offence, then having to oblige the whites to try and cross another cultural chasm and get to know another black person when they had just put all that effort into getting to know one: me.

To be obviously 'black' in language, mannerisms, dress, hairstyle, tastes and sexual desires makes many white people very uncomfortable. To express different tastes and desires mark you out. You, as a black, are not fitting in. I think 'you're not really black' is the most offensive statement a white person can make to a black person. Yet they mean it as a compliment; they mean that they feel very comfortable in your presence. You're not behaving the way black people are *supposed* to behave. Who made the suppositions?

'When we first started going out,' Clare Ince once said, 'he treated me better than any other boy I'd met. Because of the way he acted on the field, nobody believed me. Now they can see he's a brilliant father. Thomas can't get enough of him.'

Nobody believed her because people expected Paul Ince to, at best, dominate her completely; at worst, to rough her up, slap her around a few times. Because that's what black men, violent creatures that they are, did to their women. There is no evidence that domestic violence is more prevalent in black households compared to white households. Domestic violence occurs everywhere.

Anyone unconvinced about white male fear of 'rampant' black male sexuality, ready to devour white womanhood, need look no further than the sports pages. Here's the *Sunday Mirror* on the first day of the 1994 European Athletics Championships in Helsinki:

Headlined WITH THE BIG TALKING POINTS – LEGEND IN HIS OWN LUNCH BOX!, the report by David Moore opened with: 'Linford Christie and his world-famous "lunchbox" are all set to be a big, big turn-on for the ladies yet again.

'Millions of viewers, many of them women, are expected to tune in to see 34-year-old Christie repeat his starring role as the oldest swinger in town! "This is top-class sport, bound to attract a wide audience to watch Christie, Colin Jackson and Sally Gunnell strut their stuff," smiled a TV source. "But there's no denying Linford holds some sort of special appeal, particularly where the fairer sex are concerned. It's for others to guess at the reasons why!"'

As yet, there is no Olympic competition entitled: Who Has Got the Biggest Penis. Yet Britain's foremost athlete – it'll be a very long time before anybody catches up with his medal collection – is reduced by the white male sportsworld to speculation about the length and width of his dick.

The *Sunday Mirror* report continued: '[Linford] raged: "It's distasteful, disgraceful even – I am an athlete, a runner, a sprinter, not some human peepshow. People don't show me enough respect when they talk about the lunchbox. I am in Helsinki looking to win a gold medal for my country, and help put the Great back in Britain."'

The majority of the rest of the article was concerned about whether he had sex before a race or not. So nearly an entire page was devoted to Christie's genitalia. His objections to this kind of coverage are regarded as being unsportsmanlike. His demand for 'respect' derided.

'Every man's dream. An extra one and a half inches in the lunchbox department,' was the advertisement that got Jacobs the biscuit-makers into trouble in September 1996. *The Times* said: 'The poster is illustrated with nothing more suggestive than a picture of the new Club biscuit, but callers to the [Advertising

Standards] Authority have described it as smutty. The largest number of complaints has come from men in the North-East. All the complaints have been from men unhappy at the way their sex is being portrayed.' Why did white men take offence at being portrayed (in a biscuit ad) in a way that Linford (more graphically) is asked to take in his stride?

I remember seeing an old television shot of Kevin Keegan in his undies. He seemed pretty well-hung to me, but I have never seen or read any references to Kevin's lunchbox. Articles don't mention it. His sporting talent is automatically regarded as far more important. He doesn't have to ask for respect; it's a given. The sexuality surrounding white male stars is kept in its rightful place: articles written for women's-lifestyle feature pages. You'll see these articles in many places but you won't catch a glimpse of them on the sports pages, where sporting talent is discussed. Not so for black male stars.

A player like Les Ferdinand had an ordinary working-class black Londoner's background, but his *Playgirl* looks make him irresistible to all white comers. And the footballer who says *The Autobiography of Malcolm X* is his favourite book, is the man who likes to say yes to them.

The *Sun* published a cartoon in 1995 showing Ferdinand escorting a white female into his bedroom. It was titled: 'Les Ferdinand. Play Ground'. The *pièce de résistance* was the goal-cum-headboard constructed over the pillows. At the foot of the bed there was a dugout with a sign saying: 'Substitutes Bench'. Three more busty, almost naked white girls sat there smiling, waiting their turn.

Les Ferdinand seemingly, and unfairly, fitted the portrayal of the black lecher who can't keep his pecker to himself. The mockery followed the usual kiss and tell revelations of a spurned lover. Dutch model, Eva Dijkstra, had introduced herself to the player and his friends in a central-London nightclub. The affair lasted seven months. Coincidentally, sex – what she said Ferdinand called 'the bed business' – lasted ninety minutes, 'but he always checked the football results on Teletext first'.

Eva's story was revenge after she realized that Ferdinand had no intention of leaving his white live-in girlfriend, Angelea, and their nine-year-old son. A Newcastle fan said: 'He could be having an affair with Mother Teresa as long as he keeps sticking the ball into the back of the net.' Eva claimed they broke up because of his friendship with the television presenter, Dani Behr.

I once watched the young, blonde, pretty, husky-voiced Dani Behr interview Ruud Gullit on late-night TV. And I remember thinking that if female lust could kill, that man didn't stand a chance, he was a goner. Dani Behr seems to bloom in the company of footballers.

Ryan Giggs is one of Britain's most eligible bachelors – and Dani Behr's already had a relationship with him. In one of his rare interviews – he was promoting his new adverts for Quorn vegetarian meat substitutes (although he's not a veggie: 'I don't fancy that, I couldn't go without me bacon butties') – Giggs told *Today* that he was so timid he wouldn't dare chat up a stranger: 'I'm not a flirtatious person. I would never go up to a girl and talk to her unless she was part of a crowd I knew. I'm a very shy person, people don't know that but I find meeting strangers difficult.'

As the paper's woman's editor put it: 'And shy is not a word you'd associate with a party-going, paparazzi-seeking celebrity like motormouth Dani. You wonder if the quietly spoken Manchester boy ever got a word in edgeways.' Giggs said the relationship 'just came to an end. We're still friends, we still talk.'

Dani admitted to the *Sun* in November 1994 that she'd been besotted with Giggs. 'He's a cool guy. So down-to-earth, genuine and unaffected. It wasn't until a couple of weeks after I got to know him that I realized how big he is – he's bigger than a pop star! He has wonderful hazel puppy eyes. We've met our match. We're exactly the same – stubborn.'

However, the fans weren't that keen on them as an item, Dani said. They used to heckle her when she went to watch Giggs play: 'At Old Trafford they were saying, "You leave Giggsy alone. He's playing crap since he met you." Thing is, he *has* been playing crap since he met me.'

Giggs might hate it, but the newspapers see no reason why they shouldn't follow popular footballers on their annual holidays. Randy-footballer holiday stories are about as good as you can get. And as long as there are newspapers there will be girls willing to bed and sell.

There he goes, off on a Greek holiday and before you can say 'it's a goal', he's scored with a 'stunning brunette' a couple of hours after he gets off the plane. Perhaps Giggs also inherited that 'natural ability' for pretty fast moves on the female sex from his black dad. The difference is, though, whilst his dad, Danny Wilson, is still condemned for sowing his oats when he too was a randy young thing and a player, his son Ryan is lauded for all the girlfriends he manages to get through in a year. Les Ferdinand is portrayed as a womanizer; Giggs is just a bit of a Jack-the-lad. Ferdinand is clearly black; Giggs passes for white. Ferdinand is objectified as the representative of unbridled black male lust; Giggs is given the space to be subject to the whims of his own personality.

It isn't a surprise to see a mixed-race footballer with a white woman rather than a black partner. Especially if it's the mixed-race man's mother who is the white side. Whatever advances modern men think they have made in relearning how to be a parent, initial cultural awareness and knowledge is still held in the mother's powerful hands. For a white woman, passing on to her child the vital cultural and historical knowledge of his or her black side will depend on the mother's personal outlook and determination to acquire that knowledge in the first place.

I've met too many white women who are with black men but have no time for black people in general. It's almost as if their man doesn't belong with the 'rest of them'. It would be difficult for a child to escape this view even if it is not expressed verbally. What can amount to a contempt for black life can emerge simply through the way a white mother approaches her child's personal hygiene.

I don't know what I counted to but it was much more than ten when, in a newsagent's, I saw the matted, sticking-up hair and dry, greying skin of a mixed-race child accompanied by her white mother. It made me angry to see that even in the nineties the message still hadn't got through to some white women that you cannot physically look after a black child – even a half-black one – in the same manner you would a white one. The skin needs a good cream; the hair needs oils. Basic. Unless you think it's not nice, it's odd, it's too different, and you never needed it yourself, anyway. If that's what the external condition is being exposed to, what's happening to the child's mind?

Of the few black soccer stars with black women, Ian Wright's relationship with Debbie is the one most cherished by black females, because it appeared to be so normal – like one they had had, were in or could have. The Wrights' relationship reflects similar, numerous ones in the wider black world. I personally know of several black couples who first started going out with each other in their teens, and now in their thirties, are still together, whether married or not, often with children – although one or two of the men's children don't belong to their longterm girlfriend.

When sweet-faced Debbie met little tough guy Ian, she was 12, he was 16, and they were living on the same council housing estate in south London. The four-year age gap meant that was the end of that story.

Nineteen ninety, nine years later, Debbie Martin, Barclays Bank cashier, was waiting at the bus stop when Ian Wright, Crystal Palace footballer, queued up behind her. He was at the bus stop because he'd crashed his car through 'driving like Ayrton Senna'. Six months later they were engaged and living together.

Debbie is an ordinary black woman. There is nothing bimbo-ish or football-groupieish about her. Much too down to earth for any of that nonsense. Her figure is what western magazines who adore the starved look – which only those who have plenty to eat aim for – would call 'full'. Anoxeria and bulimia hardly disturb the minds of people in Africa or those of African descent. Debbie's body is very familiar to black women and men anywhere in the world.

Her kind, comforting face is a delight. Even to strangers, there is something vaguely recognizable about her. I've known a few Debbies, I grew up with one. Every street where lots of black people live has a Debbie – the nice, down-to-earth woman who was probably the first one to make you feel at home when you moved in, the one who'll always help out. Just don't take her for granted.

'Once I saw her again,' said Wright, 'it was love at first sight. My first relationship had faded. I went and lived with a girl when I was too young – my success has had nothing to do with it.'

When they bumped into each other again, Debbie didn't have children, but Ian had three as a result of that early relationship. Bradley, Bret and Shaun live with their mother, but see Ian and Debbie very frequently.

'My having kids wasn't a problem for Deborah because she knows the sort of guy I am. I never had girlfriends all over the place – I've only had about five in my whole life. She knew I wasn't the type to mess around,' he said in the *Sunday Mirror* in 1993.

'Others might not have been able to handle the kids and the fact that I'm a footballer. My name was well-known around football circles when we met again, but nothing like it is today. It would be hard to meet somebody now because I'd never know whether it's me they love or what is surrounding me – but I know it's not one of the factors why we are together.'

The two married shortly after the Arsenal FA Cup Final victory against Sheffield Wednesday in 1993. The wedding pictures are lovely. 'He hasn't changed,' says Debbie. 'If he had, I wouldn't want to be with him.'

Black footballers, Sheffield Wednesday's Mark Bright and West Ham's Mitchell Thomas, were among the tiny number of close pals who flew to Mauritius for the island ceremony in 1993. It probably helped Bright get over the fact that his side had lost the Final. At least he'd lost to such a close friend – Wright and Bright have known each other since their playing days at Crystal Palace.

Debbie and Ian could easily have appeared on *Mr and Mrs*, the old television show for the averagely-married. They're just a lot richer than the average couple, that's all. But like quite a few men, Wright is quite pleased that he has a woman who could look after the family financially if necessary. 'Deborah is independent in herself, not looking for anything from me. She has worked since I knew her. In fact, she could pay the mortgage if I stopped playing football.' They now have their own baby son.

Single mothers have a notoriously difficult time juggling the money to pay bills of any kind, as Brixton girl, Shirley Dewar, knows well. She went to school with a lot of girls who already had two or three children by the time they were 20. But when she got pregnant at the age of 20 in 1995 she didn't feel it was too young to become a mother, or too young to bear the financial responsibilities. Andy Cole, her 23-year-old boyfriend, was as thrilled as she was.

'We weren't planning a family,' Shirley said in the *Sun* in February 1995, after the pregnancy was confirmed, 'but once it sank in we were both really pleased.'

'There's Nothing Like This' was one of the biggest British soul hits of 1990. It's Shirley's favourite song because it was playing when Cole came over to ask her for a dance at Kevin Campbell's brother's wedding. Campbell was in the Arsenal first team when Cole was languishing in the club's reserves.

As Shirley remembered: 'I had no idea who he was. His name didn't mean a thing to me. We were both single and exchanged phone numbers. I called him two days later and we went out to the cinema.

'I was quite taken by him. But I thought he fancied himself a bit. It wasn't love at first sight. That just sort of happened.'

Andy was her first serious boyfriend. 'First time lucky, I guess. I'm glad he wasn't a big star when I first started going out with him. At least no one can accuse me of being with him just for fame and fortune. He didn't have a penny when we met – now he's worth millions, but it hasn't changed him. He's still the same. He's a big softie.' Shirley won't bother to pretend she's a football fan, and makes sure she keeps her own friends because she says too much football-talk drives her mad. 'I support who-ever he is playing for. I watch him on TV and sometimes go to the matches.'

If he hadn't had to dash off for a Manchester United game against Southampton – where he scored a goal – he would have been present for the birth of their son at St Thomas' Hospital in London. Having a child doesn't mean marriage is on the horizon.

'We've been together for some time now and neither of us thinks we have to get married just because we're having a baby,'

Shirley said. But she would like to put some more permanent roots down. 'If you're a footballer's girl then you have to get used to being apart. I have never known it any other way. But with a child we'll need to be together as a family.'

When Cole was at Newcastle, and she stayed at his home in north London, one of them would commute each weekend. She didn't like life in the North-East and was much happier when Cole's record transfer meant a move to more cosmopolitan Manchester.

Wright and Debbie, Cole and Shirley. Very typical of black on black relationship patterns among working-class blacks who live in mostly black communities, who meet very young, have a long relationship and children. Although Wright and Cole had moved away financially from the majority of their black peers, when it came to settling down, metaphorically, they went back home. You could say that those with very working-class black backgrounds, like Wright and Cole, are more likely to find black women to settle down with, and in doing so, buck the black star/white woman storyending. But then again . . .

'I walked into a radio's evening programme department last week,' wrote Garth Crooks in January 1997 in *New Nation*, 'to find a posse of black women silently staring into orbit as though they'd been simultaneously hit by a bolt of lightning. In fact, it turned out they were actually suffering from Ianitus, a condition that leaves its victims in a state of shock for at least two hours before exploding into a fit of uncontrollable rage.

'The attacks had developed after a tabloid newspaper revealed that Arsenal's Ian Wright was having an affair with a girl from a burger bar. His infidelity has sent black women into a frenzy, gnashing their teeth and ripping out their weave-ons. The attacks are particularly bad in north and south London.

'The man the men refer to as "The Dapper" has admitted to

cheating on his wife and Ian can't expect any sympathy from his extensive female constituency. One said in a hushed voice: "My God, how the mighty have fallen." Another exclaimed: "I'm heartbroken . . . a white woman!"'

They Couldn't Manage a Piss-up in a Brewery

After netball one afternoon at my secondary school, our games teacher, a tall, muscular woman, took me and the only other black girl in my class aside in the changing room. We were both very tall for our age (I haven't grown since) and were both excellent at games: you name it, we could play it. Miss said we had the potential to become excellent runners, and she wanted us to join an athletics club after school. Of course, we were both flattered by the attention, but I felt uncomfortable. A few days later I went up to her and refused her offer. And it wasn't just because I knew exactly what my daddy would have said had I brought it up: 'Running? Running to where? Go and sit down, my friend!' You can only appreciate the complete never-bring-this-up-again nature of that sentence if you try to say it using a heavy Nigerian accent.

You see, even at twelve years old, I knew nobody ever asked little black kids to stay behind at school for help with maths, chemistry or physics, all areas I could have done with a bit of after-school training in. So I didn't bother to tell my father. My friend didn't run round the tracks either. I'd been flattered because I thought we were amongst the few approached like that; but we weren't, we were amongst the many. We belonged to a race whose brawn was instinctively and historically thought to be of superior quality to their brain.

In October 1994, the *Weekly Journal* reported that 'The hated book [*The Bell Curve*] co-authored by a darling of the radical right which brought the subject of race and IQ to the forefront of an angry and anguished debate has been branded racist and wrong by Reverend Jesse Jackson. *The Bell Curve*, written by the late Harvard University psychologist Richard Herrnstein and conservative theorist Charles Murray, argues that black Americans average 15 points behind whites and Asian people in IQ tests, and this measure of intellectual inferiority results in high levels of crime, teenage pregnancy and poverty. Jackson has pointed out that a theory of racial inferiority has long permeated American life and been used to justify such outrages as slavery, segregation and discrimination.'

It appears that the people who inhabit the top of the football industry, or the heights of any sports institution for that matter, still believe that black people have brawn (they're good at sports, aren't they? We'll give them that) but no brains (they couldn't manage a piss-up in a brewery). Intelligence is an optional extra in a footballer. As long as he can do the business, no one cares if he's as thick as two planks. In a manager, though, intelligence is regarded as a necessity.

Jimmy Hill wrote a piece in the *Observer* in January 1994 during the run-up to the appointment of Venables as England's new manager: 'Our major problem, and the most difficult one to solve, is a lack of intelligence. Not enough thought is given to the game at any level. If a formula for temporary success is found, the tendency is to follow it slavishly. Physique, aggression and emotion become the main winning and revered qualities. There's nothing wrong with them, providing they don't override artistry, perception and deception, the weapons of a Beardsley, or a Beckenbauer or a Moore, both defenders.

'In Holland, Germany, Brazil, Argentina and Spain, football is the nation's game. In England, it still remains the game of the common man. There's nothing wrong with that, but it needs the inspiration and leadership provided by experienced common men with uncommon intelligence. When there are enough of those in the pipeline, the FA will find it so much easier to make the right appointment of a candidate as scrupulously free from sin as the Archbishop of Canterbury.'

Most of the managers in the Premiership and Football League – Jimmy Hill's pipeline – are former players. In appointing them, it was hoped that they already had uncommon intelligence, or that they were on their way to acquiring some. Currently, none of these men is a former black British footballer.

If intelligence is regarded as the vital necessary characteristic a manager must have, then most blacks are seen as being out of the game before they've even opened their mouths. Black people are still regarded by many whites as not having too much up there – a race of people without the authority to become leaders or managers because we're not acknowledged as people who can organize, who are serious, intellectual or articulate. We're not regarded as people with the good judgement or the mental faculties required for strategic thinking. Periodically, some aggrieved white pseudo-scientist, not content with wallowing in his or her perceived 'superior' IQ to friends and interested organizations, will insist on rustling up a 'study' so that we can all share in his or her claims that nature has it over nurture when it comes to the intelligence of black people.

Unfortunately, too many black people buy into one spin-off of this rubbish: believing that black people do not have the abilities to get things done. Too many blacks refuse to work for blacks who try to 'run things', opting instead to work for white people. These blacks will denigrate and undermine black establishments, while at the same time bemoaning the lack of successful black businesses. In November 1994 the *Weekly Journal* reported that: 'A survey commissioned by the "UK Black Pages" revealed that only 19 per cent of black people spend money with black-owned businesses, which goes a long way to explaining why the black economy is so weak.' Why make them better off than me is the small-minded thinking there as the black shopper goes off to make a white or Asian-run business rich. As for blacks in business themselves, instead of pooling our resources in the realization that 25 or 50 per cent of something is better than 100 per cent of nothing, we spend too much time tearing ourselves and each other apart competing against the other black on the block involved in exactly the same enterprise. You'd be hard pressed to find a Jewish, Asian or white businessperson who didn't believe in partnerships and joint enterprises as a means of gaining strength and success. We, who have so much more stacked up against us, are reluctant to pool our resources, but other races who face less prejudice or even none at all, join together as a matter of course. Too many blacks indulge in what I call the 'me–one' philosophy, as in I ('me') am the only person ('one') who must undertake this project, nobody else must get a look in.

We're not naturally seen as a race whom other people can look up to for leadership unless they're searching for a higher moral or spiritual authority – we seem to have that in bucketfuls: think Nelson Mandela. Lesser black mortals make a healthy living as counsellors, community leaders, social workers or anything in alternative therapy, under the guise of improving black self-esteem. We're the world's comfort zone: white people need only think of the kind of lives many of us have to lead, and they can feel better already. Our nurturing nature is supposed to be our strong point; our intelligence, supposedly our weakness.

If black men have managed to penetrate football to a large extent on the pitch, they're still on to a loser when they try to enter the high-stakes management game. Football management (the clubs) and the football Establishment (the Football Association, Football League, etc) are still pristinely white institutions where even black footballers with excellent pasts dare not tread.

If it's hard going on the 'shopfloor' when you're black and your colleagues and managers are white, then think of the additional burdens faced by a black person who's trying to or who has become the only one to succeed in getting to management level?

The relationship every player cannot avoid going through, whether he is single or already married, is with the manager. For a Premiership player, this meant a white man until one unprecedented dreadlocked appointment was made in the summer of 1996. And, currently, only one club, in the seventy-two-member Football League, has a black manager.

Therefore, once the overwhelming majority of black footballers walk through the doors of their clubs, the manager–employee relationship they have is with a white man. This is followed by the black player's love-hate relationships with his club's mostly white supporters. And then there are his friendships with his mostly white team-mates. Even at clubs with, for example, five or six black players, that's five or six out of a squad of thirty or more. Basically, a black player's professional life is lived in the company of mostly white people.

Do black and white really get on in the teams? There are some excellent friendships: John Fashanu and white former footballer, Glynn Mason, enjoy a very successful business relationship developed from a twenty-year-old close friendship which started in football. But the really tight friendships are black on black ones, and they are like revolving doors: Ian Wright and Mark Bright; Ian Wright and Paul Ince; Andy Cole and Paul Ince; Ryan Giggs and Paul Ince; Mark Bright and Les Ferdinand.

Whenever there are several black players in the squad, like at Chelsea or Crystal Palace, what amounts to a racial camp in the club is formed. Of course there is always the general dressing-room banter which crosses racial lines, but for the black players there will always be 'black' banter, and references to a black world and black tastes which their white team-mates will almost certainly be ignorant of. When George Graham became manager of Arsenal, he has stated he didn't like the way the dressing room ran along colour lines and worked to break it up.

However, outside the club they could do what they wished. In the late eighties and early nineties, John Fashanu was the leading light behind the organization popularly known as the 'Black Pack': a group of top black players from different teams who liked to go clubbing and partying together. It started in the eighties with players like Laurie Cunningham, Vince Hillaire, Luther Blisset, John Barnes and Paul Ince, widening to include the boxer, Nigel Benn (a second cousin of Ince's) and black boxing promoter and football agent, Ambrose Mendy (now in jail).

Later Ian Wright and Mark Bright joined in. When Dennis Wise and Vinny Jones clamoured to be let in on the fun and games, the guys changed the name to the 'Pack'. Vince Hillaire and Brendon Batson organized informal black football teams, made up of starry names, who played in charity games.

What these black groupings, both inside the clubs and between them, showed was that unless black players made the effort, they could spend their rest days and nights off still living life in a white world. It's not a question of whether they do or do not get on with their white colleagues, it's the fact that if they also spend their leisure time enjoying the pursuits and desires of their white male colleagues, then they will inhabit a white world 24/7, as the Americans say. As British football's managerial floors are all white, when a black man gets through the door he *is* entering a 24/7 white world.

The professional existence of black sportsmen and women revolves around being discovered by white people, trained by white people, and managed by white people. Black sports stars will be decorated with awards, sometimes praised, quite often virulently attacked, bought and sold, and then dumped when they are no longer of use to anyone but themselves.

They are not supposed to have careers after their exertions in the line of duty have worn their bodies out. In exercising their bodies to the limit to get to the top of their professions in the first place, the last thing the sports Establishment appears to want or expect is to have these people exercising their minds and running the industries they've made millions of pounds for. The sporting institutions can find black talent and milk it for all it's worth, but when it comes to black talent wanting a job with the institution, well, that's a whole different ball game. It's the black and white minstrel show – where blacks are just entertainers for whites.

The vast majority of black footballers, despite the glory of medals, cups, broken records, critical acclaim, and years of experience in their industry, still find themselves regarded, aged in their thirties and forties, as untested novices who will need many more years of experience before they can even think of applying for a management position. These black men will sit back and watch while the white colleagues they came up with, and who were very often not as good as they were, zoom past them and settle comfortably into a management office and the power structure that comes with it. A Sports Council report, published in 1993, said that blacks were visible in many sports, but were 'severely under-represented at all levels in the structures of sport and recreation.'

What, then, are the magical, infinitely superior leadership ingredients that whites have but blacks don't? What manner of man do you have to be to get to the top of the professional football tree? What does it take to be a manager?

The simple answer is: not a lot. That is, not a lot if you're trying to get a job with an English club. Ken Jones, writing in the *Independent* in September 1995, remarked: 'A curious thing is that any number of people in all walks of life imagine themselves successful in football management. Some take the fantasy as far as to apply seriously for vacant situations . . . Holding opinions about the game and putting them into practice are entirely different things. This applies equally to identifying faults and bringing about improvement. However, as the former England and West Ham manager, Ron Greenwood, once said, expertise is assumed automatically on retirement from the game, even if that amounted to no more than a kickabout in the school playground.'

Most of the managers in the English divisions got their first jobs without having to produce any specific qualifications (just as well because they didn't have any, sometimes not even a coaching licence). We haven't even started to force managers-to-be to undergo rigorous professional training as they do on the Continent. In Britain we enjoy a system of amateur professionalism.

Sometimes we're lucky, and after a time the slipshod system produces first-rate managers like George Graham and Alex Ferguson – men at the top of the tree because they have reaped the benefit of years of experience and failure, the right to trial and error, during long periods at a single club. The majority of the others merely bumble along from short-term job to short-term job, picking up what knowledge they can, or believing that as they were once a player they know it all already. Very little is passed on to the players under their command.

Howard Wilkinson, the former Leeds manager (and one of the longest-serving managers in the Premiership), was also the chairman of the League Managers' Association which, naturally, is very concerned about the job insecurity of its members. After the '94–95 season, in which forty-eight managers lost their jobs – more than half the managerial posts in the Premiership and Football League – Wilkinson wrote in the *Independent*: 'One problem is that every vacancy produces a hundred applicants from a huge and relatively unskilled labour pool. The majority are, in American parlance, Monday morning quarterbacks asking only a pittance for the chance to put their theories into practice. Some chairmen, particularly in the lower divisions, are ever ready to chance their arms if a few thousand can be knocked off the wage bill. So another head is lined up for the guillotine.'

Wilkinson said the solution for the future was in training: '. . . better training courses, better qualifications and a Football Association regulation that clubs can only appoint as coaches and managers those who hold the appropriate qualifications. That is precisely what happens already in most European countries. Because the labour pool is far more skilled and far smaller, a club is less likely to sack its head coach at the whim of the chairman. The pool of replacements may well be dry.'

But Britain doesn't believe in job training. The very word bores the pants off people. Training is used here to keep people away from being something else (unemployed), not to make them ready to be something else (a better employee or employer). Training is for people who've got nothing better to do. It can be seen as backward thinking, but this view is more often voiced in private than in public. But I also believe that, in Britain, people prefer coveted professions and jobs to be enclosed in mystique which, they say, no amount of training can penetrate. It's almost as if you can only be born with the right qualities to do certain jobs. Innate qualities – nature not nurture.

So we have club chairmen and boards who, alone, carry about in their minds the mysterious, undefinable characteristics of the person they want to appoint to be top dog. That way only certain people will ever be in the running, and it is extremely difficult to challenge the basis on which the decision has been made. People give jobs to people in their own image; only a small number make the conscious effort to do otherwise. The unemployment statistic for young black men in London ranges between 51 and 60 per cent, according to whichever survey you choose. Many young black men will spend weeks and months on training courses, and they'll still be unable to get a job at the end of them.

It's the chairman who'll appoint, and it's the chairman who'll do the sacking. His machinations – either cruelly drawn out or brutishly short – can often seem a like a joke falling very flatly for managers and fans alike. 'Despite his anchorage in the deadly serious harbours of money and intrigue,' wrote D.J. Taylor in the *Mail on Sunday* in May 1995, 'the Premiership soccer chairman is fast turning into one of the late 20th Century's great comic figures. There is the arrogance, the petulance, the grim reluctance to acknowledge that owning a football club doesn't automatically render your opinions more enlightened than those of the average fan.'

Chairmen and owners are wealthy, entrepreneurial, old or middle-aged white men. Men who aren't afraid of showing that the football *business* comes first, but who, nowadays, also insist that they do know more than a thing or two about the game itself.

'What people don't realize,' said Ken Bates in a September 1994 edition of the *Observer*, 'is that chairmen talk to each other a lot more than managers do. When you think I had the offer of signing David Platt, Stuart Pearce, Neil Webb, Paul Parker and Dean Holdsworth, to name but a few, and the manager of the day didn't know about them or couldn't be bothered about them. My mate from Crewe said: "If you can match Aston Villa's offer of £220,000 for Platt he's yours." John Hollins said he'd never heard of him. So much for our bloody scouting system.'

'Some people have suggested that I don't know everything that's going on,' said Jack Walker in the *Mirror* in January 1995. This was the man whose sixty million pounds of investment is credited with bringing the Championship to Blackburn Rovers. 'That's rubbish. I'm in touch. I know what's going on. And I'll tell you this: I've vetoed plenty of players. Plenty. We fix a price on a player we want – if it goes past that mark, then so does our interest.'

If black footballers find it difficult to get a foot on the management job ladder now, when it's quite clear that these jobs are a free-for-all with no qualifications necessary – BUT dependent on the whim of a white powerbroking chairman from a different generation – what hope for them if rules and regulations are brought in whose interpretation could result in their further exclusion? When coveted jobs become even more difficult to get in a shrinking workplace, whites become even more agitated and determined to prevent blacks from getting them.

Even when armed with the right paperwork, blacks still don't get jobs or work we're more than qualified for. Having observed this too many times in my own industry, the media, I decided, as I said, that true racial equality would be to have as many mediocre black people working in the industry as there are whites. Why should we have more qualifications and/or work three times as hard to get a job or hold down a job when any old white person walks into it, or performs consistently sloppily and nobody bats an eyelid?

When we do manage to break in, a single black person in a senior job always becomes a major issue for the whites who work alongside or under him or her. Why has that person got such an important job over a white candidate? A couple of blacks in a white office environment become a threat to white jobs. What I find amusing in its perversity about the 1990s' 'angry white backlash' against equal opportunity schemes is that many whites actually do feel that black and white now compete on equal terms for work, that they have an equal chance of securing work of equal standing. They assume that because they have a single black person, maybe even two, now working in their mostly white offices that all is hunky dory, so why should blacks be deserving of any more jobs. Plum jobs which they, the white person, deserves. Today's racial battles are being fought in an economic zone.

To get the plum job of manager means entry into the inner sanctum of a club. The identikit of a manager of an English club looks like this: he's white; he's male; sometimes he's had a decent, even successful career playing at club and possibly international level; and, if he's still in his thirties, he might even fancy himself as a player-manager.

Have you ever seen a senior job that you have been doing very well for a long time, written down? When it's being advertised, for example. It's a horrible jolt to the system, quite shocking. You didn't even know you were doing all those things. There's a feeling that there's no way in the world you could possibly do everything this job demands (you forget that you do do 'everything' the job requires). Senior management is trying to kill you, you decide.

The written job description of a football manager would demand: a man who is a strong leader, who has authority and commands respect from players, club officials and fans alike. A man whose tactics and strategic knowledge will defy any opposition team; a man with immense, almost divine, judgement. Any manager-to-be's organizational skills would be just one of his strong points. Whatever tactics and style the manager decides on, the players need to know what he's on about. The right man for the job would be an excellent motivator. And he must have the mental toughness and thick skin to take the attacks on his methods from the chairman, fans, media and players – sometimes all at the same time.

One of the few to be chosen will have to have an unimpeachable moral authority. 'The football manager at any club,' wrote

Trevor Brooking in the *Evening Standard*, as the storm clouds swirled around George Graham in December 1994, 'is the key man because he has the crucial role of leading by example and setting the standards for everyone under his control. His drive and personality can ignite players, supporters and backroom staff alike. Such enthusiasm can be infectious as it can help create an atmosphere which demands and deserves a successful response. Managers cannot afford any character blemishes or challenges to their integrity in case it weakens their standing when dealing with players on matters of contract or discipline. There is also the important area of attracting talented schoolboys to the club. Any adverse publicity might influence the choice made by parents when eventually deciding which club their boys should join.'

In March 1995, when Bruce Rioch was at Bolton, he told the *Mirror* that management to him was like being an adopted dad. 'That's how I view management. It's just like being a father. You are tough on your own kids, you discipline them if they step out of line. It doesn't mean to say you don't love them. It's just the same being a manager. I treat my players as if they were my own sons. I have only one rule here at Bolton, and that's don't be late. If they are then we can't get down to work.'

But while the managers may be keeping a fatherly eye on their young players, who's watching them? Even fully grown men find it difficult to handle the temptations of the game: the biggest being wads of notes in big brown envelopes. The transfer bung scandal which claimed George Graham as its sacrificial lamb led to a scurrying for cover from the intense media and Inland Revenue spotlights. Financial probity is now another vital necessity for any manager.

After the accusation that they lack intelligence, the next biggest problem black management candidates in any industry have to deal with is the accusation that they either can't handle money or that they are swindlers. Black people, and not white men like

George Graham, or the several other unnamed white managers rumoured but not yet proven to be partial to under-the-table dealings, are seen as having the greatest potential for involvement in financial misdemeanours.

A white Englishman, Nick Leeson, demolished Barings Bank with his multi-million pound fraudulent dealings, but it is the little man in an African country, who demands the financial equivalent of a pack of cigarettes to, for example, process a routine application form for a Westerner, who has led to whites using Africa as a byword for corruption. The much-referred-to huge corruption practices on the part of African governments are different only in style, not in substance, to those perpetrated in European and Asian countries. I find it just as corrupt to give a lucrative contract to a friend (no old school or club tie, no contract), as often happens in the West, as to give it to a foreign organization willing to pay the over-the-odds price you demand for it. And Eastern nations are just as adept at this as African ones – yet the Asians are regarded as thriving, go-getting countries whom 'even' the Europeans should emulate.

'You know,' a Midland Bank manager said to me, 'most bank fraud in Britain is committed by West Africans, especially Nigerians and Sierra Leonians. In fact, all along that coast, but we're noticing it is mostly Sierra Leone now. We keep a close eye on accounts opened here by people from those countries.'

Banks are said to keep accounts with African surnames under surveillance. Caribbean-descended blacks with 'English' surnames accompany their African relatives when the latter enter the bank to try to get loans. One of the chief (possibly *the* chief) complaints of black businesses is about the difficulty in trying to get seed money or development loans from white-run banks. Our businesses, as a result, are terribly under-resourced and under-capitalized, which leads to failure, and in turn to denunciation for being unable to sustain a entrepreneurial culture. Our colour makes us a risk too far. Our ambition is unappreciated and unnurtured.

When I set up a small independent television production company in the early 1990s, I was taken aback by the thinly veiled attempts to undermine the project ('Why do you want to bother with that for?'; 'That's a bit grand'), the digs and jibes struggling to be hidden behind 'jokes'. For example: 'How's all that ethnic stuff going?' The comments about 'that ethnic stuff' are particularly telling. I've been told 'not to bother with it', 'don't waste your time', 'there's no money in it', and, most frequently: 'it's ghetto programming'. Underneath all these little pearls of unsolicited advice is the notion that to want to make programmes, or write about, or indeed do anything which has at its centre the lives and experiences of black people is a waste of useful time. But why should the documentation of black lives and black loves mean a lonely, meaningless journey into a 'ghetto' as nobody, it seems, cares to understand why you are bothering them and the world with such stories, whilst, on the other hand, white lives and white loves are experiences which the entire universe can share and find deep meaning in. It appears that black lives are deemed so unimportant that they are not regarded as worth recording as extensively, frequently and in the minute detail that white lives are. Those of us who are black and who attempt to challenge this gross anomaly are condemned to ridicule, pity and hostility. But, for some bizarre reason, white people who feel the urge to focus now and then on the lives of black people do not encounter the same wall of obstacles. Indeed, many of them end up with awards presented by their white peers. It's never 'ghetto' work when it's being done by whites; it's kudos.

One senior male producer with his own large TV company told me flatly that it was futile trying to do what I was doing because black businesses didn't survive, and blacks would be better off working for better established [white] companies like his. Can you imagine anyone telling a white man or woman not to, at least, try to do something they really wanted to? Black people should be free to work wherever they can find work – there's nothing worse than being without work. But how dare anybody tell us not to try to create work and jobs for ourselves? The plantation rules OK.

I suddenly realized how discouraging a white male 'friend' of mine was: his little jokey references to how I still managed to keep going instantly became clear for the jibes they were when, with me sitting next to him, I listened to him bolster and encourage a young white woman who was intending to do what I was doing – a woman with far less experience in the industry, as she outlined herself. The final straw came when the newcomer went to get some drinks. He whispered: 'Don't tell her how rough it is, it might put her off.'

When, during a period of despondency at lack of work, I told a white, middle-aged woman with years of very senior experience behind her, that it would be nice to make at least one programme a year, she laughed, turned to her colleague and said: 'This girl is so ambitious!' A table separated us, but I could still feel the imaginary pat on the head. When this woman had been in her thirties, my age, she had already made dozens of programmes – a feat which would have been impossible if she'd been making them at a rate of one a year. More importantly, one programme a year was the minimum for personal and professional survival. It's the old double thinking which is applied to us so often: attack blacks for not having the ambition to do well, but the minute they show some get up and go, undermine and attempt to subvert them. Black people do not lack ambition – the main problem is sustaining their ambitions in the face of other people's obstacles.

Black entrepreneurs in my industry have a poor survival rate because the television and film industry does not want a viable black independent sector. The highly respected industrialist, Sir John Harvey Jones, once said that good industries looked after their business suppliers because it was in the industry's own interest to do so. The need to nurture valued suppliers does not apply to black suppliers, however.

The irony is that media and communications are very popular with today's job seekers. An industry study by Skillset, a training body, identified 32,000 places on media courses in further and higher education in 1996, compared to 6000 in 1990. (In 1981 there was only one media degree course listed in the universities handbook.) Where will the jobs for all these thousands come from? Skillset estimated that there were just 500 new jobs a year for people who wanted to work in television. If those blacks who are well qualified and who've been in the industry for years find it difficult to be in work, what hope for black youngsters starting out with or without qualifications?

I bumped into a highly intelligent black male acquaintance near my office one evening. He had some good news, he said. He was now a runner. (A runner's day: 'Four teas and a cappuccino, thanks. Oh and a round of toast, with marmalade.' 'Nip out and pop these in the post.' 'Take these tapes round to . . .') He was 30. I was enthusiastic during our conversation, saying many people start off in that most junior of posts. But I went home depressed. Yes, many people do start that way, but if they're white, they are virtually always still in their teens or, at worst, very early twenties. This guy was not only self-taught, having gone to a school where, he said, nothing was expected of him and where he'd left with nothing, but he was also putting himself through college, and starting out again. Good luck to him.

In all businesses, we're not to be trusted or relied upon. Our judgement is always doubted, forever queried. Financial institutions, any organization, actually, involved in financial dealings with black people, would much prefer to be talking to a white person, to have a white man or woman in charge of the accounting. Black people don't run things. Only whites can.

The football manager's job description also demands good man-management as a priority. It's often said that teams reflect the manager's personality, but that personality has to be one that senior players want to see themselves reflected in, otherwise the unhappy ship sinks. Generally, new managers can buy and sell players under the benevolent eye of the board. Making the right choices in the players' market means that a club needs the kind of man who is able to build and run the right team. A manager with pulling power: good players must want to sign for the club now that he's there. He must be able to spot talent at home and abroad before anybody else. As many club boards still leave managers to negotiate financial matters, the ability to wheel and deal and get the necessary players in the transfer markets is essential. You need the right team to win games, and winning is the means to the only end a manager must have: making sure the club is not relegated. Most chairmen, faced with bad results, would rather clear out the sitting manager than show the door to several players at the same time.

'There is no sadder sight in football than the bar at the Football Writers' Association annual dinner a couple of days before the FA Cup Final,' wrote Michael Herd in the London *Evening Standard* in August 1996. 'Out of work managers line up, glasses half empty, usually with their backs to the rest of the guests, as though sadness is a communicable disease. Some are in white tuxedos, others have flowers in their lapels. They talk to each other, of course, but despite football's camaraderie, you sense they are lonely people making each other lonelier. They're all in for one job or another but some were standing at the bar a year earlier. You can't help remembering that line about there being only two certainties in this life. People die and football managers get the sack.'

It took a close friend's death to put things in perspective for Ossie Ardiles, who was still in mourning months after he got the boot from chairman Alan Sugar at Tottenham. In the end, he had to leave England to find work. He'd applied to other clubs here following his dismissal, but several didn't even bother to reply.

Tottenham insisted that Ardiles was sacked because the team wasn't performing well, that he was a loser. But most managers' records don't bear close scrutiny and, normally, they happily emerge months, if not weeks later, posing at some new ground. Was it because Ardiles was foreign and a loser? As Roy Collins wrote in *Today* newspaper: 'There was a particularly nasty xenophobic taste about the humiliation heaped on Ardiles, a decent man who only did what 99 per cent of British managers do by failing to live up to expectations.'

I was sitting at home daydreaming when the radio said Glenn Hoddle was going to be the new England coach. It took a few moments before I gasped: 'Gullit!' Please, please, please. Chelsea did appoint him. Fantastic – and I'm not even a Chelsea fan. But this was the first black manager of a Premiership club.

A glorious player, highly intelligent, tactically aware, a vast football knowledge, hugely respected by fellow players and fans, a proven winner of silverware. And a black man. A black man who had popped up and pinched one of the plum Premiership jobs. Like a thief in broad daylight. Frustration and envy bounced off the walls, I think, in some unemployed and employed managers' homes: 'How the hell did he get that, then?'

Chelsea chairman Ken Bates told the *Sun* in August 1996: 'On the day Glenn left, I knew Ruud was the man to boss Chelsea. We had made our decision before Glenn accepted the England job. I have had no doubts about him since. He is an exceptional person. Now we know exactly what to expect from our manager because he talks to us all the time. He is a complete professional. The first thing he did when he came to the club was appoint a fitness trainer. Next, he separated the job of goal-keeping coach and reserve-team manager because he thought working with the keepers was a full-time job. Before Ruud, one man did both. You only have to look at his TV appearances to see what an intellectual character he is. He had never even done TV before the BBC signed him up for Euro '96, but he showed all the professionals a clean pair of heels. Then I saw him on Sky after our game against Southampton on Saturday. There was none of this "er, you know" stuff you usually get with footballers . . . I don't want to damn Glenn with faint praise but it is even more positive here now than it was before.' Positive vibrations ushered in by a young, black, dreadlocked Continental who had penetrated the heart of the English footballing élite.

The only dampener on my own personal enthusiasm for Chel-sea's new appointment was the knowledge that in England you have to be black and foreign (ie., you have no links with England) to stand a better chance of making an impression on the job, cultural and social scenes as a person 'of colour'.

For instance, the British have always preferred black Americans to black British. Numerous programmes and articles have been made and written here about the ups and downs of black lives there. On TV, the experiences of home-grown blacks are, at worst, ignored altogether, or just crammed into a little zone of programming sneaked out once a year, perhaps in the summer when the powers-that-be know people have other things to do than watch television; or even very late at night, when they know people are going to bed. In programming aimed at the majority white population, black faces and voices are kept on the periphery – adding a bit of colour but not any substance. The rare substan-tial black role in British drama is often given to a black foreigner.

Advertising companies and their clients prefer the tiny number of blacks they feature (for instance, exotic fruit drinks ads appear to be the natural habitat of smiley happy black people) to have very strong West Indian accents – usually Jamaican. How bewildering for the young black Mancunian, Brummie or Cockney who couldn't talk like that if you coached them for a year. Advertisers prefer not to have British blacks associated with their brands. We don't even give birth, as the increasing number of babies used to advertise products (eg., cars) demonstrate. How do you make a black baby look or sound foreign? It is difficult for advertisers who want to portray us as the foreigners who won't scare off the whites they want to buy their purchases. The illusion must be created that we're at a distance. Black people are over there, not over here frightening the folks.

So who could be more acceptable as the first black manager of a senior club than a black foreigner? Gullit's foreigner status would have worked in his favour. His Dutchness coming before his colour. But for English blacks, their colour comes before their (much debated) nationality. Their black skin reduces whatever professional qualifications they have achieved. Foreigner Gullit is put on a pedestal and given special status – he's not one of 'our' home-bred, ordinary blacks.

Just take the small example of his hair. To judge by the reaction to his hairstyle, when Gullit arrived in this country to play for Chelsea in the summer of 1995, you'd think white people hadn't seen dreadlocks before. Gullit's locks were marvelled over, mentioned in every article, and used in silly headlines – MASTER RASTA, THE ROLLS ROYCE OF RASTAFARIANS, DREAD-LOCKED BUCCANEER – as if he had personally invented locks.

The fact that several black British footballers, including some equally good-looking, high-profile ones like Trevor Sinclair, also wear their hair in dreads, and have been doing so for seasons, is ignored. No such fuss has ever been made over their smart looks. No, British locks are obviously peculiar, and for them only ridicule of the Skinner and Baddiel level has been forthcoming. The white sports media saw Gullit's hair as the real thing; they were seeing it for the first time because it wasn't on one of their own blacks.

'Dread Head Blues' was the *News of the World* caption in August 1995 on a picture of Gullit's face masked by the ball he was trying to head. 'Hang on,' the story continued, 'who's that taking the ball by his horns? Let's face it, there's no mistaking the identity of Chelsea superstar Ruud Gullit. Though his features are obscured here, there aren't too many dreadlocks that carry such unmistakable style.'

I was struck by the hushed, reverential tone of the comments on Hoddle's signing during his first English season. His every touch of the ball was oohed and aahed over. The man could do no wrong. Are they talking about a man who's extremely good at his job, I wondered, or are they talking about a god? Had they never come across a black man or woman who was their intellectual equal or superior before? Did they have to turn him into a god before that was acceptable to them? Now, 'arrogant' became a positive characteristic, and not the negative weapon used to beat British black footballers with.

'Ruud Gullit,' said a London *Evening Standard* article in September 1995, 'sports dreadlocks, loves Bob Marley's music and is fluent in Dutch, Italian and English. His world is not confined to football – he can debate anything from the horrors of Bosnia to a breakthrough in the search for a cure to Parkinson's disease. He is extrovert and frequently holds court amongst the other players. It is not arrogance, just self-confidence acquired while playing for Feyenoord in Holland and AC Milan and Sampdoria in Italy.'

'We are no longer buying cheap imports from eastern Europe,' said *The Times* that August, 'but men of character, status, achievement. Gullit has transcended two systems, two cultures: he captained Holland to the 1988 European Championships, with total football that still sends a tingle of satisfaction and joy through those who saw it. He, Marco van Basten and Frank Rikjaard, the three Dutch musketeers, helped AC Milan to change the mode of Italian football by seeking to entertain, and led that great club back to the European Cup.'

'When the Dutch international superstar, Ruud Gullit, signed for Chelsea Football Club,' crowed Giles Smith in the *Independent*, 'we fans rejoiced and beat the air with glee. But in the back of our minds, perhaps, was a question. Did he know what he was letting himself in for? Here was a potentially extraordinary marriage: Gullit, with his looks, his honours at every level, his Euro-flair, his intelligence, his sophistication; and Chelsea.'

Before we can be acknowledged as leaders – people in authority, whom white men and women will have to take orders from – black individuals have to be turned into almost superhuman creatures. If a black person is highly talented but, being human, also subject to highs and lows, and makes no effort to hide their feelings whatever they are, then they are targeted by resentful whites who can't understand why somebody who is just like anybody else they know, but who is black, is doing a senior job.

For a black person to be accepted in a position of seniority by whites, the hype begins. That black person has to be so fantastic, so great, so wonderful, so perfect, that it becomes entirely palatable for a white person to have to answer to him or her.

The nearest admission to the fact that Gullit was black was in the sly references to rumours that the 'Dreadcrock' had come to London to enjoy the reggae music, parties, nightclubs and concerts now that his knees weren't what they used to be.

'That is just a joke,' Gullit told the *Daily Mail* in June 1995. 'Somebody took it the wrong way because I said I wanted a certain amount of time off to go to some soul concerts in London.' Coupled with the fact that he once had a Dutch chart hit, 'Not the Dancing Kind', with a reggae band he played bass in called Revelation Time.

In fact, it was the search for football, not fun, which had brought him to the capital. He had joined Chelsea because he'd been in Italy for eight years and had won everything he wanted to, and because of Glenn Hoddle. 'The most important reason for my decision to come to Chelsea was the manager's way of thinking about how football should be played,' he told the *Mirror* in June 1995. 'He wants me to play in defence. I started my career as a "libero" and it is tremendous for me to be able to play sweeper again. That made the whole thing interesting.'

The *Guardian* heard that he was 'never a real striker, but everywhere I went they wanted someone big and strong to play up front. And then I made a lot of goals. That was my fault.'

When Gullit became a Premiership player-manager, his colour couldn't be avoided. Rob Hughes writing in *The Times* in August 1996 said: '. . . one heard him asked during the week how it felt to be the highest-profile black manager in the English game. Without a flicker of emotion, he responded: "Although you are black or white, what is important is the talent. My father, who studied economics at nightschool, told me that I would have to work harder than others for what I would achieve with my talent. For me, that was the stimulation, I took it positively. If you feel attacked by the way you are, then you have a problem; I felt proud of what I was, of the colour, everything."'

Gullit's father was a black footballer from Surinam. George Gullit, a defender (or 'stopper' as his son puts it), went to Holland, where he married a white Dutch woman. Their son was born in September 1962 in Amsterdam. 'My dad used to take me to watch him, and when I wasn't watching him I'd be playing football,' he told *Four Four Two* in September 1996. A footballer was all he ever wanted to be. 'I never thought of anything else. When I was 15, I had to make a decision.' His decision was to concentrate on becoming a good footballer: '. . . you can't smoke, drink, go out all the time. Or you can do that but you won't get to the same standard.'

The teenage prodigy's route from Dutch club FC Haarlem to World and European Footballer of the Year and captain of his national side took in clubs Feyenoord, PSV Eindhoven, AC Milan (for a world record £5.5 million) and Sampdoria. He captained his Dutch team-mates to the 1988 European Championship. His trophy cabinet includes two European Cup winners medals with AC Milan, and three Italian League Championship medals.

Gullit was hailed as the 'ultimate modern footballer – a 6ft 3in fusion of power, pace and skill', but unlike most modern footballers he has never attempted to hide his political awareness, or pretend that he is apolitical. Not even on the subject of race, which many black footballers shy away from.

When he was voted European Footballer of the Year in 1988, he dedicated the award to the then-imprisoned Nelson Mandela. Angered by the number of racist incidents he saw at Italian football matches, which were met with apathy by the Italian football world, Gullit spoke out: 'The time has come to say stop. We footballers cannot go on burying our heads in the sand.' He put forward a proposal: if, during a match, supporters began to chant racist slogans or hold aloft racist banners, club officials should stop the match unless the abuse ended immediately.

In Italy in 1993 he helped organize the 'Footballers' Day of Protest against Violence and Racism': 'We discussed it a lot with the newspapers and anti-racist organizations. What we could do to combat racism,' he revealed in the *Weekly Journal* in March 1993. 'Racism is something that comes with ignorance. People who have nothing economically – the unemployed – their ignorance leads them to point their finger at the other person. As a footballer, I am in a position to say something about it. I can also say nothing and just play football, but I think it's my duty to speak out.'

Gullit was going to a club which in the seventies and eighties had a strong National Front presence. Black footballers playing then, like Brendon Batson, hated going there. But at least the racial make-up in London was more like being back home in Amsterdam than Milan had been. 'I had missed things without knowing I missed them. London is a multicultural city, the same as Amsterdam,' Gullit declared in the *Evening Standard*.

Gullit had been in England less than a year when he was appointed manager of Chelsea in May 1996. He had similar ideas to Hoddle, but first he had to make the transition from player to manager. When a player becomes a manager, the changed relationship between the team and the man they normally shared a lark and a pint with can be difficult. Some players will refuse to accept the new power structure; others will try it on to see how far they can test the newly promoted man.

'I've had to distance myself because I must make tough decisions,' said Gullit in the *Mirror*, four months after his appointment. 'Before I took charge, I had to sit quietly in the dressing room and try to make changes discreetly. But I never knew if they would be carried out. Now I am right there in the middle, giving talks, holding meetings and showing the players what they are doing right and wrong. It's so nice to be able to express my feelings and ideas this way.'

Certain fellow players at Chelsea used to call Gullit 'Big Nose', 'Conky', 'Hooter Face'. Not any more. 'Ruud talks to the lads, he knows the lads and can be one of the lads,' said Dennis Wise in the *Sun*, as the team were adjusting to their new manager. 'But sometimes he has to step the other side of that line and make tough decisions as a manager. Put it like this. I don't call him Big Nose any more. He's Ruud, I know that now.'

The way he wants his team to play is, naturally, heavily influenced by his experiences on the Continent. To keep the game simple is all he desires, and he's learned from the best of them. His countryman, Johan Cruyff, taught him positional play, how to think two steps before anyone else. And Italian coach Arrigo Sacchi, at AC Milan, mixed Dutch and Italian football formations. Sacchi also passed on that it was important not to be insular: 'When Sacchi started as a coach, he went to Bayern Munich, to Liverpool, to Ajax, to Barcelona and Real Madrid, in the late seventies. He saw how these teams were playing. A good example of how a team was ahead of everybody was Liverpool in the late seventies. Their one-touch play was unique.'

As the new manager, Gullit plunged into the European transfer-market fever which overwhelmed Premiership managers following Euro '96: Gianluca Vialli (ex Juventus), Roberto Di Matteo (ex Lazio) and Franck LeBoeuf (ex Strasbourg) were to form the spine of his new Chelsea. 'I had one telephone call with Gianluca, one with Di Matteo and one with LeBoeuf,' said Gullit in the *Daily Telegraph* in August 1996. 'And they wanted to play in English football. The English game has a better image than the English themselves think. It's very spectacular. I know Chelsea made a very big impact in Europe with the way they played. They [the new men] know also that the English want to improve their game. That I took the job attracted them also. But also the fact that Chelsea is changing.'

According to the press, Gullit told Chelsea managing director, Colin Hutchinson, that he did not want to be bothered with all the financial and contractual negotiations involved in transfers, so they have been left in Hutchinson's hands. Gullit was more than happy with this system, which more clubs are introducing: 'I think it's impossible to manage, train, and do the paperwork. Everybody has his own specialities. I don't have an office.'

'Of course, we talk about the value of players and what is the limit we should go to,' said Hutchinson in the *Evening Standard* in July 1996. 'But all the financial matters concerning transfers are down to me. Ruud's job is to look after the players when they get here.' One of the new manager's Italian buys, Gianfranco Zola, was voted Player of the Year by the Football Writers' Association in May 1997, and Gullit ended his first season as a manager by taking Chelsea to that month's FA Cup Final. 'The first . . . [PAUSE] . . . overseas manager,' said BBC commentator John Motson as Gullit led his team out at Wembley. Gullit was the first BLACK manager at a Cup Final. His side beat Bryan Robson's Middlesbrough 2–0, winning their first trophy since 1971 and taking them into Europe.

Clearly, Ruud Gullit has very special talents and they more than helped his case when the Chelsea job came up. He had a world reputation which very few of the other ninety-one, virtually all white, English club managers could match. But would a British black candidate who didn't have as good a CV as Gullit but could more than match the other ninety-one white managers make it into a Premiership position? I feel a British-black managing a Premiership team could be a very long time away.

Gullit may be England's first black Premiership club manager, and Chris Kamara at First Division Bradford City the only other black guv'nor in English football (he'd been bought as a player in July 1994, later became assistant manager, and then was appointed manager in November 1996), but neither man is the first black manager in the England game. That title falls to a South African.

Edwin Stein, his six brothers, and mother and father made the trek from Cape Town to Paddington, West London, in 1968, drummed out by the apartheid which had seen both his parents imprisoned and put under house arrest. He was just entering his teens when he came here and, like many a newly arrived immigrant from Africa, the Caribbean or Asia, the first impression was formed by the temperature.

'The first thing that hit us was the weather,' Stein told *The Times*. 'It's one thing being warm and poor. There's nothing like being cold and poor. It was no fun.'

Unlike Gullit, there's no glorious football pedigree for Stein, only a CV demonstrating workmanlike hard graft. That's not to say that Gullit didn't beaver away at becoming a football legend; it's just that you feel that players are somehow having a harder time of it when they're employed by Edgware Town, Luton Town reserves, Harrow Borough, Dagenham and Barnet, as Stein was. AC Milan is renowned for its internal disciplines, even dictating what its players can eat (pasta and fish only) and drink (no beer), and how late they can go to bed. But it *is* AC Milan and, although its own players whinge about the club's enforcement of its dos and don'ts, thousands of players around the world would willingly bear a few health crosses for the wonder of ending up there.

But the two men are linked. When Gullit arrived at Chelsea, Edwin Stein's brother Mark had been a player there for some time. Yet another brother, Brian, is also a footballer. Indeed, he was under orders from big brother at Barnet when Edwin became the guv'nor there.

Stein was appointed manager at Barnet in April 1993 following the departure of his mentor, Barry Fry, for Southend United. He had already been on the staff of the club for twelve years, so the board wasn't quite throwing wild dice. He spent eight years as a player with the north London side, then became player-coach for four years before getting the thumbs up.

'There is still a cross-section of the public which feels that black people are great athletes but have not necessarily got the mental abilities for coaching or management,' Stein reflected in *The Times* two weeks after his appointment. 'I dispute that, but I can understand it, even if we have taken such huge strides in the last twenty years to get away from that mode of thinking.

As far as I am concerned, I want to be recognized for the work I do. It would be brilliant if my appointment gives some hope to others, but I don't hold myself up as a role model. My colour has never been a source of motivation.'

The man who had given him most encouragement down the years, Barry Fry, told the *Voice* he was as pleased as punch. 'I think it was a tremendous appointment. He deserves the job because he works hard. He played 500 games for me and did very well. He is a deep thinker and he will have no problem with the players. The only problems he will have will be in having to sell players.'

Stein's favourite player was Gullit's predecessor, Hoddle. And it was the skill and attacking play of the Chelsea side of the seventies which he tried to instil in Barnet – skill, not physique. And a good passing game.

'Football is in the entertainment business and people come to football grounds for excitement, to see flamboyance and character,' he asserted in a revealing interview in the *Voice* in April 1993. 'I want to entertain and put smiles on people's faces. This is a very important factor which unfortunately has been neglected in recent years. But there is absolutely no chance of seeing my teams playing route-one football . . . I have always been confident. I know my strengths and weaknesses. I won't be frightened to make decisions which I consider to be the most important criteria for a manager. I am confident in my ability to organize sides and can achieve the right balance in a team. I have a good eye for a player and I certainly know how to motivate them . . . People don't see me as a disciplinarian but discipline is very important to a football club, and is an area where I will be looking to implement changes. I also want to get the community more involved. I want to develop youth football to get the young kids and parents interested under the umbrella of Barnet Football club, and hopefully this will put bums on seats ... First and foremost I consider myself to be just another manager, even if I am the first black manager. I was surprised when Barry Fry left Barnet but I was not surprised to be offered the manager's job because I have done a lot at this club over the years, so the new board had no hesitation in appointing me.'

But Stein was soon off to join Fry at Birmingham City as assistant where, unfortunately, he was sacked in March 1996 following allegations of misdemeanours which culminated in charges of a late-night card game involving a player and the reserve-team manager, David Howell – who's also black – on the day of a match. Howell was also fired.

The sackings were straightforward disciplinary decisions, and the *Mirror* reported Fry as saying: 'There was no way I could defend either of them, despite the fact the three of us have been together for a good few years. Once you look at the evidence, I couldn't put sentiment ahead of the club's best interests. They simply had to go. I had baled Ed out on several occasions. This time, there was no defence.' When Birmingham and Fry parted company and Fry went on to become first Peterborough United's director of football then its manager, neither Ed Stein nor David Howell joined him.

Nobody had expected Stein to become the first black manager. That spotlight was supposed to fall on, if anybody, someone like Cyrille Regis, Viv Anderson, Ricky Hill or Brendon Batson.

Cyrille Regis is the man who was left humming 'it should have been me' when the board named their man. After Martin O'Neill left Wycombe Wanderers for Norwich in June 1995, Regis thought his call-up papers had arrived. But it was Alan Smith who turned up from Crystal Palace. Regis searched for answers. Was it because he was a born-again Christian? Was it his colour? Was it his personality?

'I've heard it said that men like Trevor Francis are too nice to be managers and I know that's being said about me too,' he complained to the *Voice* in July 1995. 'I would say that it hurts, but at the same time there is a part of me that would like to prove people wrong. Roy Evans at Liverpool has proved that it's possible to be a good guy and be successful and so did Graham Turner when he took Wolves from nowhere to the First Division in three years. My Christianity might put doubts in the minds of those who think I couldn't handle some of the things that go on in football. Then there's my colour. There's still a fear factor in this country about white people taking orders from black guys.'

In fact, 1993 was a significant year for challenging that attitude. In May the former St Lucia international, Keith Alexander, became Lincoln City's seventh manager in eight years – and the second black manager in the Football League following Stein's appointment earlier that year. And the two men also had a good friend in common. In September 1993 the *Observer*, in a portrait of Barry Fry, who was then manager of Southend, wrote: 'The phone rings. It is Keith Alexander, one of his former players at Barnet and now manager of Lincoln. Alexander wants help. Fry . . . agrees to lend him a promising reserve striker and rings the Football League to set it up.'

Only Brian Clough could have given Viv Anderson the following invaluable order when he was at Nottingham Forest and attracting racist attention from white players: 'Go and call him a white bastard, then kick him back.' When Anderson took charge of First Division Yorkshire side, Barnsley, it seemed that for once a senior black player's career was mirroring a senior white player's: twenty seasons in the game as a professional player; winner of a League Championship and a League Cup medal; and two European Cup medals with Nottingham Forest. Then there was his own special, personal entry in football encyclopaedias. 'Spiderman' (nicknamed because of his long legs) had been

England's first black player. The occasion was the England v Czechoslovakia game at Wembley in November 1978.

The *Sunday Times* match report on a Tranmere Rovers v Barnsley game in September 1993 said of Barnsley's 3–0 win: 'Their player-manager, Viv Anderson, has added his own ideas to Mel Machin's good teachings and Barnsley are playing a diamond midfield that worked wonderfully well on this bright afternoon. After 10 minutes Rovers lost the centre and from then on were doomed ... Anderson has already become the pragmatic manager: "We're getting clean sheets now. That's important; we worked hard in training and the lads applied those lessons today."'

But Anderson was only in the hot seat for that one season in which Barnsley finished 18th. When his friend Bryan Robson was handed First Division Middlesbrough as his first managerial position at the end of his playing days, Viv Anderson gave up his manager's post to become Robson's assistant. I thought it was a bit of a shame – apparently, according to Brendon Batson, they'd had some sort of pact. A shame because eyelids don't bat as much at blacks being deputies, at being the bridesmaids but not the brides. We've had to be thankful for small mercies in the form of men like Barry Fry, Graham Taylor and Bryan Robson, men with mindsets open enough to encourage, support, recommend and promote black players who want executive posts. Indeed, without Graham Taylor where would Luther Blisset be?

Here was a man whose excellent career included playing for clubs in all divisions, 14 England caps, and a year with AC Milan for the 1983–84 Serie A season. He also had a full Football Association coaching badge. But could he get a job in management? Rejection after rejection: 22 applications and not even an interview. 'Sure, you get frustrated,' he revealed in a 1994 *Times* profile (occasioned by the fact that this great black pioneer had been at Bury, Mansfield Town, Southport, Derry City and Wimborne Town the previous season and was now at non-League Fakenham Town: average home attendance 150), 'but it lasts only a few days. I've still got my businesses to look after and that helps take your mind off other things.' His businesses were a sports shop in Bournemouth and a promotions company in Watford.

Acquiring a top job is popularly thought to depend partially on 'who you know' with some influence, but it seems black people can know as many influential people as they care to but it won't do them any good unless one of those people is predisposed to hiring blacks in senior positions in the first place. Many of us waste a lot of time listening to white people making all the right noises but ending up performing the same old time-honoured practice of not giving us work despite our qualifications. It's not what you say, it's what you do. It was his former manager, Graham Taylor, who made Blisset Watford's assistant manager in February 1996 when Taylor returned to their old club as general manager. They renewed a relationship which had begun nearly two decades earlier at Vicarage Road.

A former black star at nearby Luton Town was forced to leave the country to find employment as a manager. Midfielder Ricky Hill played nearly 600 matches for the club and got 3 England caps, but it was an American club that gave him a job as a coach. 'I've had to leave England to get work,' he told the *Voice* in 1995, 'but I'd like to be given the chance to prove myself here.' Hill had been voted Coach of the Year at Tampa Bay in his first season and took them to two national finals, but as the paper reported, he was still pining for Bedfordshire. 'The Luton post is not available right now, but I'd love a chance if it came up. I see it as a marriage. We're separated but I'm looking for a reconciliation. I spent 15 happy years of my adult life at Luton and want to see them prosper again . . . I played alongside the best and some of them have managers' jobs now, people like Bryan Robson, Ray Wilkins and Ray Clemence. And I'd like a chance too.'

'I left in '85,' explained Keith Connor, Britain's former triple jump record holder and Olympic hero, to *Today* newspaper, 'because they didn't want a black man involved in the coaching system. It's as simple as that. I wasn't going to stay around in a country that considered blacks first-class athletes, but second-class citizens. When you think about the expertise and experience I had to offer, it was an extraordinary insult to me and my kind. This was at a time when 60 per cent of the British athletics team was of Afro-Caribbean origin.' *Today* said Connor was snapped up by the University of Texas and then was soon head-hunted by the Australian Institute of Sport. 'It's crazy,' he said, 'everyone wanted me except my own country.'

Brendon Batson, as Deputy Chief Executive of the Professional Footballers' Association (PFA), is often trotted out when the lack of black officials in the industry is commented on. He's been associated with the PFA since he was 20, but he'd wanted to be a manager when he stopped playing, only he couldn't get a job. He had one interview out of several applications. And that one response was from Cambridge United, one of his old clubs. If he'd sat and waited to be approached in the way, for example, Bryan Robson was approached, he'd still be waiting.

I define a black token as somebody who, years after his or her original appointment, is still the sole black person in the institution which hired him or her in the first place. These people are not tokens for simply being the first black person through the door; it's the institution which is guilty of the act of tokenization by failing to employ any more blacks.

During Batson's time at West Bromwich Albion under Ron Atkinson – a manager who has never had a problem fielding black players – the line-up also included Laurie Cunningham and Cyrille Regis. As this was the seventies, they were known as 'The Three Degrees', after the chart-topping black female group. Atkinson had three black players at a time when most clubs didn't have one. Cartilage injuries took Batson out of the game when he was 31. Perhaps he was thinking of all those rejection letters and telephone calls he'd received when he predicted in *The Times* in 1993 that: 'The acid test will come as the more prominent black players come to the end of their careers and send off their management CVs. There has been a natural progression for Edwin, but would a black Steve Coppell get the Crystal Palace job or a black Graeme Souness at Liverpool?' Or a black Robson at Middlesbrough. The sixty-four-million-dollar question. We won't have the answers for another four or five years when Barnes, Wright and maybe Des Walker start looking for a second career. If they choose management, will they get jobs? Or will it still be glass ceiling time – blocked by the perceptions of those who hire and fire in the boardroom before they've even been tested in a managerial position?

What happens to John Barnes will be important because he is the leading candidate for a black manager out of our present crop of black footballers who are nearing the end of their playing days. Not that he'll need the money to secure his family's future: he would be one of the growing number of managers – ie., Souness, Gerry Francis – who are financially secure.

Barnes threw a big hint in the general direction of the Liverpool board and their famous boot-room promotion scheme: 'In the last year, I have thought about being a manager,' said Barnes in the *Observer* in August 1995. 'When you're young you think it would be an impossible job, then when you get older you realize it's not what it's cracked up to be. Being liked by everyone is a problem if you are a manager because you have to make some hard decisions and your relationship with people changes. You have to distance yourself. I would like to think I could manage players I have played with rather than go to a club where I don't know anyone.'

'I've told the gaffer,' said Paul Ince in a *Mirror* interview in April 1995, 'I wanted to be a manager. I fancy managing a club. I might get Ryan Giggs in as my number two. Or maybe I'd let Ian Wright do the team talks. No, on second thoughts, if I did that he'd get the whole team sent off!'

In January 1997 Ian Wright told the papers that he'd shelved the idea of teaming up with Paul Ince to run a club. The *Mirror* reported: 'Paul and I wanted to do it for fun – a job in which we could express ourselves. But soccer is so serious now a manager can't separate his job from his family. It's constant 24-hour pressure. That's why it's something I would never do. Incey and I fancied doing it together. But you can no longer have the kind of fun we would have liked. There is too much at stake.'

But you don't have to become a manager, there are plenty of other influential jobs – still in virtually all-white hands – to do with the game which black players at the end of their club careers can consider: television and radio commentators, presenters and reporters, newspaper and magazine columnists; sports consultants; football coaches and trainers, scouts, referees, physios; players' agents and managers; authors; union officials.

Wimbledon's Robbie Earle told the *Observer* in March 1997 that he'd like to end his playing career at Selhurst Park. 'Everyone says nothing you can do afterwards beats playing, and I can easily believe that.' Nevertheless, said the *Observer*, 'Earle has been making preliminary moves towards a future in the media ("Who wants to hear Alan Hansen talking about defensive mistakes all the time?") and early indications are that his infectious good humour could carve him out a television career at least as successful as his football one. Which, of course, isn't over yet. "I've got one or two vague ideas for the future, but they can take a back seat until I've finished playing," he said.'

Broadsheet and tabloid newspaper sports desks are all-white enclaves which very rarely use black freelance journalists and writers. In her 1995 London School of Economics Ph.D study of blacks and Asians in the British media, Dr Beulah Ainley found that: 'Of the estimated 4000 national newspaper journalists only 20 were black or Asian, with each newspaper having its token 2 or 3. For the provincial papers the situation is far worse; of 8000 newspaper journalists only 15 were black. In most newspaper offices in Britain there is not, or never has been, a black or Asian trainee journalist or reporter. This is particularly worrying, especially in areas such as the Midlands, Manchester, Liverpool and Leeds, where a relatively large number of blacks and Asian people have settled since the 1960s.' It's even more worrying given the power sports journalists have to influence the opinions of football fans by the way they portray black players.

Apart from the odd report from Garth Crooks on *Match of the Day* and *Football Focus*, and infrequent guest summarizer spots from one or two black players, television and radio sport is also mostly free – both in presentation and production – from a black presence. Therefore sports, an area where black people have made great inroads, is still written about and presented by mostly white people (and mostly white men at that). Freelance Asian journalist and author, Mihir Bose, told the *Guardian* in December 1996 why he thought this was: 'It is surprising that whereas in television you have Trevor McDonald as the standard bearer and an increasing number of black and Asian television reporters who are covering the field in all topics, in newspapers that's not the case. This goes back to the fact that generally, the English, having created the sport, are very disinclined to believe that anybody other than the English know about the sport and can write about the sports they have created. It's cultural stereotyping and I think it's very difficult for sports editors to overcome that.' But what about the black British and black English? Is this yet another instance of their colour coming before their nationality?

Of course, there is always the option to chuck the whole lot in. Millwall defender Tony Witter told London's *Evening Standard* in 1995 that a non-footballing second career wasn't the end of the world. 'A lot of players look for coaching jobs when they pack up but when I retire I don't want anything to do with football. I'll go back to working for myself and hopefully providing a good living for my wife and little girl.'

Whatever Happened to . . .

A council towerblock in Leeds. Endless stairs and poky, stifling rooms. His body had lain there, in his tiny flat, for several days before anybody noticed the smell and somebody called the police. The neighbours said he had had a drink problem. He was 53 years old. Shame, they said, but there you go.

A few ageing fans and long-lost friends popped up afterwards to say how much they'd liked him, how he'd entertained the crowd, how he was a gifted, wonderful footballer, how much he'd meant to them when they were boys – how he'd been their hero. Now that he was dead, they remembered him. His life's significance lay in how it had touched their own existences.

When he was alive – a lonely, wandering, spiritually battered alcoholic – he was living in poverty, and forgotten. He could see how, in his middle age, people regarded him as a drunken scrounger and a boring good-for-nothing.

He could have died an impoverished, lonely alcoholic in South Africa; he didn't have to come all the way to Britain to end up that way. But it was the dream of being able to carve a comfortable life out of his love, football, and the possibility of becoming a star, which lured Albert Johanneson to Yorkshire from his home in Germiston, a township near Johannesburg.

It was 1961 and Leeds, under Don Revie, were building a team for the glory years to come. A local teacher had spotted Johanneson's talents in Germiston. He came to Leeds on a three-month trial and stayed. At Leeds, they called him the 'Black Flash'; he called everyone, from fan to captain to manager, 'Sir'.

In more than one sense, Johanneson's reasons for coming here were no different from those held by the thousands of black immigrants who also arrived in the UK in the late fifties and early sixties. The appalling thing is that, as in Johanneson's case, too many of them are also facing a lonely, poor old age in a land that wants to forget about them. No one knows how many are in this predicament, because nobody bothers to count – to notice them might mean something would have to be done.

'Albert Johanneson, who went by the nickname "Yoyo",' the *Guardian*'s obituary said, 'played on the left-wing in the first of the successful Leeds teams to emerge under the management of Don Revie in the early sixties. A natural athlete, he brought a combination of speed and artistry to an attack which looked to Bobby Collins and Johnny Giles for its ideas and Jim Storrie and Alan Peacock for its finishing.'

Johanneson's claim to FA fame is that in 1965 he became the first black footballer to play at Wembley. Liverpool beat Leeds in that FA Cup Final, but Revie and his men were welcomed back home by a quarter of a million people. Johanneson stayed with the Yorkshire club for nine years in total before being given a free transfer to York City. His life went downhill fast after that, although his drinking had started when he was a Leeds man.

Norma, his wife, and their two children, left him in the seventies – she eventually went back to Jamaica. He lost his house, his belongings, just about everything. At one point, later, he was reduced to doing a bit of tidying up in a clothing factory for a man who, as a child, regarded Johanneson as his football idol. 'It was heartbreaking for me to see him do this,' said the factory owner. God knows what Johanneson felt.

'The last time I saw Albert,' recalled former Leeds star and teammate, Peter Lorimer in *Remember Albert*, 'the lady at the telephone came out and said, "Albert wants to see you," and I knew what he was looking for. I knew what the position was, and I've got to admit that I was busy. I said, "Oh, you can tell him I'm busy." Because like most people, you know, I'd helped him a few times.

'At the end of the day, are you doing him any good by giving him some more money to just go and have more drinks, with people laughing at him walking about the city, sometimes in a drunken stew? It's not a very nice thing to see. If he doesn't have the ammunition, he can't have the drink. So maybe, in your own way, you thought you were doing him a favour.'

But Johanneson knew for himself that things weren't as they should be. One day, he went to his solicitor and gave him a small casket. In it were his treasured League and Cup medals. He told his solicitor that he was scared he might, in a moment of weakness, pawn or sell them. He wanted his medals put away in a safe place. 'If anything happens to me,' said Johanneson, 'please give them to my children.'

The tragedy of Johanneson's middle years is one which black people in particular want to avoid at all costs. Seeing the disillusionment, pain, bitterness and tiredness etched on the faces of middle-aged and elderly black people on England's streets signals to younger blacks what could lie in store. Generally, the white elderly do not walk about in the same way, do not carry the same expressions. They are usually more at peace with the prospect of impending death in their country.

My father came to this country in 1961 to study law. He never did go back home to Nigeria, and he never became a lawyer. He died in London in May 1983, aged 66, lonely, and full of unfulfilled dreams. I would give anything to have my father fat, drunk and sitting comfortably in an armchair with his Players No. 10, cursing at *Match Of The Day*.

Insecurity and poverty breed sickness and death. For a black person there's also the thought of being poor, old and helpless, and therefore at the mercy of the white people and white institutions who look after the elderly and the infirm. Many black people's mistrust of a white-run medical profession was rendered palatable by the number of blacks who had entered nursing on arriving in Britain as immigrants. (Although there are as yet no reports of white British doctors having used impoverished black workers for a study of syphilis, as the Americans did with 399 people for 40 years before being caught out, British blacks are aware that their health needs – both physical and psychological – are still not fully understood. In what was akin to a Nazi experiment, the black American men from Tuskegee in Alabama were not told they had syphilis during the decades the white doctors in the US Public Health Service kept them under observation. 'Many,' said the *Guardian* in May 1997, 'passed it on to their partners and most died. An antibiotic jab could have cured them.' Twenty-five years after a newspaper broke the story, President Clinton apologized.)

In April 1997, the Manufacturing Science and Finance Union, which represents many community nursing staff, unveiled the results of a study which showed that the number of black and Asian nurses in the NHS was falling sharply. The *Guardian* reported: 'Fewer than three in every 100 nursing staff under 25 are from an ethnic minority. Fewer than one in 100 is black. Among staff aged 55–64, however, more than 11 in every 100 are from an ethnic minority and almost nine in every 100 are black.' What is preventing young black women from entering the profession which their mothers' generation went into? When, in January 1997, the Labour MP for Hackney North and Stoke Newington, Diane Abbott, accused the NHS of racist practices that were forcing black women out of the service they'd played a vital role in building up in the 1950s, the Conservative Health Minister Gerry Malone, the *Guardian* reported, called on the Labour leader Tony Blair to take disciplinary action. The previous month Ms Abbott had attacked a hospital in her constituency for employing 'blonde, blue-eyed Finnish nurses' at the expense of local black nurses. She was forced to apologize after coming under strong attack from the media and the Royal College of Nursing. She told the *Guardian*: 'I only wish they would put as much energy into speaking up for black nurses.' So, when the MSF released figures showing concrete evidence of the concerns voiced by the black MP, I waited for somebody to apologize to her, or at the very least, comment that she had pointed to what was a deepening problem for the NHS. There was a deafening silence from the media, government ministers and the health service. Like I said in my introduction, when we say something is wrong, nobody listens; rather, we're accused of making breathtaking claims. When the statistics back up our concerns, those in charge hope nobody will notice, and too many others keep silent.

Younger black people have seen and are seeing what has happened and is happening to their parents, grandparents and other elderly relatives, friends and strangers. And it's for that reason that I want to punch people who criticize black people, and especially black sports stars, for wanting to rake it in. How dare they! Have they never seen the black elderly on the streets of Britain? Those waves of immigrants, whom my parents were part of, are now in their old age, still in the country they thought they were in only temporarily, in order to make a bit of money to retire 'back home'.

Blacks don't need surveys to tell us we have a hard time finding and keeping work when we are young, fit and able; the people who should be told don't want to know. The *Observer* reported on one government survey in February 1995: 'The survey of those who took Youth Training courses between December 1992 and January last year shows that only one in four young blacks found jobs, compared with a third of disabled trainees and half of whites.' Being black, in white eyes, is about as disabled as you can get. In London, the figure for black male unemployment between the ages of 16 and 24, is 62 per cent. For white men of the same age, the figure is 20 per cent.

In August 1996, an official Labour Force Survey on 'how Britain's ethnic minorities are faring in the labour market' was analysed by a Professor of Economics at Manchester's Metropolitan University. Derek Leslie concluded that: 'The pay and prospects of British-born ethnic minorities continue to lag behind their indigenous counterparts at work – but at least they are doing better than their foreign-born parents . . . minorities are denied job opportunities and promotion that their qualifications and experience ought to entitle them to.' But we're supposed to be comforted by the fact that we're not always having to do the dross work and earn the dross pay that our parents did.

'The survey,' Leslie wrote, 'studies unemployment levels – where the news is rather bleaker – occupational status, earnings and so on for the various minority groups based on information from 60,000 households.'

The rather bleaker news? 'There is another more sinister disadvantage suffered by the ethnic minorities. They have much higher unemployment rates. For example, in the spring of 1994, male ethnic minority unemployment was 25 per cent compared with 11 per cent for whites. For the black groups aged 16–24 the rate was an astonishing 51 per cent, and 37 per cent across all ethnic minorities.

'In a low-employment economy, which for Britain now seems to be a way of life, marginal groups suffer disproportionately.'

Fifty-one per cent across Britain; 62 per cent in London. The figures don't surprise blacks; neither do they move the government, who do nothing about the huge waste of black talent and black lives those figures represent.

Imagine then the terror at the prospects of employment when

we are older, having lost work and been unable to find more. It's a terror which wraps itself around a black person's throat in a way no white person can comprehend.

For years before his death, Albert Johanneson was unemployed. Former Leeds midfielder Bobby Collins, regarded as one of Revie's best signings, also played in the 1965 FA Cup Final. He went on to become player-coach at Oldham, and manager of Barnsley. Today, he's hooked on golf in his retirement. 'Football has been a wonderful life for me,' he told the *Mirror*. 'I turn out occasionally for a team of ex-Leeds players even now. I'm a bit greyer now, but I still get the same buzz from having the ball at my feet.'

Eddie Gray also used to play with Johanneson, having gone to Elland Road straight from school in 1963. He became manager of Leeds in 1982, was sacked in 1985, and then returned ten years later to become part of the coaching team, first under Howard Wilkinson, then George Graham. 'My only regret is that I stopped playing in 1983 when I was still player-manager. I should have played on until I was forty,' he said, also in the *Mirror*. He moved on to manage Rochdale, Hull City and Whitby Town. Before going back to Elland Road he combined coaching in local schools and soccer camps with radio and TV work.

Gray also plays with Bobby Collins in the ex-Leeds United XI. 'We play strictly for charity these days, so everyone is on his best behaviour. Most of the players from the Revie era still live in the area so we see a lot of one another. We joined the club as kids and grew up together.'

When Birmingham bought Gary Sprake from Leeds in 1973, for £100,000, he became Britain's most expensive goalkeeper. Before that he'd made 381 League appearances for Leeds – no other keeper has played more games for them. He also played with Johanneson when he joined the club in 1962. Sprake was forced to leave Birmingham and football because of back problems when he was 30. 'I wept when they told me I would never play football again, and it took me some time to accept it.'

Divorce, unemployment and a driving ban took place during the miserable period which followed four operations. These days, according to the *Sun*, he's living contentedly in Solihull with his girlfriend. And when he's not working at a college as 'a sort of Mr Fixit, finding and arranging work for the unemployed in the area', he's playing golf, relaxing in his garden or listening to the radio. He doesn't go to football matches.

Whatever happened to? Where are they now? Do you remember XYZ? Whatever became of him? What's so and so up to these days? What will be the future answers to these questions for today's generation of black footballers? Will they be forced to dig a hole big enough to bury their ambitions in, and eke out a living as best they can? Or will they be able to make as much money as possible today to buy security and dignity tomorrow?

John Charles was born in East London's Canning Town in 1944. His first job was a £7-a-week groundstaff boy for West Ham, and he went on to become the Hammers' first black footballer, playing for them from 1963 to 1970. After the club released him he decided to retire from the game – he was still only 26.

He told the *Sun*: 'I was on £65 a week at West Ham and my father-in-law, Ernie Gingell, said I could make more in the greengrocery game. So I worked on market stalls in Gravesend, Southend and Slough. I turned in football altogether. I'd also had a lot of hamstring trouble and just got fed up with it. Once I got into the greengrocery lark, I really loved that. I became my own guv'nor and met different people. It was nice.

But in the mid-nineties Charles found himself on the dole and suffering from drink problems after his fruit and vegetable business collapsed. 'I'm right off the booze now,' he said in

September 1994. 'I won't drink again. It would frighten me too much. I had a drink problem then started drinking more heavily when the business went wrong. I was drinking ten pints a day.

'My business went down the pan because of the recession and I'm out of work now and not sure what, if anything, I will be doing in the future. I'm not qualified for anything else. I had a breakdown because of the business collapse. Everything got on top of me. I was shocked when they admitted me to a mental hospital. It frightened the daylights out of me. I thought I was just going in for a check-up at an ordinary hospital.

'Ronnie Boyce and Frank Lampard came to see me, and Jimmy Greaves took the trouble to call and spent twenty minutes on the telephone, which was very kind and a marvellous boost. Jimmy used to have a drink problem and he was in the cracker-factory too, so he understands what I've been through.'

Although life in Kumasi, Ghana, wasn't as hard for Tony Yeboah as it is for many Ghanaians, he knew he had to use his footballing skills to make his fortune. To do that he had to leave Africa. As the Leeds player and Ghanaian international recalled: 'We were lucky because we were always well looked after, but I knew football was my way to become rich and have nice things for my family. I have seven houses out there, and several sports shops, so I think I will be a businessman when I finish football. I was always determined and single-minded. I knew I wouldn't become rich from playing football in Ghana – I had to go to Europe.'

Even those of us with decent jobs and/or salaries measured in European terms (the burgeoning black British middle class) never lose this virtue of our race. We, or our families, were without for too long, and we know too many black people still without. The white British working class also understand this perfectly: they share this healthy attitude towards wealth.

Many white people and very few blacks ask me what the 'I' in my company's initials stand for. When I'm in an obliging mood, I tell them. It's 'International'. Black people love it. Whites have a problem with it (they're often informed: 'It's my initials'). That's because I can always spot the ones who are going to snigger. They're the kind who are thinking: 'International?' What an uppity little black girlie. Who does she think she is? I've never heard any white person question a white female producer in my industry, who also has 'International' after her surname, about her impudence.

I suspect that the reason the middle-class white people I come up against feel uncomfortable with my company (not just its name) is that they're uncomfortable with the notion of a black business person. A black person who wants to be in charge and make money. That's not what we're supposed to be like, is it? We're supposed to *be* paid and *be* looked after (preferably by State handouts). We're not playing the game if we start doing it for ourselves.

Without blacks parading ourselves as victims of our black skins, how can a white person feel superior? Even when he or she is a failure, a white person can still feel legitimately superior to a black, because failure is the only thing we are expected to achieve, whilst if you're white, at worst you've still got an evens chance of success.

Look at the vitriol and suspicion which surrounds any black Briton who has managed to make some money for him or herself. It's extremely interesting that white Britons accept and expect black Americans can be rich. But like in so many other areas where comparisons can be made between the achievements of black Britons and black Americans (e.g., the music industry, especially British rap), they don't want their own home-grown brand trying to ape the success of their transatlantic cousins.

It doesn't matter which sport they're in, black stars will nearly always be depicted as greedy. Stan Collymore, Brian Lara, Chris Eubank, Linford Christie and Colin Jackson – all greedy. While white stars tend to be portrayed as only being paid what they are worth, and the bigger the fee, the more big-willied and deserving the white man. For top white footballers, their clubs and managers bear the burden of their high price tags. But for black stars, the players are held personally responsible for their 'greedy' valuations. Cole, it seems, is destined to be linked for ever with the £7 million price tag, whilst nobody mentions £5 million and Chris Sutton in the same breath, nor, after a season at Newcastle, Alan Shearer and £15 million.

Stan Collymore knew all about 'greedy' tags and called the £8.5 million valuation put on him by Frank Clark in 1995 ridiculous. Clark replied in the *Sun*: 'What we ask for Stan is none of his business. He cannot dictate the value we place on him. I've got to do what is best for Nottingham Forest. That is why the fee has to be well in excess of the current record. If Stan doesn't want to play, I have got to get as much money as possible so I can bring in quality people who do.'

'The fee for Stan is £8.5 million, not a penny less and not a penny more. I want it in hard cash,' insisted Clark in the *Daily Mirror*. 'Once Everton or Liverpool come up with the money, they can talk to Stan. Until they do, he is in quarantine. Stan has consistently refused to tell me he wanted to carry on at Forest, so I must consider my alternative team plans.

'Of course, if nobody is ready to pay the price we are asking for Stan, the boy has got a big problem. You never know, he might end up coming back to beg us for the contract we promised – it might end up as his only option.'

Collymore knew that if he was sold at that price, it would be him, and not Clark or Nottingham Forest who would be called greedy. The manager and the club would merely be seen to have executed a good deal. Which is what happened when Collymore asked for his 5 per cent cut of the transfer as outlined in his contract with Forest. Forest refused, saying that the player had requested a transfer, which made his cut null and void. Collymore and his agent, Paul Stretford, insisted that the club chose to sell him.

'Stan has certain confidential clauses within his contract,' said Stretford in *Today* in June 1995. 'It is my belief they should remain that way, but others do not share that view. I would like to stress that two clubs made a record bid for Stan and Forest accepted that money.'

But Collymore is regarded in the business as a money-grabber – someone who always wants more if anybody comes in with more money. It didn't take long for somebody to tell the papers about Collymore's 'confidential clause'. The headlines went to work: DON'T PUSH ME COLLY!, SULLY-MORE, COLLY: I WANT MY LO£&Y!, MORE LOLLY. Collymore's cut was a 'massive' £425,000; he was now a 'rebel striker'.

'I don't wish to label Stan as greedy,' said Clark in the *Mirror*, doing exactly that, 'but enough is enough. My directors are backing me every step of the way on this one. The Forest board have been very annoyed at some of the comments Stan has passed about this club, his team-mates and me.'

Clark said Forest would reluctantly pay Collymore's £150,000 signing-on fee from when he joined them from Southend, and offered a percentage of what the player wanted from the Liverpool transfer: 'We maintain that it is Stan who has broken his contract and we possess bags of evidence to prove the point if it goes before an independent inquiry. Perhaps Stan should remember that getting any percentage of the £425,000 would be better than receiving 100 per cent of nothing.'

But Collymore retaliated in the *Mirror*, feeling he had a right to all the money: 'It was obvious from the start Forest were not fighting to keep me. They never stood in my way. If it was Alan

Shearer and Blackburn, other clubs would have been warned to keep their hands off. Instead, nearly everything Clark has said has been with one aim in mind – to push my transfer price up and up.'

Three weeks earlier, when he was celebrating his first appearance in an England line-up, Collymore had said to reporters at the news conference: 'It is about ambition, not money. I would rather be on half the money and winning things, rather than three times my salary and desperately unhappy. I want trophies, not bucketfuls of money. When I was a kid dreaming of being a footballer, I dreamed of winning things, not earning fortunes. I want to be financially secure, but if you win the Championship or the European Cup, the money will come.'

Collymore was forced into revealing that he'd turned down an extra £500,000 in wages offered by Everton to join Liverpool instead. 'This proves I'm not being greedy,' he said in July 1995. 'People make out footballers are greedy, but that's not fair. If you look at people like Andre Agassi and other top tennis pros, they earn a lot more than we do. Everton offered me a more lucrative deal than Liverpool, but my decision was football-motivated, not finance-motivated. I'm not a greedy person, but, if something is in a contract, it should be honoured.'

Columnist John Sadler, writing in the *Sun* in November, shouted: 'Admit it, Colly – you don't deserve royalties.

'Princess Di and Stan the Man wouldn't have realized until yesterday that they share something in common. Both have a bare-faced cheek and neither seems to appreciate the fact that they're on to a bloody good thing.

'The bad odour of her *Panorama* performance of self-pity and self-promotion is to be followed by his pursuit of a twisted sense of justice and fair play.

'Tomorrow, in London, he will argue his right to almost £600,000 from Forest, claiming he did not ask to leave. It is an important case – one which, if Collymore wins, will further erode the authority of clubs, the ability of managers to manage and directors to direct. It will leave English football at the mercy of greedy players whose consciences, more and more, seem to be governed by cash. Forest's admirable manager, Frank Clark, a man of high integrity and a reputation for honest endeavour in an industry smeared by sleaze, has appealed for Collymore to tell the truth at the tribunal.'

The Premier League inquiry decided for Forest: Collymore had waived his right to the 5 per cent by making it known that he wanted to move. Collymore went to the Football League's Independent Appeals Tribunal. They upheld the verdict.

The huge resentment over Cole's £7 million transfer to Newcastle was as large as the immense joy when Shearer knocked Collymore and sent Cole flying off their 'unearned' pedestals when he become the country's most expensive player. The white media decreed that Shearer wasn't greedy. Indeed, money didn't come into consideration when he was thinking about whether to stay at Blackburn or not. (I'm sure his earnings potential following Euro '96 just wasn't a factor. Just as when he said he would be staying at Blackburn into the next millenium, they all sighed and said, 'What loyalty.') At the same time Collymore and Clark were getting down to their 'greedy' name-calling business in June 1995, Alan Shearer was promising Blackburn the world – and they were paying for it. But no one was calling it anything as ghastly and undignified as greedy.

Steve Millar reported in the *Mirror*: 'Alan Shearer last night committed himself to Blackburn until the year 2000 with an £800,000-a-year contract. The staggering deal, sealed in just 60 seconds, means the England striker has turned his back on the billion-*lira* lure of the Italians. Shearer's deal brings him £3.5 million in wages alone, with an estimated £50,000-a-year bonuses. But money was never Shearer's motivation as he sat down to talk with millionaire owner, Jack Walker, and chairman, Robert Coar.'

'Course not! The caption under the beaming player and Uncle Jack, his beaming, filthy-rich boss, read: 'That's The Spirit.' Shearer was gone a year later for £15 million. But he was only going home to Newcastle, as any man had a right to; he wasn't leaving Blackburn for the money. The *Sun* decided that the player would be earning £2 million a year – but that wasn't Shearer being greedy, that was 'Shearer's incredible loadsamoney deal'.

Michael Parkinson wrote in the *Daily Telegraph*, under the headline KEEGAN'S £15M COUP BRINGS NEWCASTLE MORE THAN A PLAYER: 'Anyone doubting the sense of paying £15 million for Alan Shearer should ask the 30-odd thousand fans who will pack the ground for his debut what they think. Another 30-odd thousand who cannot get a ticket will say the same thing. The signing of Shearer is Kevin Keegan's greatest coup. Not only has he bought a marvellous player, but a grown-up, mature professional, who will be an inspiration both on and off the field.'

The black man Shearer dethroned as the country's most expensive player, Stan Collymore, reflected in the *Mirror* in August 1996: 'It was a millstone that affected me badly. Good luck to Alan. I don't envy him.'

Shearer replied: 'Stan forgets that I had this problem before, when Blackburn paid all that money for me. It had no effect then, and it won't now.'

Andy Cole knew nothing about the machinations going on behind his back.

A January day in 1995. Midway through the season, and Alex Ferguson was tired of being messed around by Frank Clark. He'd already tried three times to get hold of the Forest manager, and each time the man wasn't there. Now, Alan Hill, Clark's assistant, had returned a call to say Clark had gone for the day as he wasn't feeling very well. The message was he'd call Ferguson the following week.

Ferguson didn't get where he was by sitting around waiting for people to call him at their leisure. He dialled a Newcastle number. Kevin Keegan did answer his phone.

'It was a shot in the dark,' Ferguson recalled in the *Mail on Sunday* in January 1995. 'I was after Collymore. If I had been able to speak to Frank Clark, I might have been able to sign him. But it's amazing how things can turn out in this game.'

Earlier in the season, Ferguson had also tried to get Keegan to part with Cole, but had been told where to go. The word was out that Collymore was more likely to don a Manchester United shirt. Both Cole and Collymore are Paul Stretford's clients.

Stretford was on his way home the day his secretary put Keegan through following Ferguson's surprise call. '[Kevin] told me he had received a bid which he thought was good for the club. It included a player coming from Manchester United and he thought the deal was the right thing for Newcastle and Andy Cole. That was the first mention of his name and I was thunderstruck. I was stunned into silence long enough for Kevin to ask if I was still on the line.'

Stretford's next call was to Cole: 'Don't go out, I'm coming round on some business.' Cole still didn't have a clue. Stretford got into his car and drove from his Wilmslow office, near Manchester, to Cole's Newcastle home.

'Nobody was more shocked than me by what happened,' said Cole. 'I had no quarrels with the boss. He had no reason to sell me other than he thought he was doing a deal that was best for Newcastle.'

'He couldn't believe it,' said Stretford. 'Moving from

Newcastle was the last thing on his mind. He hadn't long signed a four-year contract. He hadn't been scoring, but he was working hard and enjoying his football.'

Cole was going through the longest drought he'd ever suffered: nine successive games without a goal. A depressing, death-like situation for any striker. Confidence is low, and morale-boosting support and encouragement until the spell passes – as it will – is all that is needed. His manager sold him.

As the *Times* put it: 'Long-term doubts about the shin-splint condition that has restricted Cole's recent goalscoring form, and other concerns relating to his attitude, suggest that £6 million and Keith Gillespie may be a fair trade-off.' Cole didn't even get the chance to say goodbye to the fans who'd loved his record-breaking 41 goals for Newcastle during the previous season. Cole's cold comfort: if you've got to go, you may as well go to Manchester United.

It's not as if black players are asking for and getting money which white players are not. Nobody decried Germany's Jürgen Klinsmann's £1 million renumeration package when he made an expensive one-season appearance for Tottenham (terms which Bayern Munich virtually doubled when they enticed him home); but Colombian Faustino Asprilla's rumoured £1.5 million annual salary at Newcastle is an 'outrage' and 'absolutely obscene'. His personality suddenly became a big issue, especially compared to his light-skinned fellow South American on Teesside.

The *Daily Mail* reported: ASPRILLA'S ONE BIG HEADACHE: 'Tino Asprilla sounds like a powerful, exotic cocktail – and the Colombian striker possesses the lifestyle of one. A Molotov. Juninho first set elegant foot in the North-East a few weeks ago, a diffident young man, whose first call for help, you imagined, would be to his mother; this South American import, for whom Newcastle are understood to be willing to pay up to £30,000 a week, dances to a more disturbing, demonic rhythm altogether.'

Indeed, England's white and black players share the same agents. Men like Eric Hall, and Paul Stretford, have to wheel and deal on behalf of both white and black. Both races want the same. It's just that black players 'demands' are highlighted in the media, and these financial issues are repeatedly referred back to.

All players expect good basic wages, good signing-on fees (spread over the duration of the contract) and very good bonuses, especially loyalty bonuses. But the majority do not get anything like £15,000, £20,000 or upwards, the figures much loved by the sports press.

There are bonuses for goals scored; for wins; for points won; for becoming Champions; for every appearance notched up by a player; for doing well in Europe . . .

Then come the personal sponsorship and endorsement deals with companies like Nike, Umbro, Predator, Patrick; sports clothing, sports drinks and, obviously, boot deals. Which may come on top of modelling contracts, personal appearances and ghosted newspaper articles, signed by the player.

There are also the 'perks': wonderful accommodation, luxury cars and, if you're a foreigner, regular first-class air fares home. And there are pay-parity clauses so that you can renegotiate the whole lot when the latest flavour of the season arrives and tries to knock you off your pedestal. And, finally, depending on whether the player hangs about long enough, he might be promised a testimonial for services rendered.

All of which is just a little bit different from life as a footballer in 1961, when Albert Johanneson landed on these shores. That year Jimmy Hill, as PFA chairman, was about to launch what would have been the first players' strike – in order to force the clubs to scrap the maximum wage of £20 a week (£17 in the close season). When Fulham started paying Johnny Haynes £100 a week, the game was up. When Brian Clough broke the million-pound barrier to buy Trevor Francis in 1979, the transfer game was up, up and away.

Currently, Newcastle may top the big spenders' league with their £60 million worth since 1992, but even poorer Premiership clubs have to keep up in the wages department.

'Wimbledon are no paupers when it comes to contracts,' asserted John Fashanu. 'They cannot afford to be if they want to keep the best. No one should expect Premiership players to be on Second Division wages, even if the club does only get crowds of around eight thousand.'

In April 1997, Imperial College's Dr Stefan Szymanski revealed that black footballers 'are losing out in the wages league'. The *Daily Mail* reported that Dr Szymanski compared the total wage bills and final League positions of 39 League clubs between 1978 and 1993. He found that 'those with more black players achieved higher League positions but had a lower wage bill. "Because there's a competitive market for players, wages reflect ability and so spending on players translates directly into performance," Dr Szymanski explained. Premier League clubs were among the worst offenders, spending about £70,000 less per black player.'

Nobody really knows what soccer players truly earn – apart from the agents and the players themselves. Everybody else just has to take part in a guessing game. But the courts have to be told the truth (don't they?). During the first trial, in January 1997, of the three soccer stars accused of match-fixing, Winchester Crown Court heard that during his time with Wimbledon, Fashanu 'received gross salaries of £186,000 in 1991–92, £200,000 in 1992–93 and £192,000 in 1993–94,' said the *Daily Telegraph*. 'In August 1994, he transferred to Aston Villa and received a £200,000 signing-on fee and a weekly wage of £3000 as well as match bonuses. David Barnard, chief executive of Wimbledon FC, told the hearing that Fashanu had been a leading scorer for the club. He said Fashanu's final contract in March 1994 allowed him to choose whether to play and train while he pursued his business interests. He received a weekly wage of £90, £5000 a match and £1000 a goal.'

The court was told that Bruce Grobbelaar was said to have been paid gross salaries of £162,000 as Liverpool's goalkeeper in 1991, £137,000 the following season, and he received £130,000 in 1992–93 and earned £159,000 in 1993–94. The Wimbledon keeper, Hans Segers, received gross salaries of £72,000 in 1991–2, £85,000 in 1992–93 and £87,000 in 1993–94.

When Derby County's Dean Sturridge wanted a judge to lift a driving ban in April 1997 following his disqualification for speeding, he told Stafford Crown Court that he 'couldn't afford a chauffeur – even though he earned £3000 a week, plus £600 win bonuses. He saved £600 a month and put £1000 in a pension,' reported the *Mirror*.

Arsenal have one of the highest wage bills in the Premiership. As George Graham put it in the *Mirror* in 1994, the year when salaries rose by an average of 19 per cent and, according to accountants Touche Ross, swallowed 80 per cent of gate income: 'There are a lot of players who don't like working hard. They are very quick to demand big salaries, but it's amazing how few volunteer for extra training or coaching. We get lots of criticism, and our bill is big, but it's more equal. There is no player at this club earning twice what anyone else is. The differential is close. You would have to be a Pelé or Maradona to be earning two or three times more than a teammate, but that happens at other clubs.'

Indeed, there are players who would be quite happy to remain in the Premiership as reserves and never get a game, rather than go down divisions and get regular first-team appearances.

'This is a labour-intensive industry,' said Gordon Taylor. 'People don't pay to watch directors, they pay to watch players.

But no one is tying the clubs' hands and forcing them to pay big wages. We don't expect a club to pay more than it can afford.'

'One day,' said Conservative Chancellor Kenneth Clarke, 'this country will decide that good businessmen are entitled to be paid at least as much as good footballers. Personally, I am in favour of good footballers being paid quite a lot. A guy who runs his business successfully, who is as good at running a business as a footballer is at scoring goals, should be paid.'

Sport is the only business where black people have, literally, the muscle, undisputed talent, and power to put bums on seats, glue eyes to the set, and put shirts on people's backs. Economic power. And that demands payment for what we are worth to the industry we represent. Proper payment for a change. Yet, even though we are demanding what any white person would expect *per se*, we are deemed to be grasping.

Mike Tyson, 'the biggest attraction in boxing', was paid £16 million for his comeback fight in Las Vegas against Pete McNeeley in August 1995. As the *Sun* reported: 'There will be many who think it is an obscene sum to get for a maximum 30 minutes of sporting activity. Yet no one who lives in this city is complaining about the vast fortune Tyson will pick up – because everyone will be lining their pockets this weekend thanks to Mike.

'With tickets ranging from £130 to £1000, the sell-out 16,000 crowd will put more than £8 million into MGM's coffers. The money those people spend on hotels, food and drink is expected to come to at least £5 million. The waitresses benefit by the extra tips they get, and one said she will be more than £1000 better off by Monday.

'Van Heffner, president of the Vegas Hotel and Motel Association, said: "You can always feel the electricity building up to a major fight, and this is no exception. Having Tyson back means our community will benefit by millions of dollars. Everybody does well – stores, restaurants, bars and car-hire businesses."

'If the forecasts are correct,' the article continued, 'the casinos will benefit by up to **£200m** [the *Sun*'s highlights] as the high rollers lose at the tables. The Tyson–McNeeley clash is also expected to beat the pay-per-view television sales record, which belongs to the Holyfield–George Foreman title tilt in 1991.'

ONE GIANT LEAP FOR DOW JONES was Jeff Powell's headline for one of his *Daily Mail* columns in March 1995. 'Two little words have whipped the world's largest democracy into a frenzy of expectation which will transform not only the sporting landscape but the television ratings and even the stock markets of America.

'When the greatest basketball player of all time announced on Saturday, "I'm back," the United States braced itself for a second coming which would come second here only to the ultimate resurrection. Since the Messiah himself has yet to re-materialize, America will settle for the return of Michael Jordan. Ecstatically.

'Jordan's personal fortune was secure already. For the privilege of retaining his registration, Chicago have been paying him $3.8 million a year not to play. A nice little earner but no more than pocket money compared with the $30m a year he accrues from his sponsorship contracts.

'The mere rumours of a possible Jordan comeback played a substantial part in lifting the Dow Jones – the FT Index on Wall street – to record highs at the end of last week. This was achieved through the five major companies whose products he endorses. They enjoyed a staggering, combined rise in share value of $2.3 billion. Nike, whose Air Jordans are their top selling sports shoe, went up by $200m. Sara Lee, for whom he endorses Hanes underwear, rose by $500m; Quaker Oats (Gatorade) by $100m; General Mills (Wheaties) by $500m; and McDonald's by a phenomenal $1bn.

But that wasn't the end of it: 'Also polishing their lenses in anticipation of an unexpected windfall are NBC, Turner

Broadcasting and the local Chicago cable station, who share the TV rights to Bulls games,' wrote Powell.

When, in June 1995, Les Ferdinand made his £6 million (estimated £15,000 a week) move from QPR to Newcastle, a tiny club, formerly in the Diadora League, also came into the money. Hayes collected £600,000 – 10 per cent of the transfer fee – as a result of the sell-on clause their chairman, Derek Goodall, cleverly inserted into the contract when the club sold Ferdinand to QPR. Goodall was once bitten, twice shy. Ten years earlier, he'd sold Cyrille Regis to West Bromwich Albion for £10,000, only to see him transferred to Coventry for £300,000, and not a penny winging its way back to Hayes.

'It's like winning the lottery, a real windfall,' said Hayes' financial director, Trevor Griffiths in the *Guardian*. The club has an average home gate of 500. 'The cash secures our future. It would take years and years to earn that kind of money and it's head and shoulders over anything a non-League club has received from a knock-on fee.'

GIVE ME A LARA MORE LOLLY! The *Daily Mirror* called the West Indian Brian Lara the best batsman in the world after he set a new Test record score of 375 against England in Antigua in April 1994. Warwickshire had signed him up cheaply – for £40,000 – prior to Antigua, but five months later, and following his 501 for them against Durham (the highest score ever in first-class cricket), Lara expected a bit more.

'But they have offered me only another £15,000 to come back in 1996, after the West Indies tour here next year,' an aggrieved young batsman complained. 'I like it at Warwickshire, but county cricket is hard work and that really isn't enough after all I've done for them. I'd be better off sitting on a beach back home in Trinidad. I would still like to play for them, but they'll have to come up with a better offer than this.'

Lara had boosted Warwickshire's membership to record levels

and had helped them to two Lord's finals. As Brian Scovell wrote in the *Daily Mail*: 'His impact was unprecedented. Besides increasing attendances everywhere he played, each of the counties made extra cash from the sale of Lara souvenirs. Gloucestershire's biggest one-day crowd for seven years earned them £15,000 at Sunday's league match when Warwickshire won the title.'

But the sponsors came calling. HOW LAID-BACK LARA PERKS UP WHEN IT COMES TO PAY TIME announced the *Daily Mail*. In the *Telegraph*: 'Yesterday's papers were full of pictures of him in pinstripe suit and bowler (compare with Chris Eubank posing not long ago in morning dress and monocle),' wrote Geoffrey Wheatcroft. 'He had just signed a promotional contract for an unconfirmed but assiduously leaked £500,000 a year with the fund managing company Mercury Asset Management. This is in addition to the half-million which he will earn this season from sponsors to whom he is already contracted. It makes him much the highest-paid cricketer of this or any age, though nothing like the highest-paid sportsman.

'Today, vicarious comfort is all most professional cricketers can take from Lara's sudden enrichment. It would be churlish to begrudge it. It may encourage youngsters to take up the game, both here, where so many State secondary schools have scarcely heard of cricket, and in the Caribbean, where athletically gifted boys are tempted by the bright lights and megabucks of soccer, boxing or even baseball. But if it is wrong to begrudge, it is not easy to welcome the crashing sound of cash registers drowning the thwack of leather on willow.'

We can't have young black men dressing or looking like city or country gents, can we? The reason blacks are painted as greedy, money-loving people is because of the white belief that we should be grateful for every penny we are getting in the first place. Don't we know already that the majority of us are poor, on the breadline and destined for a life of poverty? Remember, is the attitude, that you haven't come that far from black cultures who would be quite happy using beads and baubles as money anyway.

One subtext is that black immigrants would rather die than return home to an African economy. (Literally prefer death. Think of self-starved black immigrants demanding sanctuary in a French church, and then screaming and fighting with police as beautiful white actresses demonstrate on their behalf to prevent their forced removal from the church back to Africa.) Another is that we should count our lucky stars that we are earning a low salary in the West because we're in plentiful supply. We come cheap. Our self-valuation is at such a low that too many would be willing to die to join those of us with a presence in Europe. White people so undervalue us that, if they could, they would give us away.

We're painted as hustlers, who if we do earn real money, are wont to spend it wastefully, like children. Chris Eubank is publicly chortled over and thrown in our face as the ultimate example of the tastelessness and vulgarity of black people who come into money.

'King of bad taste Chris Eubank,' said *Today*, 'yesterday unveiled his new £200,000 Aston Martin [red] – then signed a cheque for the insurance 17 times larger than his next opponent's average purse. The premium alone on the 200 m.p.h. 6.3 litre Volante is a staggering £25,000, which dwarfs the fee Irishman Sam Storey received from his last fight.

'Eubank said: "I should be praised for giving guys like Sam a good payday, not criticized for taking on unworthy opponents. I should be acknowledged as a provider, not disrespected by the media." The WBO super middleweight champion raised some eyebrows in the Dorchester car park where his car nestled uncomfortably with the Bentleys.'

As black people, we know what drives our Eubank of this world. Every black neighbourhood has a Eubank to treasure and laugh *with*. What he demonstrates is simply a more in-your-face version of the black virtue to put your money where your mouth is. As Eubank said in the *Sun* in October 1994: 'Money and fame has allowed me to be honest, to do what I want to do and be what I want to be. That's why I dress the way I do. Wearing my hacking jacket, jodphurs, paddock boots and carrying my gold-top cane makes me look good and feel good. The monocle is the icing on the cake.'

The white *schadenfreude* over the possibility of Eubank's financial collapse following his defeat by the Irishman, Steve Collins, and the loss of his World Boxing Organization super-middleweight title, was quite sickening.

EUBANK MAY BE LEFT HUNTING FOR SCRAPS said the Guardian. 'This is the cruellest of ironies for Eubank – and a delicious one for those who could not abide his arrogance when he lorded it over everyone in the sport, from commentators to promoters to opponents. The man who, while at the top, consistently derided boxing as an ugly bloodfeast, a job he did solely for money, now finds his bargaining chip, the otherwise worthless WBO belt, swept from his grasp. He has debts and a lifestyle to support; all of a sudden he may have to start really fighting for a living. Where once he dictated the terms, he now finds himself part of a complicated scenario, one that involves several of the main players in the business.'

CAN EU BELIEVE IT? wailed an affronted *News of the World*. 'He lost his title. He quit the ring. But he still blows £20,000 a week.' And to make matters worse, the black boxer had got ideas above his station: 'Only Christopher Livingston Eubank, you presume, would have the effrontery to pay £40,000 for the title Lord of the Manor of Brighton.'

Generally, if we do run into money problems, we are upfront about them. A white British characteristic is to hide financial difficulty until it is so awful and so huge that there is no alternative but to have it out in the open. (Nick Leeson. Paul Merson. Peter Shilton.)

Peter Shilton was once Britain's highest-paid player when Derby were paying him £250,000 a year. In 1992, the former goalkeeper was appointed Plymouth manager. In October 1994, he was outed by his bitter chairman, Dan McCauley, in the *Sun*. 'Like a mug I tried to do something to help, and he slapped me in the face straight away. I've never felt so humiliated in all my life. His situation must be far worse than even I envisaged.

'He says he hasn't got financial problems, but cash-flow problems. He must have come to me seven times for advances, though, to be fair, I did offer last time. I would estimate they totalled £100,000. It won't happen again. I realized after only two months that Shilton wasn't quite what I expected. It was over money. There were several phone calls before I agreed to help.

'I don't know why he doesn't speak to us. We have a financial adviser on our board, and he could go to one side and talk things over with him. He doesn't want us to know the real story and just drifts on. Like many footballers, he bought houses in different areas. Most sell when they move on – he probably kept them as an investment.

'And a lot of people have been caught out on property. Why he feels that's a stigma and can't discuss it, I don't know. Perhaps there's more behind it. But he doesn't seem to want help. He says he's under pressure, but he has his salary, presumably rental from houses, income from other sources, and he must have a pension after playing so long. It's hard to imagine where his money goes.'

Today reported that the former England star owed nearly half a million pounds. Other papers said the figure was around three-hundred thousand. In October 1995, he narrowly avoided bankruptcy.

It's frequently claimed that our overwheening ambitions show us up when we try to set up businesses. We are too ambitious even when we are doing or want to be doing just what others are. It's OK for Terry Venables to open and run Scribes, his trendy club in West London. It's OK for Venables to be involved in myriad business interests, and write books galore. This is applauded. It's OK for any white retired player who feels like it to run a pub or a hotel anywhere in the country. But how dare Victor Umbogu open a sports bar. How dare Fashanu try to turn himself into a businessman. How dare Du'aine Ladejo set up a production company. How dare Linford Christie set up a sports agency. Getting a bit above themselves.

After an analysis of the 1991 census (as noted, the first to include a question on race) by academics, an Oxford University professor, Ceri Peach, pronounced in the press in June 1996: 'One of the most telling summaries of the differences between the Caribbean and Asian settlements in Britain is that the Caribbeans faced what I term an "Irish future" while the Asians faced a "Jewish future".

'The implication of the statement,' the professor continued, 'is that the black Caribbean population is working class, waged labour, State-comprehensive-school-educated and council-housed; while the Asian population will become self-employed owner-occupiers and white-collar workers with professional qualifications.'

Beggars stare at blacks walking past, and there is a slight, but significant change of tone when they ask us for money. They expect the money; the action may be one of begging, but the tone is more demanding, as if they have inside knowledge. It's a tone which says: You'll give me some because you're closer to where I am than white people are. White beggars clearly haven't noticed how few black beggars there are. I saw a teenaged black girl beggar with a girlfriend sitting in a central London doorway with a blanket thrown over their knees. They were giggling and chatting, and clearly having a bit of fun. Perhaps someone had dared them to do it. As I approached, the white girl whispered to her black friend, and they giggled some more. 'Got any change?' the white girl said, laughing. I directed an extremely pointed look at the black girl, making sure she knew I was taking a very close look at her hair and the state of her skin. She looked away, and I kept on walking. I never saw them there again.

The concept of 'shame' is very strong amongst black people generally, and almost pathological amongst Africans. To do that which would shame yourself, your parents, family, village, town, country or race is virtually a capital offence; the execution of which is borne by yourself. Nigerian drug dealers caught abroad would rather serve jail sentences in foreign countries than at home where they would have to see the unbearable reality of their crimes in the eyes of their people. Didn't that girl have shame? No shame at all. She knew I wanted to slap her, and pull her off the pavement. Drag her by her disgraceful hair to the nearest wash and blow dry.

I knew it would be him. Who else? Didn't he sum up for many whites the typical black footballer? He was a big, pacy, aggressive striker. And arrogant, they said. He came from a broken family background, had sexual liaisons, lived in expensive property, drove luxury cars, and revelled in his social cachet. He loved money and pursued his business interests as determinedly as he played his game – in 1994 *Business Age* magazine said he was worth four million pounds. He was supposedly the acknowledged master in demonstrating how you can play football and make money from outside interests too. He said he had confounded the image of black people as financially inept, or corrupt swindlers, or people who were like children when it came to handling money. The public didn't even have to know about football to be aware of him because he was also visible on television as a presenter of one of ITV's most popular programmes, *Gladiators*. UNICEF made him an ambassador. He travelled the world and had it all, it seemed. He was successful in capital letters. But, in his perception, he said '*they*' were out to get him. Was it because he was black? Or was he just another example of the media destroying the god they had created? I refer, of course, to our leading black footballer, John Fashanu, the London-born English player of Nigerian parentage, who was arrested and charged with match-fixing together with two 'other' foreign players, Zimbabwe's Bruce Grobbelaar, and Holland's Hans Segers, in British football's trial of the century. All three men were acquitted. Whatever the rights and wrongs of the case, the central question remains: did pride come before a fall, or did they big him up to knock him down?

By the start of the 1997–98 season, Stan Collymore had transferred to Aston Villa for £1.5 million less than his record 1995 Liverpool fee. His critics followed. Andy Cole was still at Manchester United, but still having to prove himself to those who doubt any run of good form is permanent. And Les Ferdinand was sold by Newcastle to Tottenham for six million pounds, the price Newcastle had bought him for originally. He had been reluctant to leave. Alan Shearer was still the most expensive player.

For black footballers who have put on a fight akin to an invasion of England's pitches, in some respects, to gain representation and to make an outstanding impact on the English game, success is never unqualified, uncontroversial or long lasting. There are always 'difficulties', 'problems' and 'controversies'. Is that all the present and the future hold for the black British population whose lives here too many white British people still regard as an invasion of their pitch? Each of us will have to find the answers to that one.